Configuration Management

The Missing Link in Web Engineering

For a listing of recent titles in the *Artech House Computing Library,* turn to the back of this book.

Configuration Management

The Missing Link in Web Engineering

Susan Dart

Artech House
Boston • London
www.artechhouse.com

Library of Congress Cataloging-in-Publication Data
Dart, Susan, 1957–
   Configuration management: the missing link in Web engineering/Susan Dart.
     p.   cm. — (Artech House computing library)
   Includes bibliographical references and index.
   ISBN 1-58053-098-2 (alk. paper)
   1. Web sites—Management.   2. Web site development.   3. Software configuration
management.
   I. Title.   II. Series.
TK5105.888 .D37   2000
005.2'76—dc21   00-059389
                                             CIP

British Library Cataloguing in Publication Data
Dart, Susan
   Configuration management: the missing link in Web engineering. —
(Artech House computing library)
   1. Web site development. 2. Web sites—Management. 3. Software configuration
management.
   I. Title
   005.2'76

   ISBN 1-58053-098-2

Cover design by Igor Valdman

© 2000 ARTECH HOUSE, INC.
685 Canton Street
Norwood, MA 02062

International Standard Book Number: 1-58053-098-2
Library of Congress Catalog Card Number: 00-059389

10 9 8 7 6 5 4 3 2 1

To A. Nico Haberman, for teaching me well
To Leslie, who died much too soon
To Karola Yourison, for being a wonderful friend

Contents

Understanding the Many Views of
Configuration Management   73

Preface

The Internet is a fabulous invention that is changing our lives at every level: from our personal lifestyles to the way world economies operate. We feel the presence of e-commerce and e-business via a variety of Internet-connected devices in our offices, homes, transportation vehicles, and shopping areas, not to mention in wearable Web devices.

All of these options imply massive amounts of Web systems development and maintenance. Unfortunately, much of this work is being done without benefit of good software engineering principles. This worries me deeply because I see too many Web site crashes and problems with system upgrades, along with unrealized potential. Companies are up against a Web crisis in which they are unable to develop and grow their Web systems at the rate that is needed. They are in chaos, making too many mistakes and running around like headless chickens wondering what to do next. And it is only going to get worse as Internet devices and uses continue to pervade the world.

My aims in writing this book are to articulate and raise awareness about the Web crisis and then provide a solution in the form of configuration management (CM). I show how various companies have addressed their Web problems using CM. The software industry long ago realized the value of CM. The Web industry is hitting all the same software problems and more (such as increased speed of change along with the variant explosion challenge). CM now becomes even more critical, not only at a technical level for developers and managers, but also at an economic level because it offers tremendous business value to companies by enabling them to not only survive in the Internet economy, but to thrive in it!

Acknowledgments

No book can be written without the assistance of many people. This book represents a snapshot of my experience in configuration management. I owe much of my knowledge and wisdom to every person that I have come into contact with in my career: my colleagues, my nemeses, my advocates, my employers, my teachers, the tool vendors, my clients, the case study contributors, the attendees at my seminars, and the people who read my papers and gave me feedback. I thank you heartily as you have all contributed in some way to this book.

No book can get published without a kind and patient publisher. I thank Artech and its entire staff, including my editor, Viki Williams, Ruth Young, Rebecca Allendorf, and Julie Lancashire for being incredibly kind and patient and for taking me to great restaurants in London.

No book gets published without a good technical review, so I'd like to thank Darcy Wiborg-Weber very much for taking the time to review this material and provide good feedback despite her very busy schedule of developing CM tools.

No book can be completed unless the author stays sane. So I'd like to thank Karola Yourison for being a wonderful long-distance friend and nurturing me through the strains of earning a living and writing a book. Her tremendous support, her wisdom, and her many weekend phone calls to me kept my spirit high.

No author can write a book unless she's been taught to write, so I must thank my mother Valerie for ensuring that as an impoverished young girl, I got the best education she could afford. I also thank my brother Victor for being a person of strength.

Contents

The Internet Is a Fabulous Invention, But...

"Oh, what a tangled web we weave ..."
—Sir Walter Scott

Imagine a spaceship hovering over planet Earth. Inside is a friendly alien using special instruments to gaze at the Internet—the World Wide Web (WWW). From space, the WWW "appears as a swirling sphere of light . . . as a global efflorescence . . . the radiant chrysalis from which will spring a new global economy" [1]. The alien travels forward a little in time to glimpse what the WWW will become. It sees that the "Internet is not merely a radiance of connections; it is a mesh of constant invention. . . . The Net is a seine of collaborative production . . . it has fallen into the hands of a billion learners and value creators. . . . The Internet is a network of networks of learning curves and melodies seeking their points of harmonic resonance. It triumphs by proliferating the slopes of learning, the songs of searching, the quests

1

of curiosity that are at the heart of wealth creation" [1]. The alien is happy with what it sees, and flies away.

I adore the WWW! As a consumer and business professional, I marvel daily at all the benefits of simply being connected to the Internet. As a computer scientist, I feel proud of the people in my profession who created it and continue to expand its abilities. The WWW is an invention that is transforming the world on the scale of an industrial and social revolution.

But I am also troubled and worried. As a practitioner, a software engineer, and a project manager, I see the maintenance shock that descends on companies when trying to maintain their Web systems. I see stunned companies. Once the thrill and excitement of their new Web site—the e-commerce or e-business package—goes on-line, a paralysis, a frustration, a feeling of being overwhelmed by the volume and speed of changes, inevitably sets in. They did not envisage such speed!

Along with this *velocity of change,* they did not envisage another significant requirement: *business and technical operation synergy.* That is, the tight bonding between strategic business decision-making and the technical operations of the company requiring the immediate execution of those decisions. The Internet has exasperated this synergy.

In the old days—the pre-Internet days of software development and maintenance—software companies typically functioned in a certain way. For instance, the executive team would do 5-year strategic planning. They would go to some off-site location, typically a fancy resort, and spend weeks developing the 5-year plan. Frequently this planning was done in a mildly euphoric, inebriated state since it was such tedious work. When they got back from the plush resort, the executives would then disseminate the plan throughout the company. It would take months for the company as a whole to put the necessary procedures, schedules, tools, hardware, people skills, resources, standards, and processes in place to support the new plan. But now, pure Internet companies are changing these rules, which in turn affects all companies—including the bricks-and-mortar companies—that provide an Internet offering. Pure Internet companies realize that it is impossible to do any kind of serious, long-term planning. Certainly 5 years is too long a period to even envisage for the Internet economy!

What they do now is short-term strategic planning. For instance, they realize that they can only imagine the next few months, and they do weekly strategic planning. So, every Monday morning, the executive team meets. In their euphoric (yeah—love the stock price!) but tired (overworked) state, they review certain information: the traffic monitoring statistics for their Web sites from the last week; the competitors' Web sites; and their strategic plans from last week. Based on subsequent analysis, they may simply change their key strategic decisions. For instance, the marketing vice president may decide that new products or types of transactions or partnerships have to exist immediately because the competitor just released new features on their Web site.

Once this meeting is over, the team then takes the new decisions and strategies back to the rest of the company and begins implementing them. They cannot afford any lag in their execution because they know the competition is just a click away from them. So, all the work schedules and tasks get adjusted immediately. No longer is there any comfort-zone time delay between the decision making and their execution. No longer is there any opportunity for managers to focus on getting their staff to "buy in" to the new decisions. The company must respond immediately; otherwise, it could easily lose its market share or even go out of business.

Hence, this means that for all software and Web development, the content authors and software developers have to respond immediately. It means people must adapt straight-away and their tools and development environments must do so also, not to mention the processes and procedures. There essentially is no time to change—everyone and everything must "switch over" to suit the new decisions.

The serious implication then for companies doing Web development and maintenance is that their environments must be very flexible and instantly adaptable to change. Of course, the only way to achieve such a Utopian ideal is to automate everything. That way managers go on-line and make the process changes and everyone falls in behind, guided by the process controls of the tools. *It is only through the use of tools and automated processes that companies have any hope of achieving the efficiencies, flexibility, and immediacy of change needed to support the velocity of change required by the Internet.*

But what kind of tools? Because Web development is just like software development, the tools we used in the past for good software engineering are needed: requirements, testing, quality assurance (QA), help desks, distribution, design and modeling, workflow, and so on. One vital tool that many software companies found out about the hard way (through their software quality problems) was that of configuration management (CM).

CM helps a company control the creation and evolution of its software, along with the processes involved. CM takes on even more significance now in the Internet economy. Not only is it a major technical solution for enterprise development and maintenance practices, but it is now elevated in importance and assumes or generates tremendous business value for companies. It helps companies avoid many Web site mistakes (such as publishing bad content) and enables companies to quickly recover from crashes (by being able to rebuild sites or roll back to previous versions). CM assumes much more business-critical status because of the dramatic upsurge in the speed of change and because of the synergy between business decisions and technical operations. This book is essentially about the incredible value and criticality of CM for Web development and maintenance.

The Internet is not going away. It is only going to get bigger, bolder, and faster. Without CM, companies will struggle. My goals in writing this book are very grandiose indeed. In short, I want to save the world's companies from encountering a Web crisis—the inability to maintain their Web systems while growing the business at a fast rate. In the next chapter I discuss in detail the nine key challenges that companies must address in order to avoid a Web crisis. We do not need to suffer its consequences. We have learned a lot from the software crisis. In the old days, the software industry knew it had software problems. Those problems boiled down to the inability to deliver quality software on time, with all the changes required and within budget. This kind of crisis could easily befall all companies doing Web development and maintenance. To see the beginnings of a Web crisis, you only have to look at all the Web site crashes because of server upgrade problems or bad content displayed on Web sites.

We should learn from the early software crises and not relive all those problems with Web developers, content authors, and new tools and languages. If you look inside the companies doing Web development today, you see a great sense of urgency. This urgency is creating frustration and a sense of being overwhelmed. Web developers are expected to work 24 hours a day. They wear pagers at all times because they could be called on to do Web fixes or upgrades at any time.

There are at least five drivers or causes of this urgency, which will be discussed further in the next chapter. Essentially though, they are (1) competitive issues, (2) societal forces, (3) being successful too quickly, which results in (4) too many avoidable mistakes, and (5) the need to choose the right development processes. These drivers affect the kind of Web development and maintenance environment and resources that companies provide. Hence, it is important for companies doing Web development (which eventually will be every company on this planet) to recognize the driving forces and adjust their environments to them.

The beginnings of maintenance problems

Consider a typical Web system. A medium- to large-sized system may consist of 20 Internet Web sites, one of which may be a private intranet site and the others, global Internet sites. Each site represents a particular e-commerce product targeted to a specific market niche. These sites share a significant amount of code and content because they are essentially the same product. About 80% is common code and content, meaning 80% of the same material is shared across all sites. The other 20% is tailored or unique to each site. Hence, if a change has to be made, much of the decision-making involves deciding the ramifications of the change. For instance, should the change be propagated to each site if it affects the common, shared code, or is it specific to the site-dependent code? How are the updates published simultaneously to all sites?

Now scale this up to thousands of Web sites/products, and thousands of changes ranging in priority from urgent show-stopper bugs to low-priority "wish list" changes. Quite a bit of work is involved in making the changes, including the decision-making about the change (who, how, why, when, cost), the speed with which the change has to happen, and the mechanics of doing the change, testing it, and publishing it on the appropriate live sites. The decision-making, mechanics, and speed all have their elements of complexity. On top of that, imagine that the Web sites are subject to government or industrial audits. How does a company keep track of all the pieces? How does a company make all the changes without making any mistakes, such as publishing the wrong version of the content?

Then imagine having to redesign the Web sites on a regular basis in order to keep customers coming back, or having to merge and create new sites—all while maintaining (fixing bugs, adding enhancements) the existing sites. A tremendous amount of work must be done in parallel, requiring significant technical and managerial coordination and synchronization.

Then, add to those factors the variant explosion problem. For instance, each site represents a variant of the original, common code and content. So, at any time there are 20 variants that are live. Well, actually, there are more because each site must cater to all versions of browsers (in fact, all versions of Internet Explorer and Netscape Navigator, among others). Thus, each of the 20 variants has multiple variants themselves because they must support all versions of those browsers. Even further, those products are designed to run on non-PC (personal computer) devices such as smart phones (phones that can connect to the Internet). Now, each variant and its browser "subvariants" must support further variants that will be accessible through all the "micro-browsers" for the smart devices—and all versions of those micro-browsers. Thus, the variant explosion continues as more devices are added to the product line. A company could very easily be supporting at least 200 variants of one product at any point in time.

No company can manage this variant explosion problem manually. Tools and techniques are needed to assist. That is where CM comes in. At a high level, CM is a disciplined approach to managing the evolution of software/Web development and maintenance practices (e.g., the publish–fix–test–publish cycle) along with their products (e.g., Web content plus the back-office applications and tools and variants). CM tools provide all the support that assists the developers (programmers) and content authors along with the project managers and team leaders. CM has been around for at least 30 years, and there are now very mature CM tools in the commercial marketplace.

Unfortunately, very few companies with mission-critical Web systems are using CM tools today. Some are developing their own CM tools and techniques because they are not fully aware of the commercially available CM tools. In fact, they may never have heard of CM at all. The purpose of this book is to make the Web community aware of the Web crisis they will face if they do not employ CM as part of their development and maintenance infrastructure. And then, given that awareness, what are the best practices for a company in selecting and deploying a good CM solution?

The Web crisis consequence

Many companies are heading toward a Web crisis. This crisis involves the proliferation of quickly "hacked together" Web systems that are kept running via a continual stream of patches or upgrades developed without any rigorous or systematic approach. With the Web there is the speed and the ease of making mistakes. "Bricks-and-clicks" (the bricks-and-mortar companies that provide their products and services via the Internet) and pure Internet companies cannot afford to make mistakes because downtime means lost business. For instance, eBay was the first company with Web problems that got the mass media's attention. Its Web site went down, resulting in a loss of at least $5 million in revenue, more than a 29-point drop in stock price in one day, and a tarnished reputation.

All companies will eventually do business over the Internet. The world cannot afford to have faulty Web systems, or Web systems that crash or have any downtime. We live in the Internet economy now. The Internet is not a fad. It is a way of life and is a major part of the world's economy. It drives the stock markets and makes—or breaks—millionaires overnight. In March 2000, the Nasdaq stock market indicator hit 5000 [2], confirming further that technology companies now drive the U.S. economy.

I see a reemerging pattern from the "old software" days. That pattern concerns companies concentrating on creating new software without thought of maintaining that software. Everyone in the world can see the side effects of the emerging Web crisis—Web sites crash and serious mistakes are made because wrong, inconsistent, or stale content was accidentally published to the live sites. Software companies can no longer hide their software maintenance problems from the world because now all problems are visible from the Web site.

In the old software days, it was an acceptable fact that companies released products that were buggy [3]. They could always say to the client, "Hey, we will fix that in the next release. And that will be in three months' time." With the Internet economy, that response is no longer acceptable. If the Web site has a bug, serious financial and litigation consequences could result and a client may be lost since the competition is just one click away. Because the customers can see the Web site, they expect your company to be able to fix the problem right away.

If one projects forward in time into the next decade, nine key challenges are evident for companies concerning their Web system development and maintenance. Table 1.1 summarizes them and they are discussed in detail in Chapter 2. Although CM is not the entire solution to the nine challenges, it is the core support capability that is needed to address all challenges well. I believe that a good, well-automated CM solution will give a company 80% protection against the Web challenges. Without CM as a core part of a company's IDE (interactive development environment), a company will struggle to survive because it will make mistakes that can be avoided and will waste time "firefighting" or

Table 1.1
Nine Key Challenges Facing Companies With Web Systems

Speed of change
Variant explosion
Dynamic content
Process support
Performance effect
Scalability
Outsourcing
Politics
Immaturity

recovering from those mistakes rather than moving forward and expending time on creative endeavors like new products, Web sites, or partnerships.

Survival is no longer good enough for companies. If you look at pure Internet companies like Amazon.com, you see that they are not just surviving, but thriving. That is, they keep growing. They didn't just stick with selling books, but moved into selling movies and music, conducting auctions, and so on. Jeff Bezos, the CEO of Amazon.com, has said that eventually they will be selling everything imaginable (apart from live animals and guns).

Then imagine way out in the future when the world learns how to digitize everything. What would it be like if we could digitize pasta and send it through the Internet? as Nicholas Negropointe, a visionary of our digital future, proffered.

To do business over the Internet, companies have to be able to thrive. They have to really know how to do business and to grow in the face of continual and constant change, and be able to execute plans quickly. A key enabler to this is CM. Companies need to structure their Web development and maintenance activities and environment around CM.

There are different ways of doing just that. One is by simply buying a good off-the-shelf CM tool and inserting it into the environment with appropriate processes. Another way is to wait until the heavy-duty Web content management vendors [4] (such as Vignette and Interwoven) add it to their tools so that CM is embedded. But this will take time, time that companies cannot afford to waste without some kind of CM support. Creating good, automated CM facilities is quite complex and takes many years. Most of the CM vendors have taken nearly 10 years to perfect their capabilities, so I expect the same kind of maturing period for the Web content management vendors.

CM is not merely a technical solution to development and maintenance problems. It has tremendous business value, and consequently needs to be considered a key strategic issue and core competency for a company. It is such an incredibly powerful support system that, by itself, can save the world from the Web crisis. In Chapter 3, I discuss further what configuration management really is and the value and benefits it offers companies.

CM is typically not considered a "sexy" topic, and you will not hear it discussed with loving affection around the Silicon Valley bars unless surrounded by CM aficionados. What you do hear about, though, are all the problems the companies are having because they do not have CM. Metaphorically, I view the value of CM as similar to the value provided by the pylons of a large bridge. The pylons provide insurance in the sense that the bridge will not fall. But they also enable structures to be built on top of them, such as multiple tiers. The bridge can also withstand the prevailing conditions such as traffic loads, weather patterns, or accidents. But if the pylons are not solid or are improperly designed, then each user of the bridge is at the mercy and whimsy of the weak points in that bridge. Users take their lives into their hands each time they cross the bridge. It is like asking a truck driver to drive his big, heavy truck over a makeshift, rope bridge while praying that the rope bridge holds. Just like the truck driver, no company wants to function on prayer alone. A company needs to function with good engineering principles, processes, techniques, and tools to support them.

The Web changes everything

The Internet economy changes the rules of business such as the 5-year strategic planning that I mentioned earlier. Companies are abandoning their 5-year strategic plans. They must write and rewrite their business plans every quarter or even every week: "Now the fast eat the slow" [5]. "Net speeds force all sorts of cultural changes. Hierarchies flatten out. Budgeting cycles get compressed. Decision-making gets pushed out to the front lines. And customer expectations, not the executive board, guide the next big project.... The prosperity of a firm is directly linked to the prosperity of its network" [6]. Carly Fiorina, the chief executive officer of Hewlett Packard, said in March 2000 at the Governors' Conference in Washington, DC, that even the role of the CEO has been changed and what we used to consider as power (the owner of the knowledge) has greatly changed.

The Web offers challenges at many levels: business, process, people, and technical. The ways of doing business have changed. Companies must find better processes to support these business changes. Users are now in control because if they are not happy with their "Web experience," the competition is just a click away. Technical solutions must be found to support the business changes and the speed with which they happen.

On the business side, companies need to know how they can maintain all their Web systems while continuing to grow. They need to thrive in the face of constant change and growth. It is not good enough to just survive now. The old software model of, for instance, scheduling new releases of products every quarter, is not acceptable anymore. Customers and business partners expect everything now; immediately! That is a consequence of the Web: 24 x 7, meaning up and running and ready to do business 24 hours a day, 7 days a week. There are no notions of downtime and asking customers to wait. The expectations and the speed and timing of business have changed. Everything we know about software development and maintenance then has to be adjusted to these new expectations.

Speed has changed everything

The speed of doing business, making decisions, responding to customers, fixing bugs, and designing enhancements increases dramatically with a Web system. Everything must now be done in a much faster manner. Decisions must be made quickly: when and how fixes and enhancements are made to the Web sites along with when and how fixes for upgrading the network infrastructure are made. Developers must speed up the release cycle for fixes, bugs, patches, enhancements, and site redesigns.

Even the way in which product brands and advertising are treated or executed is different. Internet companies are willing to scrap their investments in brands and start all over because franchises are being established at a much faster pace [7]. For instance, E*Trade Group Inc.'s strategy is "built around the need to shine in the overcrowded e-broker market. To stand out, the company fashioned itself into a financial portal, complete with stock quotes, financial news, and company releases for free. The core idea? Be the place that empowers the small investor to trade like a pro" [8]. Now it is the Web experience that defines the brand. If the customers/users of the Web site are happy with the service, they like the brand/company and they will continue.

In the third quarter of 1999, $5 billion in venture capital funding was pumped into Internet businesses in the United States, which is double the entire amount for 1998. "The result: multiple brands fighting for dominance. . . . On the Web, brands are born, force-fed to maturity at a terrifying rate" [7].

E-commerce systems can be up and running in 90 days. E-commerce is changing traditional bricks-and-mortar businesses. For instance, the financial market sector is a booming Internet business. As an example, the city of Pittsburgh, Pennsylvania, was the first city in the United States to auction $55 million worth of municipal bonds directly to investors over the Web [8]. It cut out the middlemen and appealed directly to the buyers, thereby eliminating steep underwriting fees, and helped cut the city's cost of issuing bonds by paying a lower yield at the same time, saving the city at least $1 million. There was a feeling of controlling their own destiny. Such e-commerce means investors have access to more offerings, more information, and better pricing than they have ever had. Electronic trading is also significantly changing how traders operate. Pension funds, mutual funds, and insurance companies have much better transaction data along with the reduction in trading fees and improved performance.

Not only has the Internet changed the way we do business, but in itself it generates new business, such as new opportunities for customized products in foreign markets for electronic trading. There will be an "explosion in secondary trading. This will create more liquidity in the market, making it less volatile. Every investment bank must reinvent how they think about their business. . . . Technology is changing the balance of power. There is a shift in the bargaining power from the sell side [dealers] to the buy side [institutional investors]. . . . Institutional investors see electronic systems as a tool to increase productivity and manage more money" [8].

Companies have to adjust further to the level of control that their clients wield. The customer is in control [9]. If they do not enjoy their Web experience, they easily click over to the competitor. Customer expectations have changed. They expect everything now and they expect to have control over everything. Companies are being forced to take a much more responsive approach to the customer. Industry's idea of customer satisfaction has to be adjusted to suit the Internet economy.

A company must be flexible in all aspects: its planning approach, its line of products, and its customer response services. They must keep pace with the customers' whims and fancies, along with technological advances. Creative ways have been found as in [5], for instance:

- Solutia, a chemical company spin-off of Monsanto, has its strategists plan for four different short-term outcomes for each initiative, enabling them to change and act fast when they have to rather than being blind-sided.

- Sun Microsystems's CEO holds weekly "whack-o-meter" sessions to assess ways that rivals might "whack" Sun in the marketplace. This enables Sun to react quickly.

- Accompany, an on-line buying club, has their executives communicate strategy shifts in group e-mails. They only hire people who thrive on ambiguity.

- Bluefly.com, an on-line discount clothing outlet, tunes up its sales budget weekly to synchronize with strategy changes.

- Portera Systems, an e-services firm, does weekly sales analysis and adjusts strategy based on those analyses, resulting in software changes every few weeks (rather than every 18 months).

The message for companies is that every level of the company (its business, process, people, technology) must be prepared to change in an instant. Thus, every executive decision a company makes has ramifications on its Web development and maintenance environment—and vice versa. Web development is also quite different from traditional software programming in that it is a more asynchronous style of programming. I discuss the differences further in Chapter 2.

Companies that embraced the Web created new opportunities

Companies embrace the Web in various ways. Some try "Webifying" or putting a browser front-end on their products and legacy applications.

That is what most bricks-and-mortar companies do in order to get their Internet offerings out there as quickly as possible. They quickly realize, though, that adding a front end is not the ideal situation and they end up redesigning a pure Internet version that will give them the performance and usability needed.

Other companies create from scratch their e-commerce or e-business system. Some fail at releasing their Internet offering and just give up. Those that fail usually find an alternative way of embracing the Web, such as by mergers or partnering. Many companies catch "Web fever" out of necessity or out of excitement. We will end up having all companies being bricks-and-clicks companies at some point in time. Today we still have pure Internet companies that came into existence with the advent of a viable Internet and appropriate technologies.

Pure Internet companies, such as eBay, came into existence apparently very quickly. Some bricks-and-mortar companies, such as Charles Schwab, have rushed to the Internet. Others have lagged behind, such as Merrill Lynch and Wal-Mart, while others, such as Christie's and Levi Strauss, decided not to tackle e-commerce. The laggers had to catch up quickly and the others decided it just did not make a lot of sense to them [10]. They found that selling on the Internet is a complex proposition. There were lots of logistics: Build a distribution center or outsource it; develop a complex Web system for complete inventory and distribution management; have better customer service call centers; and sort out how to deal with returned merchandise.

Some companies decided not to expose all their brands initially due to industrial politics such as union issues. Others realize that the technology is not yet ripe for their particular type of commerce; for instance, getting the right sizes in jeans from Levi Strauss or buying the right engagement ring from Tiffany's.

Partnerships are becoming popular because companies need to attract millions of new customers to prevent any slowdown in their growth [11]. Company evaluations are predicated on fast growth and the ability to financially leverage their large audiences through commerce, advertising fees, and other services. Companies such as Kmart are using retail as a way to get new users to sign up for its new on-line service, BlueLight.com, which is a free Web service. Regardless of how it happens, companies achieve many benefits by making the move to the Web, especially if they are the first mover in their industry.

The typical benefits that any company, especially bricks-and-mortar ones, can achieve by a Web presence are summarized in Table 1.2 [12, 13].

The Web will revolutionize every business. Table 1.3 shows the benefits that car companies such as Ford, GM, and BMW are reaping from the Web [14, 15], and Table 1.4 shows benefits that the banking industry is espousing [16].

In the car industry, I consider a particular Internet offering to be a business miracle. Ford, GM, and DaimlerChrysler have agreed to join forces to create a single automotive parts exchange that runs on the Internet [17]. To me, this is a miracle because I cannot imagine this happening between these fierce competitors at all before the introduction of the Internet. It will be the world's largest Internet company. Economists, looking at such a deal, are now realizing that business-to-business e-commerce will add about one-quarter percentage point to the annual growth of major industrialized countries during the next 10 years. This attests to the power and potential of the Internet.

IBM has already done considerable analysis on the return on investment (ROI) that a Web presence gives them [18]. A Web presence will allow IBM to:

Table 1.2
Typical Benefits of Embracing the Web

Increasing competition and globalization
Growing interactivity
New opportunities
Efficiencies and cost savings
Enhanced market and customer reach
Real-time activity
Match supply to demand on a day-to-day basis
Improved customer service
Cut cost of selling products and offerings
Cut cycle times and improve flexibility in order to cope with radically different demand patterns created by growth of e-commerce
Cut time to market by tying every element of the front and back office together using the Web
Sales force can tap data instantly, helping them to customize and close deals in hours rather than days
Unit sales rise significantly and head count falls by same percentage

- Save \$750 million by letting customers find answers to technical questions on its Web site;

- Handle a portion of internal training over the Internet instead of in classrooms, saving \$120 million;

- Expect \$1 billion in savings in total per year with the Web;

- Save \$240 million on the goods and services it buys;

- Apply the Web to all business operations: logistics, procurement, training, and so on;

Table 1.3
Benefits of a Web Presence for the Car Industry

Suppliers are linked on-line, which allows them to offer far greater possibilities than just improving communications.
Factories can build to order, eliminating billions of dollars in carrying costs.
Dealerships can report warranty problems live from their service shops so plants can correct any assembly-line problems immediately.
Suppliers can control inventories at the main plants, thereby ensuring "shelves" are constantly stocked.
Factories can apply the Web to the entire auto production process.
Billions of dollars in revenue can be generated.
Costs can be reduced.
Site can spin off as a separate Internet company.
Everyone can access all information via an intranet, instead of having to get copies of print, microfiche, and CD-ROM forms.
Employees can better cope with large volumes of diverse and time-critical information.
Management difficulties with decentralized processes are eliminated.
Publication can be delayed until the last possible moment so that a company can incorporate the very latest information.
Market-specific configuration of manuals is possible.
The overall process, from planning to delivery, is bound together seamlessly, providing a better quality product and higher customer satisfaction.
GM can turn its one-time customers into buyers of long-term services (OnStar) with predictable monthly revenue streams.
BMW can provide Internet access in its cars via built-in phones and devices.

Table 1.4
Benefits to the Banking Industry With a Web Presence

Changes financial dynamics of banking industry
Reshapes relationships between bank and customer
Transfers power (as information) into the hands of the customer
Lowers the cost of entry for new banks and increases competition by making product comparison simpler
Allow banks to survive
Allows nonbanks to create their own distribution networks at a tiny fraction of the cost of building branches
Allows more complex products to be sold than over telephone networks
Defines a new role for themselves

‣ Plug in at least 6,700 suppliers to its on-line procurement system;

‣ Provide ubiquitous access to information.

This list of benefits and IBM's ROI along with the issues I discuss in Chapter 2 convince me that the main focus for all companies now must be their Internet presence. *No company should treat its Web site as simply just a list of documents,* though Web sites require serious software development and need to be given the appropriate respect. Also, no company decision should be made without considering the ramifications on Web maintenance. Every improvement made to the Web development environment has ramifications on the business strategies. They are all tightly bound together now. You cannot, nor should you, separate these issues.

We already have enough experience to know that companies that ignored the Web or failed in their Internet offerings are paying a price.

Companies that ignored the Web are paying the price

Companies that have ignored the Internet bandwagon have paid a price for that decision. For instance, "Galvanized into action by a tech-driven stock market and its humiliating lapse in letting the competition jump ahead in the battle for the retail on-line market, Merrill is in the process of remaking itself" [19]. Merrill Lynch is building an electronic replica of its global capital markets businesses, which employ more than 17,000 people and take in more than $6.5 billion in revenue in a year. "Like so many other financial services companies, Merrill is under siege from the Internet" [20]. The rapid growth of electronic trading systems is forcing fundamental, structural changes in the markets. "More than any other company in Corporate America, the brokerage Goliath is feeling the Internet's destructive force. . . . The brokerage industry is absolutely feeling the pain more than any other industry. . . . Traditional companies such as Merrill Lynch are at a disadvantage when a disruptive technology like the Internet blasts through" [20]. Merrill Lynch had to make a key strategic decision about where to expend its resources. No company wants to develop technology that cannibalizes its thriving bricks-and-mortar business, but the forces made it so. Wal-Mart, the world's biggest retailer, is another example [21]. Nimbler rivals beat Wal-Mart in e-commerce. Merrill Lynch and Wal-Mart had to play catch-up.

Some companies even opted out of developing an e-commerce solution. Christie's, the famous auction house, was beaten by Sotheby's and Amazon.com. Companies have been slow to adapt or incapable of adapting to the Internet or of creating an Internet presence. An example is Time Warner, which overcame this deficit by its merger with AOL, which has the Web presence and more than 40 million subscribers [22]. This merger was the biggest ever (until the Vodafone-Mannesmann merger). No doubt, we will continue to see even bigger mergers (which will in turn create more complicated Web development environments that have to function under more pressures).

Traditional brick-and-mortar companies, such as the giant retailers, were surprised by the Internet. "E-commerce evolved much quicker than anticipated . . . sales picked up so fast that traditional retailers were forced to speed up their e-commerce offerings . . . old-line merchants are starting to 'get it' by experimenting with different business models and cleaning up their sites" [23]. E-retailers have struggled with the quality of their Web systems. One of the main issues has been technical problems with their Web sites [24]. New business models also have problems. For instance, on-line book sellers decided to download for free the release of a new Stephen King novel. More than 400,000 copies were sold in the first 24 hours, after recovering from the server crash at Barnes & Noble's site. Amazon.com was getting 1.5 hits per second on the book [25]. Companies have to find better ways of maintaining their Web systems.

We need Web engineering

We need Web engineering. The industry cannot mature by using "cowboys" to "hack" code and content and to do server upgrades without well-defined processes. Well-understood maintenance cycles such as that shown in Figure 1.1 in conjunction with change tracking cycles as in Figure 1.2 must be put into place. We must move beyond the simplistic two-step Web publishing cycle shown in Figure 1.3 of (1) fix the bug and (2) publish it. Tightly integrated tools that allow us to access the metadata across tool repositories and automate workflow across tools are needed.

We need to blend in all the best practices from the software world. After all, Web code and content are software and they need the same respect. People developing and maintaining code and content and databases must be treated like software engineers. Arthur C. Clarke has his definition of an engineer, which as I remember goes something like: "An engineer is someone who can create something for $50 which any fool could create for $100." The sooner the Web industry finds its engineering techniques, the better. And it will achieve its potential. Louis Gerstner Jr., IBM chairman, said in 1999 something to the effect that the true revolution coming from the Web is when the Web can get integrated with your business processes. That can only happen when we have engineering practices and tools comfortably in place.

Considering the business side of the Web with financial analysts from Wall Street, who can affect a company's stock price, it is the maintenance and business operations that matter over the long haul. "In the final

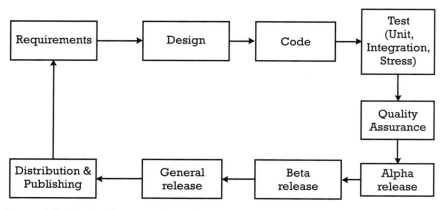

Figure 1.1   Typical best practice software maintenance life cycle.

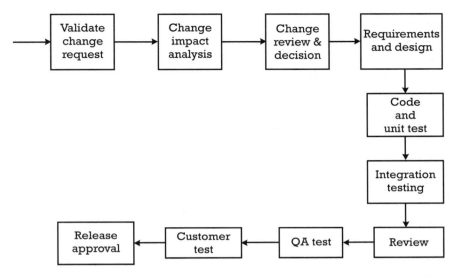

Figure 1.2   Typical change request (i.e., to fix a bug or provide an enhancement) life cycle.

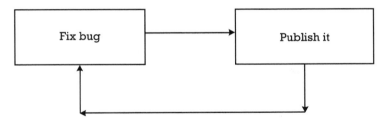

Figure 1.3   Typical, but dangerous, Web maintenance life cycle.

analysis, we can't allow ourselves to be seduced by revolutionary new technologies and Web services absent of solid business models and profit margins. Eventually, all companies will have to justify their stock prices on some multiple of earnings" [26].

Companies are busy now

Companies with Web systems are busy now dealing with basic infrastructure issues: getting enough servers and developers, focusing on network speed and performance, doing server installations and upgrades, providing secure access, analyzing traffic monitoring results, hiring staff, and planning for e-business. At some point, the complexity of Web system maintenance will hit them. The process of maintaining and growing large Web systems is a complex one. But it can be done in a pain-free and cost-effective manner. The case studies in Chapter 6 will give you examples of how it can be done. All of the companies discussed there use CM tools and practices.

From my experience and from watching many Web companies, I have come to the conclusion that the key elements to achieving good Web maintenance are these:

1. Use CM as the core or heart of development and maintenance.

2. Automate as many processes as possible.

3. Integrate all tools as tightly as possible.

4. Define Web development standards to guide developers and content authors.

The rest of this book focuses on CM, the problems it solves, and the value it adds to companies. Because of Web development, the business value of CM is being elevated. CM used to be sold as a reactive technical solution to development and maintenance problems. But now the proactive business value of CM can be seen. For instance, CM helps a company:

▸ *Eliminate mistakes:* Wrong content does not get published on a Web site.

▸ *Recover from site crashes:* Recreate the Web site, or roll back to an earlier version of the site.

▸ *Automate quality:* Ensure workflow is followed via automatic notifications and approvals.

▸ *Optimize teamwork:* Enable teams to function effectively at all times in their safe workspaces where they control code mergers.

▸ *Manage change complexity:* Allow companies to control changes to everything in a manageable way without chaos.

▸ *Adapt to process changes:* The maintenance or release cycle can be changed easily via the GUI or browser based on the current business strategy.

▸ *Enable survival and growth:* Growth rate is a requirement for the Web. Bricks-and-clicks companies will not be competitive without CM. CM is the glue for addressing all Web crisis challenges.

The future and some good advice

Companies are growing larger because of mergers. Pre-Internet, the client–server world gave us many distributed, disjointed development environments and tools. The trend to mergers creating incredibly huge companies will push the industry back into a more centralized, enterprise-wide focus. This will have a profound effect on their software and Web development environments. Companies will make more enterprise-wide tool decisions leaning toward a uniform tool set rather than group-specific ones that encourage a plethora of different tools.

I encourage you to get the best possible CM solution for your company so that you can garner its benefits while avoiding the Web crisis. Do it now. Buy the best tools. Cheap tools sometimes create more headaches than they are worth. Better tools cost more. What price are you willing to put on the success of your Web system?

Do not be afraid to automate processes. Good tools that automate processes and are tightly integrated will take time to deploy. Put your best people on these activities. You cannot afford to have your Web systems fail. Get the best development and maintenance environment possible. This will take time and resources. In the meantime, put top priority focus on your CM solution. Yes, you need your Web tools such as HTML editors and testing tools, but as soon as your CM is in place, the potential for mistakes is immediately reduced and you have a solid foundation for all future development along with maintenance of legacy systems.

You merely have to look to some statistics to realize that the challenges will escalate. Michael Dell, chief executive of Dell Computer Corp., predicts that there will be $4 trillion in annual Internet business transactions and 500 million Internet users by 2003 [27]. Similarly, Vinton G. Cerf, "father" of the Internet, predicts that by 2006, more than 900 million electronic devices will be linked to the Internet, equaling the number of telephones in the world [26]. Behind these transactions and devices, much Web development and maintenance will have to take place.

Be proactive and win!

Companies need to be proactive and include CM as part of their infrastructure. Do not make the typical mistake of being reactive, of ignoring CM until the Web crisis problems hit. The consequences, recovery time, and lost time cannot be removed. Your competitor can use your lost time to overtake you as market leader. Prepare well for the future now because at some point in time, technology, network infrastructure, and security won't be the battle. Technology will become ubiquitous. Content will be the battleground. If you have a solid maintenance support system via use of CM, then your company can easily pass through the battleground without too much collateral damage.

An outline of each chapter

This book is not about the low-level technical details of Web coding (such as how to write efficient Java code) or of CM implementation (such as how to branch and merge five variants). Such answers are readily available from books or a Web tool or CM tool vendor. Most of the how-to technical issues already have answers that can be easily found because CM has been around for about 30 years. My goal with this book is to raise awareness and highlight the key business issues and technical challenges that have not been brought to industry's attention. Those are the issues that get companies into trouble. My goal is to point companies in the right direction by avoiding the common pitfalls, by pointing out the issues that they need to take into account, and by optimizing their efforts to get the best possible CM solution. I see companies making typical mistakes that can be easily avoided.

This book explains how to articulate your Web needs and problems and then define your CM requirements so that you can choose the best CM tool and deploy the best CM solution throughout your organization.

This book does not tell you which is the best CM tool or vendor because there is no such thing. A tool is good when it suits the needs of users, and there are so many different kinds of users and needs in the world that every tool has its value. Also, I do not want to focus on specific tools because it is the CM concepts that are important and timeless. Those concepts are implemented in the tools in different ways. CM tools will evolve, vendors will get acquired and products dissolve, and eventually, the CM industry per se will "die" or, rather, CM will become ubiquitous. By this I mean that eventually IDEs will have embedded CM capabilities along with their software tools. Thus, CM will eventually provide the infrastructure for integration with a full suite of tools (requirements, testing, traffic monitoring, site administration, help desks, software distribution tools, and so on). Eventually, CM will be a fundamental capability in IDEs rather than one you have to add.

This chapter is designed to whet your appetite about the spectrum of issues covered in this book. It is also designed to lay the groundwork as to the importance of e-commerce and e-business to the world and how it has changed the way we used to do business and, hence, why companies must be proactive with their CM solutions. The Internet is not going away. It is only going to get bigger, bolder, and faster. Without CM, companies will struggle.

Chapter 2 focuses directly on the nature of the Web. It explains further why the Internet is no fad. I look at the four phases that companies go through in developing and maintaining their Web systems, along with a detailed description of the nine key challenges that companies face in addressing the Web crisis. Categories of problems or mistakes are presented that indicate a company has hit some kind of Web crisis. I look at what is driving companies to a Web crisis point, along with the complex nature of Web systems themselves. The chapter concludes with how Web programming is different from traditional software programming.

Chapter 3 gives a detailed discussion of what I mean by configuration management, why the world has so many interpretations of CM, why CM is not a "sexy" topic, the business value and benefits of CM, why companies are driven to a CM solution, signs that there are CM problems, and the role it plays in standards such as the Capability Maturity Model Integration and ISO 9000. I focus on the operational areas of CM, including version and configuration control, configuration item structuring, construction of configuration items, change management, teamwork support, process management, auditing, and status reporting.

Chapter 4 focuses on the key aspects related to CM tools and the vendors. It shows the spectrum of users and, hence, the spectrum of products. The two types of tools—evolutionary versus full process—are discussed. It ends by answering commonly asked questions such as which tool is best and what the ROI is for a CM tool.

Chapter 5 presents the key steps involved in selecting a CM tool and deploying a CM solution. It walks you through the important strategic issues that must be addressed, including defining the CM problems, capturing the CM benefits and vision, doing a readiness assessment, developing the requirements list, performing risk management, assigning selection criteria and a rating system, developing a Request for Proposal for a vendor, choosing the tools finalists, doing a proof-of-concept pilot project, making the tool decision, and finalizing the selection process, which, in turn, becomes the start of deployment of your CM solution. It also discusses the importance of the tool selection team and what such a team should look like, and how to develop CM processes.

Chapter 6 contains the fun stuff. It is a collection of eight case studies that show how some well-known brick-and-click and pure Internet companies use CM tools in their maintenance practices. The companies are Carclub.com, eCampus.com, EDS, Lockheed Martin, Lycos, NASD, OneSource, and USinternetworking. The tools they use include eChangeMan, ClearCase, Harvest, PVCS Dimensions, Perforce, PVCS Professional, StarTeam, and Continuus. The chapter also contains the summation of what could be called best practices for Web engineering based on what the companies in the case studies have learned, along with my experiences.

The Appendix presents checklists and templates that a company can use to help it through the key steps involved in CM tool selection and deployment, and planning for its CM solution.

Why I wrote this book

My goals in writing this book are very grandiose indeed. As I said earlier, I want to save the world's companies from encountering the Web crisis. We do not need to suffer its consequences. Let's apply all the lessons learned from traditional software development. We now have developers and content authors who may not have had any experience in traditional software development. They are doomed to repeat all the mistakes and suffer all the failures of the pre-Internet software developers.

I also have many specific reasons for writing the book:

1. The Web, from a business viewpoint, is relatively new and there is a need to articulate all the problems and challenges it presents from a business and technical viewpoint. You can easily find books that tell you the technical side of creating a Web site. At the time

this book was written, there were no books that gave guidance on maintaining large Web systems. My goal is to articulate all the business issues that companies have to face along with showing how technical solutions (such as CM tools) can support them through those challenges.

2. Companies and software vendors keep making the same mistakes: Companies are picking the wrong CM tool, or they pick the right tool and it becomes shelfware. I see weaknesses that can be readily improved. People keep asking me the same questions: "Which tool should we pick?" Or "We chose a tool but it hasn't worked out for us." Vendors ask me: "How can we sell an enterprise-wide CM solution? How can we get developers to accept our process-oriented tool?" I answer the most commonly asked questions.

3. To raise awareness about the crucial need for CM in Web development and maintenance.

4. To make it clear that there are many solutions, by way of CM tools, to address all your Web teams' critical development and maintenance needs.

5. To show you the many benefits and inherent value of CM and how your company and your Web team can tap into those benefits.

6. To stop companies from wasting time and making avoidable mistakes.

7. For those companies who already understand the need for a CM solution, to show them how they can optimally, and in a pain-free manner, pick a CM tool and deploy it. Or, if you have already picked a tool and it has become shelfware, to show you how to get back on track with it and deploy it.

8. To help companies avoid the common CM pitfalls.

9. To present techniques for making maximum use of CM tool vendors. I have worked with many of them and have gleaned many insights.

10. To help advance the state-of-the-art, or maturity level in companies for Web development and maintenance.

The audience for this book

This book has been written to address a wide audience based on the needs I have seen in industry:

- Executive management such as CEOs or managing directors who need to make strategic decisions as to where to expend resources, how to get the most value, and how to avoid the Web crisis;

- Technical managers such as vice presidents of engineering, product marketing managers, and information technology managers who need solutions for improving development and maintenance efforts;

- Project managers such as CM managers, product managers, and quality assurance managers who need to know how to select and deploy a CM solution;

- Developers who want a broader perspective on Web development and maintenance, want to know what is possible perhaps beyond what they currently do, and want ideas on how to "sell" CM to their management;

- CM vendors who want to give their prospects and clients an independent opinion about CM and guidance on how to sell the CM solution internally to their management and project teams;

- Venture capitalists who want to be able to evaluate the engineering practice of start-ups.

Key messages from this chapter

To repeat what I said earlier: No company should treat its Web system as simply a list of documents. Web systems are serious software development and need to be given the appropriate respect; otherwise, the consequences can be disastrous. Also, no company decision should be made without considering the ramifications on Web maintenance. Conversely, every decision made about the Web development environment has ramifications on business strategies. They are all tightly bound together now. There is synergism. You cannot, nor should you, separate these issues.

Companies must now take a more holistic approach in their decision-making.

References

[1] Gilder, G., "The Brightest Star," *Forbes ASAP*, Oct. 4, 1999, pp. 29–34.

[2] Krantz, M., "Nasdaq Tops 5000: Record Ushers in a Brave New World," *USA Today*, Mar. 10, 2000, p. 1B.

[3] Minasi, M., *The Software Conspiracy: Why Software Companies Put Out Faulty Products, How They Can Hurt You, and What You Can Do About It*, New York: McGraw-Hill, 2000.

[4] Dart, S., "Webcrisis.com: Inability To Maintain," *Software Magazine*, Sept. 1999, pp. 50–57.

[5] Stepanek, M., "How Fast Is Net Fast?" *Business Week e.biz*, Nov. 1, 1999.

[6] Kelly, K., *New Rules for the New Economy: 10 Radical Strategies for a Connected World*, Middlesex, England: Penguin Books, 1999.

[7] Morris, K., "The Name's the Thing: Dot.com's Are Spending Like Mad to Establish Identity," *Business Week*, Nov. 15, 1999.

[8] Gutner, T. "How the Internet Is Reshaping the World's Largest Financial Market," *Business Week*, Nov. 15, 1999.

[9] Shapiro, A. L., *The Control Revolution: How the Internet Is Putting Individuals in Charge and Changing the World We Know*, New York: The Century Foundation, 1999.

[10] Quick, R., "Why Some Rebels Are Holding Off Selling On-Line," *The Wall Street Journal*, Dec. 20, 1999, p. B1.

[11] Swisher, K., and N. Wingfield, "Behind the Wedding of Bricks and Clicks: Need To Woo More Customers," *The Wall Street Journal*, Dec. 17, 1999, p. B1.

[12] Price, C., "Business-to-Business Sales Set to Soar," *Financial Times*, Oct. 20, 1999, p. EB1.

[13] Rosenbush, S., "Rewiring Lucent in a Rush," *Business Week e.biz*, Dec. 13, 1999, pp. EB44–50.

[14] Newing, R., "Global Logistics Nightmare Solved With Java Platform," *Financial Times*, Oct. 20, 1999, p. EB2.

[15] White, G., "GM Will Connect Drivers to the WWW," *The Wall Street Journal*, Nov. 3, 1999.

[16] Mackintosh, J., "Customers to Benefit From Internet's Explosive Impact," *Financial Times,* Dec. 1, 1999, p. ITReview-4.

[17] Simison, R. L., F. Warner, and G. L. White, "Big Three Car Makers Plan Net Exchange," *The Wall Street Journal,* Feb. 28, 2000, p. A3.

[18] Sager, I., "Inside IBM: Internet Business Machines," *Business Week e.biz,* Dec. 13, 1999, pp. EB20–40.

[19] Spiro, L. N., "Merrill's Battle," *Business Week,* Nov. 15, 1999.

[20] Gasparino, C., "Merrill Faces a Challenge With Web," *The Wall Street Journal,* Nov. 4, 1999, p. C1.

[21] Zeller, W., "Someday, Lee, This May All Be Yours," *Business Week,* Nov. 15, 1999.

[22] Boston, W., "Bertlesmann Looks To Get Up to Internet Speed: AOL-Time Warner Deal Spurs the German Giant To Shed Conservatism," *The Wall Street Journal,* Feb. 3, 2000, p. A18.

[23] Stoughton, S., "Revenge of the Retail Giants," *Boston Globe,* Mar. 6, 2000, p. C1.

[24] Grant, L., "E-Retailers Need to Debug Shopping," *USA Today,* Mar. 8, 2000, p. 2B.

[25] Sefton, D., "Frightfully Slow Download at 'Bullet' Speed," *USA Today,* Mar. 16, 2000, p. 1D.

[26] Perkins, A. B., and M. C. Perkins, *The Internet Bubble: Inside the Overvalued World of High-Tech Stocks—And What You Need To Know To Avoid the Coming Shakeout,* New York: HarperBusiness, 1999.

[27] Bredemeier, K., "A Close Look at a New Medium," *The Washington Post,* Mar. 14, 2000, p. E2.

Contents

The Nature of the World Wide Web

"Spiders use Webs to attract their prey, to hide from them, and to camouflage themselves...."
—Susan Dart

In Chapter 1 I gave an overview of how the Web is changing the way we do business and, in turn, is demanding a better supporting development and maintenance environment. This chapter drills deeper into the nature of the Web. I explain further why the WWW is here to stay and how market indicators show that we are in a new economy—the Internet economy. Then, by examining how companies react to their Web systems, we can see how they become aware that they are embroiled in a Web crisis. Companies typically go through four phases: excited, stimulated, stunned, and grateful. Companies that get stuck in the stunned phase are making too many mistakes—sure signs of a crisis point. I look at what is driving the Web crisis and, by examining the architecture of Web systems, highlight why Web systems are complex to maintain. After that, the nine key challenges that companies must face in order to avoid the Web crisis, are presented along with how configuration management (CM) is a key part of the solution. The chapter ends by explaining how Web programming is different from traditional software programming resulting in an even more crucial need for CM.

The Internet rules!

The Internet is not a fad. The president of the United States, William J. Clinton, said on television that in 1999 high-tech companies employed 8% of people in the United States yet resulted in 30% of growth in the U.S. economy—a sure sign of the power of technology stocks. And 1999 was an incredibly good year for the U.S. stock markets. Many new millionaires resulted. People go to where the money is, and clearly, right now, it is in the Internet.

Addresses for Web sites now pervade our daily lives. Just look at TV or print advertising these days—the advertisement always lists the product's or business's Web site. No longer do we have to phone a company to find out about its products and services. We simply log on to its Web site and find all the information we need. The placement of advertisements on the Internet is a serious indicator of the power of the Web.

I also look at other indicators around me. For instance, in the United States I look to the East Coast and the West Coast. On the East Coast, I see what the Wall Street stock exchanges are doing with technology stocks. In November 1999, the Nasdaq composite index, which is an indicator of all stock traded on the Nasdaq stock market, hit the 3000 mark for the first time ever. The very interesting part is that the Nasdaq composite, which has been around since 1971, took 27 years to reach 2000, then only 1 year to reach 3000, and less than 6 months to reach 5000 [1]. Since then, investors have been saying that technology is the future of the United States, even with all the market fluctuations.

I also look to the West Coast for indicators, to Hollywood, to see what kinds of movies, television shows, and entertainment sites are being developed. For instance, all the movie studios have their own entertainment portal sites [2] and television stations are developing "sitcoms" (situational comedy series) based on life at Internet start-up companies [3]. I also look at the kinds of relationships people have. For instance, the Internet frenzy is shaping the nature of all kinds of relationships. Many relationships are created over the Web via e-mail and maintained by instant messaging systems. "An epidemic of secrecy pacts is spreading through personal relationships, passed between lovers, friends, relatives, roommates, even business partners" [4]. People involved in any kind of relationship with someone who has any ties to a computer company are being asked to sign nondisclosure agreements (NDAs). NDAs surface at dinner parties, religious sessions, sushi bars, picnics, in marriages, on the psychiatrist's couch, and even on romantic dates. "It's one of the critical items for a date: car keys, credit cards, condoms, and an NDA" [4]. Even Bill Gates required his carpenter to sign an NDA.

In short, the indicators I have mentioned tell me about the strength and viability of the Internet economy. Then, of course, so do all the business values, benefits, potentialities, and statistics offered by the Web, which were discussed in Chapter 1. An Internet Policy Institute, intended to be the leading "think tank" for the Internet, has been started. It gets its funding from major Internet companies (such as America Online and Network Solutions). Also, books have been written saying that the digital economy will escape the boom-and-bust cycles of industrial production [5]. Life looks very rosy for e-commerce and e-business systems, in theory.

The beauty and potential of the Web

As I began to write this book, I started to think about the incredible benefits, beauty, and value of the WWW. In Chapter 1 I discussed how various industries are benefiting from the Web along with some ROI (return on investment) statistics. The benefits show us the role the Internet plays today and also titillates us with its huge potential for the future. I am spending time mentioning the benefits and potentialities because they show that the Internet is here to stay. Hence, companies had better prepare well for it.

Table 2.1 summarizes the possibilities of the WWW. We can communicate globally with any person and with any device in theory. Data can be generated that was not possible before the Internet, such as marketing statistics. People have a venue, on a worldwide scale, for freedom of thought and expression. For instance, during the war in Kosovo, people were able to get world news, which was unavailable to them locally, via the Internet. We can collaborate with anyone around the world now, such as by sharing documents via a Web site. We can experiment with ideas and explore our curiosities. For instance, millionaires are using the

Table 2.1
Potential of the WWW

Communicate globally with any person or device.
Generate data not possible before the Internet.
Foster freedom of thought and expression.
Collaborate with anyone around the world.
Explore our curiosity.
Innovate and create in new ways.
Play games on a global scale.
Change the way we sell and what we sell.
Generate new business and legal models.
Build a virtual world.
Operate at our own convenience.
Improve business practices.
Keep anonymity.
Break business cartels.
Make businesses more cost effective.
Provide new distribution channels and methods.
Make information available at the touch of button.
Switch between competitors very easily.
Achieve personal autonomy.
Act as a solvent to break down old practices.

Internet to find spouses. The Internet allows us to innovate and create in new ways. We can play games on a global scale, such as having the world chess champion play against the entire world (and win)! Going on-line changes the way we sell and what we sell. We can easily generate new business and legal models. People can build a virtual world, such as with pornographic sites. We can operate at our own convenience, picking our own time to do business. Business practices can be improved by automating and integrating facets of business, as with supply-chain systems.

The Internet allows us to keep anonymity if we desire. Business cartels can be broken and new distribution channels and methods can be installed. Any information is available at the touch of a button. We can switch between competitors very easily. The Internet enables personal autonomy, such as getting our own message out to the world. It can act as a solvent, breaking down old practices. "It is conventional wisdom that electronic commerce is an economic solvent. It dissolves old business models and rearranges relationships among buyers, sellers, and anyone in between" [6]. E-commerce will also be a political solvent resulting in the development of new public policies, such as new copyright laws, tax laws, and litigation issues such as recognizing electronic signatures as equal to pen-and-paper signatures. I think it is clear by now that the Internet will essentially be ubiquitous and become a part of our everyday lives.

The Internet erases time and distance. Any barriers to entry are virtually nonexistent. For instance, small and developing countries are finding they can "play ball with the big guys." The initial capital investment required to set up a Web site is tiny. Smaller countries get on the same playing field as larger ones by "leapfrogging" to developed markets.

It truly is the dawn of a new era in human potential. I am convinced that the Internet will be a part of our everyday lives, from our business office to our home, while in transit, and to our hobby and entertainment arenas. Everyone will be attracted to it for one reason or other. The implication of all that has been said thus far is that there will be lots of Web systems suited to every kind of device or personal computer. This means that just about any kind of Web development then becomes mission critical since it must support our real-time needs. Hence, the Web companies had better get the right development and maintenance environment together with the right supports. Web development needs to be taken very seriously. Everything good that we have learned about software engineering must be applied to Web development and maintenance. Given how fast everything is moving, companies need to proactively prepare for this pace and prepare to avoid a Web crisis.

We need to make sure we know how to efficiently create and maintain our e-business (business-to-business) and e-commerce (business-to-user) applications. Companies face few difficulties when creating simple Web sites. Many tools, such as Microsoft's FrontPage or MacroMedia's DreamWeaver, have been designed for consumers or businesses to easily create Web pages. There are also toolkits for creating intensive e-commerce or e-business systems.

E-commerce vendors are offering complete suites of products centered around an application server. For instance, Bluestone Software offers their Sapphire/Web application server plus a suite containing pre-built components for constructing e-commerce storefronts. Components include catalog management, user registration, shopping cart, search engine, credit card processing, taxation, order checking and shipping, personalization engine for tailoring content, and an XML-based integration server that links data sources with partners. A fully functioning e-commerce system can be created in 90 days.

A company can simply outsource its Web system's development to a third party. Many good books are available to help people develop Web sites [7–13], sort out their Web strategies [14–18], understand the kind of change the Internet economy brings [19], learn about Internet psychology [20], and find advice on Web engineering [21–24], which is still an undeveloped field. But guidance is lacking on the "right" kind of Web engineering and team management practices for maintaining the Web and even on how to initially create a Web system that is amenable to maintenance. Web teams are learning the hard way—by making mistakes and feeling the resultant pain from that.

The phases of Web acceptance

Companies typically expend a lot of time, money, and resources to get their initial Web system up and running. Note that I am using the term "Web system" as the generic phrase for an e-business or e-commerce system and to capture all the aspects of a Web site: its content (the stuff that is visible when browsing the site), the Web applications (the code and the back-office applications such as the database access systems), and the Web infrastructure (such as the servers, the protocols, the languages, and the tools used). Actually, the computer industry does not have standard terms for Web "stuff" yet. When talking about Web systems, one never really knows what the other means by the term *content*. Does it include data and code that are generated dynamically in response to a user's request?

This terminology is actually an important issue because, as you will see in the case studies of Chapter 6, most companies end up defining their own terminology in the sense that boundaries are defined on their Web development and then the appropriate tools and processes (or workflow or life cycles) are put in place. For instance, many companies say, "Let's define Web content as the static HTML text for a Web site. Then we can let the marketing team make changes to content as frequently as possible." But the boundary is set at Web code, such as JavaScript. Any changes to Java code can only be done by the software teams and only after the appropriate change request has been submitted.

Hence, terminology and its definition can determine how companies set up their structural organization and roles and responsibilities.

Let's go back to the phases of Web acceptance. Once a company gets its Web systems up and running, I typically see it go through various phases as the system goes into maintenance. There are four phases:

Phase 1: Excited;
Phase 2: Stimulated;
Phase 3: Stunned;
Phase 4: Grateful.

(Forgive me for anthropomorphizing companies, but it enables me to present a snapshot of the well-being of a company at certain points in time.) The first phase, *excited,* sees companies enthusiastic and thrilled about the prospect of the new Web system and doing business over the Internet. When the new site is published, everyone runs to view the site and play with all of its features.

The second phase, *stimulated,* begins when the company starts to see the results of its customers using the site. The company tracks the usability of the site, its performance, the traffic patterns, and the success rate of the transactions. The findings stimulate new ideas about how the e-commerce or e-business could be improved, generate new product suggestions, weigh user interface and performance improvements, and accumulate new data (such as traffic statistics) that did not exist before the Web site did. The attitude is one of "That's a great idea. How can we do more?"

A company is in phase 3, *stunned,* when it has an uncomfortable feeling of being overwhelmed. A kind of paralysis sets in on the company for a short period of time followed by frenetic activity. It has become so overwhelmed by the downtime of the Web system and/or the volume, frequency, and speed of change to its Web system, that business within the company comes to a halt for a short period of time because everyone has to digest this feeling and put plans and actions in place to counter it. Then they panic and start their chaotic maintenance activities again. Essentially, they have hit a Web crisis point [25, 26], as discussed below.

Phase 4, *grateful,* begins when a company starts to feel that it has control over changes to its Web system. It has recovered from its paralysis. Now it can track the changes, make better and faster decisions about the kinds and timing of changes, and plan its site redesigns. Yes, Web sites *must* be redesigned within a particular time frame, such as every quarter, for various reasons described below in the Web crisis drivers section. The way to get out of phase 3 and move into phase 4 is by implementing a good configuration management solution, which will be discussed further in Chapters 3 and 4. Otherwise, companies remain stuck in the stunned phase and live in a constant "firefighting" mode. They expend all their energy surviving the Web system, rather than thriving with it.

Initial focus for companies concerning their Web systems

The initial reaction of companies that reach the stunned phase is to focus on infrastructure. That is, they look at ways of improving the network performance by adding more reliable servers. They tighten their security features, and invest heavily in traffic monitoring tools and improving customer service. These are, of course, very worthwhile and required. But most companies ignore the management or control of the software side of their Web systems: the content, applications, tools, databases, and all the versions and permutations of those. As a result, they have a significant gap in their arsenal of support tools and techniques. This, in turn, leads to many mistakes that will cost them dearly and could have been avoided in the first place. Then, combine this with the need to redesign systems and retool systems, and the complexity adds up.

Companies have found that Web site redesign and multisite integration are very important factors to improving the customer Web experience. For instance, Autobytel redesigned its site because it had outgrown its space, similar to what happens in a department store. There has to be constant growth and evolution to meet the demands of the customer. Other companies such as e-GM, which has at least 150 consumer sites around the world that were initially created without common navigation, are integrating those sites and making them easier to work with. A natural part of Web site evolution is the requirement for faster sites and more personalized sites.

To create a Web site, many bricks-and-clicks companies merely stuck on a Web front-end. Once the Web system was up and running, it didn't take long to realize that the system had to not only be redesigned, but also retooled as new technology appeared.

Consider the overhaul of schwab.com's Web system [27]. As the leading Web broker in 1999, Charles Schwab decided it had to redo its systems architecture. Originally, it quickly built its on-line trading business and aggressively added capacity to meet the demand for e-trading, which involves more than 3 million active user accounts. Its original system was never designed for the transaction loads, account growth, and rapid application development required of the market leader. Also, its subsequent acquisitions and partnerships required more flexible systems that could easily exchange data internally and over the Web. Client–server systems and mainframes do not work in an environment where lots of partners are using the Internet to communicate. Pure Internet companies like competitor E*TRADE have the advantage in this area since their Web systems were built from scratch as Web trading systems rather than as a result of turning non-Internet trading systems into Internet trading systems. Schwab is now migrating away from mainframe-based COBOL applications to Java ones.

All of these factors—Web site mistakes and the natural evolution of Web systems—make for a nonstop maintenance effort in a world that is constantly changing. Companies must maintain their live systems in parallel with their redesign and retooling efforts.

Mistakes are made too easily and are very costly

Many Web mistakes have been made, and Table 2.2 categorizes the typical mistakes that are made regarding Web content. Content gets published that is inappropriate for that site, is published at the wrong time, is inaccurate, is confidential and should not have been published, has become corrupted or is stale (out of date), has not been authorized to be published, has not been tested before being published, or is inconsistent with existing content. For instance, large companies often have inconsistent content because each group (for instance, marketing, human resources, accounting, software teams) publishes its version without any centralized coordination or synchronization of the content.

Table 2.2
Typical, Avoidable Web Mistakes

Inappropriate	Wrong timing
Inaccurate	Confidential
Corrupt	Stale
Unauthorized	Untested
Inconsistent	Wrong version

Until companies have the appropriate controls and techniques in place, we will continue to see more of the types of mistakes listed in Table 2.2. While the beauty of the Web is that information is available immediately, in real time, it also means that mistakes are visible immediately and on display to the world. A company cannot afford to have its mistakes visible to the world. For instance, in 1999, eBay experienced several outages of its Web site [28] that cost it at least $5 million, a drop of nearly 30 points of its stock price in one day, and a bad public image concerning reliability. The public reason given for the outage was server upgrade problems. Such problems indicate to me a configuration management problem—the wrong version of code or content installed on the wrong version of server.

Apart from eBay, we have seen other examples of mistakes or weaknesses on Web sites that have tarnished companies' reputations. Check-Free, an on-line bill and payment service affecting customers of at least 21 banks, found its high-volume transaction processing software had a bug. This caused a blockage in service when volume peaked [29]. Encyclopedia Britannica's Web site was down for several weeks after it went live because it couldn't handle the volume of users. Merrill Lynch went live with its e-commerce knowing that all the features could not be implemented, thereby costing it the leadership in the full-brokerage service marketplace. It was too slow [30] in getting its system up and running. Its competitor, Charles Schwab, became the market leader. As a result of moving quickly, schwab.com saw its stock price go up more than 700% over 3 years [31]. Then again, schwab.com had outages as well.

The NorthernLight.com search engine site went down. While originally thought to be a systems upgrade problem, it was found that a worker had accidentally drilled a hole in the electrical conduit [32]. So, while not really a software problem, NorthernLight thought it was. It took the company a while to track down the cause. But the company paid a big price: It experienced a 4-hour outage plus bad timing since its competitor (AltaVista) was making announcements about new products. NorthernLight had to work on regaining its reliable reputation.

SAP, Europe's biggest software maker, garnered a bad name and embarrassment because of installation glitches at some large customers' sites [33]. SAP released its Internet version of SAP, mySAP.com, but the late start has been costly [34].

Election results from the East Coast in the United States were published on the official Web site before the polling booths for the West

Coast were closed. This is illegal because results cannot be made public until all polling booths around the United States are closed, which is done to avoid affecting the voting pattern on the West Coast. The Internal Revenue Service in the United States posted a policy on its Web site without doing a spelling or semantic check on the content, thereby creating the wrong impression. Yahoo!, the biggest search engine portal, lost the trust of more than 4 million of its subscribers because it changed a policy about user content once it merged with GeoCities [35]. Raytheon filed a lawsuit against 21 of its employees for posting confidential information on a Web site [36].

Of course, not many mistakes are publicized by the news media, but outages of the "big players" are typically tracked. Companies obviously do not like their mistakes being publicized, especially in the Internet economy where stock price can drop or rise based on the quality or reliability of a Web site.

Most of the mistakes are avoidable because, if the right checks and balances are in place—that is, if the right testing and review processes are followed—then these mistakes would not happen. For instance, inappropriate content (such as bikini-clad women on a Web site for Arabic businesses) or inaccurate content (such as spelling of a product name) would not be published if reviews and authorizations were done. Confidential content would not have been published if a high-level manager had to sign off and validate content before publishing. Corrupt content would not exist on the site if the appropriate regression testing had been run when new content was added. Untested content would not go live if the right tests had been run on it. Content would not get stale if the company could track the versions of the content and set some kind of expiration date. Inconsistent content (such as the Web site content for the London office of a company not matching the content on the German site or the Spanish site) could be avoided if global consistency checking procedures with sign-offs were in place. The wrong version of content being published could be avoided if a valid configuration of content pieces is identified and only valid configurations are published.

Now, to many Web teams it is clear how the problems can be avoided, but, because of the pressures and urgency of Web changes, there seems to be no time to follow good maintenance procedures. That would be true if automation were not available to us. But with CM automation, the cycles are enforced to the degree required and in the time frame needed. Notifications are automatic and quick. People know what they need to do, when, and how.

Some managers and developers worry that CM will slow down the fix cycle dramatically. If the CM solution is well automated with minimal manual steps, then this concern has no basis. What typically happens, though, is that a company gets out of synchronization with its teams. The teams disconnect. For instance, the developers go about their coding without doing CM, and when they are done, they throw the code to the CM team saying, "Here it is." Many companies end up doing CM backwards. They do the CM after the development or changes have been made. This is not an efficient approach and is prone to mistakes.

As I will discuss in the next chapter, different kinds of configuration management tools with different degrees of automation are available that suit the various needs of companies.

The Web crisis

"For the most part, Web crashes are the result of human error, flawed predictions, and the frantic pace of trying to keep up with on-line competitors" [37]. The mistakes are indicative that a company may have reached a Web crisis point. The Web crisis [38] is the proliferation of quickly "hacked together" Web systems that are kept running via a continual stream of patches developed without any rigorous or systematic approach. In short, it is doing Web maintenance in an insane, uncontrolled manner without following, and automating, all the good software engineering practices that we learned from the software crisis [39].

The software crisis highlighted that software companies were generally incapable of delivering quality code on time and within budget. Internet companies can easily fall into the same kind of crisis because they face the same issues that traditional software companies faced. Along with the software issues, Web development teams also face more dynamic factors, including:

- Responsiveness to the "Web experience";
- Real-time expectations;
- Modus operandi of continual change;
- Speed of change;
- Limitations of performance and scalability.

Companies doing Web maintenance have to be very responsive to the users of their Web site. The "Web experience"—using the Web site—must be a pleasant experience for clients. If not, the competition is just a click away. The user is in control, or rather, is in the driver's seat regarding how the Web site should operate. If the user is not happy, the Web site has to be improved. Users also now have much more stringent expectations on the company. If they do not like what they see on your Web site, then they expect you to change it—and change it immediately. Customers expect everything to be done in real time, meaning immediately. If it's visible on your site, they expect you to be able to fix it immediately.

Being open to the world, the Web site is open to many suggestions for changes: Change requests can come from all the users, from the need to redesign the site for good reasons (such as you want users coming back so you change the site) or bad reasons (site has reached its limits of scalability—how do you add more pages and where do you put the hyperlinks?), from making mistakes and having to correct them (such as replace the copyright sign on every page), from corporate mergers that require product/site mergers, from the need to grow at a fast pace (such as adding more sites where each site represents a new product), and from the need to maintain multiple sites in parallel and propagate the right changes to the right site. Web teams have to work in a state of constant change. There is no notion of downtime—the Web site is operational 24 hours a day, 7 days a week.

Web teams have to respond to performance bottlenecks on the site. For instance, at the Olympics, user response time was not acceptable. The site took four clicks (dynamic page traversals) before the user found the information they wanted. This sounds OK, but when a million users at one time all over the world want access, 4 million dynamic pages must be generated. So IBM redesigned the site to bring it down to two-page traversals [40].

Changes also result from scalability problems. For instance, most newspapers [41] face the challenge of dramatically increasing the size of their Web sites. Consider that they add a full newspaper each day of the year to their sites. That could amount to thousands of pages per day. They have to decide how to structure the site in the face of such rapid expansion along with structuring the hyperlinks—how deep can the links go and across what pages can they traverse? Newspapers can very easily reach a point where it is impossible to know how to add the next day's paper to the site.

What is driving the Web crisis?

The crisis is being driven by many factors. These drivers are determining the type of Web development and maintenance environment and practices that companies are putting in place. The working atmosphere around Web systems becomes frenetic, chaotic, and very pressurized. There is an overwhelming sense of urgency. Developers have to live with pagers permanently attached to their bodies (well, almost). Understanding the nature of the drivers can help companies focus better and provide more supportive environments for developers and managers.

I classify the drivers into seven categories:

1. Competition drivers;

2. Success drivers;

3. Pain drivers;

4. Process drivers;

5. Skill set drivers;

6. Technology drivers;

7. Societal drivers.

Competition drivers come from the desire to keep up with or surpass the competition. I've talked enough about how companies have fallen behind or missed their "window of opportunity" for an Internet offering. Their competitor got there first. Now they have to catch up somehow. Competition arises simply from the explosive growth of the Internet and the urgency each company faces in order to present its applications and products on the Web. The Internet "gold rush" is attractive because everyone wants to become a millionaire overnight by means of an outrageous IPO (initial public offering) of an Internet company. Also, the need for a company to thrive is crucial. As I said earlier, bricks-and-clicks companies cannot just be content to survive; they must thrive. That is, they must have a certain level of growth because that affects their stock evaluation. A lot of that growth has to do with the coming of the device commerce that Web systems have to support. I discuss device commerce, i.e., Internet devices, later in this chapter.

Success drivers refer to the problem of being successful too quickly due to incredibly fast growth. Too many customers too soon can overload a company. On top of that, coping with technology changes creates new pressures for Web teams. In Chapter 3, I give an example how, over 4 years, a company that gets too successful too soon experiences problems.

Pain drivers concern mistakes or limitations companies must face. For instance, companies cannot meet deadlines; they cannot release multiple fixes or enhancements simultaneously; they do not know what went into a release or Web site or whether there are missing features or wrong versions of features or content in their products or on their Web sites (developers fix the same bug and overwrite each other's fix, and no one knows what has been tested on the Web site or what was distributed to the customer); companies cannot quantify the quality of their released products or their Web sites (for instance, has 80% of the code or content been tested?); managers have no visibility into the status of work (for instance, who is working on what change; why, how, and when will they be finished?); and companies cannot recover quickly from Web site crashes since they cannot easily recreate the site or roll back to a previous version. All of these issues are painful to companies.

Process drivers relate to getting the workflow right to suit particular needs. For instance, companies must be certified ISO 9000 compliant in order to get certain contracts. Similarly, most U.S. government contractors must be assessed at Capability Maturity Model Integration level 3. Most industries have some kind of audits that they must pass, requiring certain practices along with documentation. Some smart companies want to know what exactly is the best practice for Web development and maintenance. It is not evident to them yet. In the same vein, companies want to know which tools they should deploy.

Skill set drivers concern finding the right people to do the work. There is a significant lack of skilled developers for Web systems. Web programming is different from software development in various respects (as described later in this chapter), so it is not easy to convert experienced developers over to Web development. The new programmers have no software experience at all. They come from various disciplines and got into Web programming, perhaps because they found an HTML editor that they could easily use. Take the shortage of seasoned Web developers and couple that with the fast growth rate of Web systems and the urgency, and companies are justifiably worried about getting their work done.

Technology drivers concern the fast pace of change of technology. We have to deal with "moving targets": changing tools, languages, and browsers as well as dynamic content. The natural evolution of Web sites demands retooling in order to use more efficient languages and tools to meet the performance and functionality demands users require.

Societal drivers are not that visible yet, but will soon be. For instance, because of the Internet, there are many more millionaires in the United States today. And these people want to do something of value to society with their money. Several have set up university and educational systems via the Internet. Michael Saylor, founder of MicroStrategy, is using $100 million to found a free on-line university [42] for making certain kinds of education available that were previously unattainable to people, perhaps because of cost. In February 2000, in the United States, a Governors' Conference was held. The governors control all the policy and budgeting issues for all the states in the United States. At that conference, various chief executive officers spoke to the governors explaining how the government and entire education system could be revamped using the Internet. Thomas Friedman also expressed to the governors that the "government must become as efficient as AOL" through use of the Internet. Governments are starting to develop Web systems to support their communities.

All of these drivers combine to create great pressures on companies to maintain and evolve their Web systems.

Web systems can be very complex

For companies with simple Web systems, I see few problems. A typical scenario is that they have a small intranet site (an internal network) for employees to use for collaboration and presentation of the latest version of documents for corporate procedures and standards. They typically have a Webmaster who publishes any necessary updates to the Intranet site. This person is also responsible for the public Web site, which actually contains a subset of the content on the intranet site since some of the information is confidential. Webmasters typically set up a daemon program that runs, say, every 15 minutes and will automatically publish the content updates. Anyone in the company can publish to the intranet, but the Webmaster acts as the gatekeeper for publishing to the external Internet site. This approach works well for simple Web systems.

But for complex Web systems that could be large intranets and that contain high-profile e-commerce and/or e-business, there are tremendous complexities—complexities that arise because of the nature of the

Web system, the volume and frequency of change requests, the mission criticality of the Web sites, and the high volume of user traffic. For instance, stock trading systems such as Nasdaq [43] or Schwab's site, or ticket reservation systems, or auction sites like eBay all transact millions of dollars in hours with millions of user hits in minutes. On a heavy business day, Nasdaq can get 20 million hits. Content must be completely accurate every second, and it can change within seconds. Boeing [44] has more than 1 million pages hosted by more than 2,300 intranet sites on more than 1,000 servers.

Figure 2.1 gives a simplified picture of how complex Web systems can be. A Web system can be composed of, or interact with, all the resources shown in Figure 2.1. Let us walk through this figure. Consider the human users. They interact with the Web system through their PCs (personal computers) using a browser. Each user has his or her own version

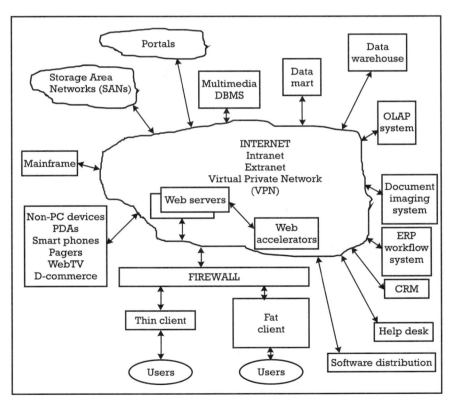

Figure 2.1   A complex Web system. (After [26].)

of a specific browser (maybe Microsoft Explorer or Netscape Navigator as two examples). Each user has either a thin client (application code resident on server) or a fat client (application code resident on their PC). All user requests (human or device) go through some kind of firewall that monitors security and sets access rights. The requests are executed by the Web servers, of which there could be many. (Nasdaq uses eight servers for every database server [45].) For very high-speed Web sites, accelerators or dynamic caching mechanisms [40] are added to Web servers. Dynamic caches store the most frequently accessed pages. This is a tremendous performance advantage when you consider that a high-performance site, such as for the Olympics [40], instead of having to generate 4 million pages each minute, only has to generate 2 million.

The Web sites being accessed could be in different kinds of networks. It could be an intranet. It could be an extranet, which is just like an intranet but is intended for a company's suppliers so that they can collaborate and have access to the latest version of data (such as an inventory) for their e-business. Or the network type could be a VPN (virtual private network), which acts like an intranet but uses public leased lines with secure encryption facilities. It is handy for a company's remote offices to use without the company having to make a full investment in a network infrastructure.

The Web system can incorporate, or access, typical business applications such as ERP (enterprise resource planning) systems for workflow/process enforcement; document imaging systems for controlling documents or forms libraries; OLAP (on-line analytical processing) systems for performing multidimensional analyses on databases; CRM (customer relationship management) systems that enable companies to track their clients, such as with a sales representative tracking all sales and prospects in his or her region; help desk systems that the company uses to respond to customer requests such as bug fixes; software distribution systems that the company uses to track and distribute versions of its products to its customers; and, of course, any legacy applications that exist on the mainframes.

The Web system can also incorporate, or access, storage and database systems such as data warehouses, data marts, multimedia database management systems, and SANs (storage area networks). A data warehouse is a virtual database where, in reality, many different databases are made accessible via a common interface. Data marts are warehouses that provide business-specific interpretations of the data. SANs are networks of databases offering terabytes of data. They provide a virtual data store with multiple servers built around redundant, high-volume storage devices. They enable multiple organizations to share data.

All Web systems will eventually connect into some kind of portal. A portal is a full-service hub. Portals range from typical commercial portals to business-specific portals. Commercial portals such as Yahoo! or AOL provide mail services, access to on-line communities, customized news, search engines, and directories. Business portals, or on-line exchanges, are communities of companies in the same profession that use the Internet to transact business and "cut out the middleman" by going direct. This is happening in many businesses from the steel business, to farming, to fishing [45]. Such portals allow businesses to exchange purchase orders, request quotes, and generally resolve any over- or undersupply issues very quickly.

Also part of a Web system is what I call *D-commerce*, or *device commerce*. By this I mean all the non-PC devices—smart devices that make up our everyday lives and can connect to the Internet. These are mobile phone, pagers, WebTV, and PDAs (personal digital assistants) such as 3Com's Palm Pilot VII or HandSpring's Visor. They also include devices such as on-line vending machines and grocery trackers. For instance, Coca-Cola has vending machines that can be monitored from a central location via the Internet. As the ambient temperature of the vending machine changes, Coca-Cola can adjust the price of the drink—higher in hot weather since demand will be high, lower in cold weather since demand will be low. Internet-connected devices allow companies to have dynamic pricing models, something that couldn't be done before the Internet. General Store International, an on-line grocer, gives its customers a black box that sits on their kitchen counters and keeps track of food staples running low [46]. When you run out of milk, for instance, you scan its code across the black box, which sends a message to the supermarket that you need some milk and then automatically places the order and has it delivered.

Wal-Mart is looking at non-PC devices for its in-store customers that will be linked to the Internet. This availability is aimed at customers who have not shopped on-line before. Wal-Mart may give the device away free to its customers, which will attract them to the Internet sites [47].

All of these devices have different kinds of browsers—microbrowsers in a sense, since they cannot display all the content from a Web site that a PC browser could. New companies have sprung up (such as Spyglass) whose sole business is developing these device browsers and utilities for automatically converting between browsers. Japan has miniaturized its Web sites (i-mode sites) so that Web content is accessible via cellular phones [48].

A Web system must cater to all forms, types, and versions of browsers in the marketplace. That is, many variants (parallel or concurrent versions) of a Web system have to be created simultaneously to support the WWW. It is one thing to create all of these variants; it is unimaginable as to how to maintain all of these variants with respect to their changes. Any piece can change—the browser, servers, any box in Figure 2.1, the protocols, the middleware, and the tools and languages used to create them. At the same time, new development (enhancements, content redesign, retooling) must go on too. The management and processes required to achieve safe, error-free maintenance are beyond manual comprehension and control for large Web systems. That is why configuration management practices and their automation are required. Chapter 3 presents CM in further detail. Now that we know about the kinds of resources that can go into a Web system, let us examine the internal architecture of a Web system in more detail.

Web system architecture and terminology

Trying to talk about the boundaries of a Web system is like trying to catch a cloud. It is nebulous and almost intangible. In fact, the computer industry really has no standard terms or architectural concepts to delineate a Web system. If we look at a spider's web, for instance, in theory there is no boundary to it. The spider can make the web any size or shape, just as Internet Web developers could also do.

Generally speaking, a Web system consists of fundamental pieces, as shown in Figure 2.2:

1. *Content:* Content consists of the data we see via the browser on the client machine along with the code behind the scenes that executes the user's request.

2. *Application server:* This server executes actions on the content.

3. *Web server:* This is the transaction server, the middleware, and the link into the Internet. Common ones are Apache, IIS (Internet Information Server), and Enterprise Server.

4. *Database server:* This includes the database and its applications.

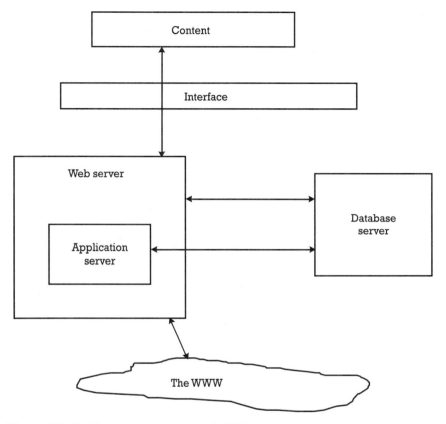

Figure 2.2 Architectural components of a Web system.

5. *Interface:* The browser or the API (application program interface) makes up the interface.

Low-level details about how to create a Web system can be found elsewhere [22]. The important thing for this book is to know that many pieces make up a Web system and different teams typically work on different pieces. That is the essence of the maintenance problem—trying to create all the right versions of pieces that work together and then trying to update them in synchrony and publish them simultaneously, in parallel to all the Web sites. Again, CM is the means to enable this.

As the Internet industry matures and we gain experience from developing and maintaining Web systems, we will begin to see patterns form, and hence types of Web systems. Once we understand the types of Web systems, we can then assign the right tools, processes, and engineering techniques for developing and maintaining them. It will take another decade before we see clear patterns that will result in better Web engineering techniques and best practices. Right now, though, I do see the beginnings of those patterns for Web systems [26]. Those patterns are summarized in Table 2.3.

1. *Informational:* Information sites with read-only usage, commonly called *brochureware;* for instance, content that gives details about a company and its products. First-generation Web systems were of this type.

Table 2.3
Types of Web Systems

Type of Web Application	Description
Informational	Brochureware sites that just present information
Delivery system	Download content (e.g., plug-ins)
Customized access	Access to selected services via a customized interface
User-provided content	User provides content, such as by filling in a form to register for a seminar
Interactive	Two-way interaction between sites, users, and resources such as a company and its suppliers
File sharing	Remote users collaborate on common files such as schedules
Transaction oriented	User buys something such as travel tickets or does on-line trading
Application service provider	User rents an application such as a virus program or disk backup facility
Database access	User requests access to database information such as looking up a catalog of parts
Document access	Access to on-line documents, such as corporate standards
Workflow oriented	Access is based on a process or workflow such as order entry automation
Automatic content generator	Automatic content generator by robots or agents that scour the Web for information, such as the best price on a car

Source: From [26].

2. *Delivery system:* The site can download content to users or a resource; for example, download upgrades or plug-ins.

3. *Customized access:* Access is via a customized interface or based on user preferences; for example, my customized view of my Internet service provider's home page or my favorite portal.

4. *User-provided content:* The user provides content by filling in a form on the site; for instance, a subscription to a magazine or registering for a company's seminar.

5. *Interactive:* Two-way interaction between sites, users, and resources as in business-to-business exchanges.

6. *File sharing:* Remote users collaborate via common files stored on the site; for example, a team that coordinates on-line schedules or reviews documents.

7. *Transaction oriented:* The user buys something such as books or airline tickets.

8. *Application service provider:* The site represents rentable applications; the user rents an application on a per user, per month, or per transaction basis, such as a virus scan program or a testing suite.

9. *Database access:* The site uses databases that the user can query, directly or indirectly; for example, a supplier looks up a catalog of parts.

10. *Document access:* The site provides access to libraries of on-line documents, such as the set of current corporate standards.

11. *Workflow oriented:* The site ensures that the process or workflow is followed, as in supply-chain management or order entry automation.

12. *Automatic content generator:* Robots or software agents automatically generate content. For example, "bots" scour the WWW to bring back specific information, such as a best price on products.

As Web sites evolve beyond the first-generation brochureware types, they end up being combinations of some or all of the classes listed.

Nine key Web crisis challenges

Figures 2.1 and 2.2 show why Web systems can be complex. When I look at the bigger picture and examine the business and corporate environment in which teams develop the Web systems, I come to the conclusion that there are nine challenges facing companies doing Web development and maintenance. Those challenges are listed and described below in detail:

1. Speed of change;

2. Variant explosion;

3. Dynamic content;

4. Process support;

5. Performance effect;

6. Scalability;

7. Outsourcing;

8. Politics;

9. Immaturity.

Speed of change challenge

As I mentioned earlier, the speed of everything changes with a company's entry onto the WWW—business planning, decision-making, execution of plans, response to change—all because expectations have changed. Also, the means to do things faster now exist. Bill Gates's phrase "change at the speed of thought" is very apt.

Once Web systems go into maintenance mode, large systems typically experience a dramatic increase in the volume and frequency of change requests (fixes, enhancements, customer specials, emergency patches) compared to traditional software applications. For companies with multiple e-commerce systems, changes occur to the common code as well as the site-specific code. Changes need to be published to a live site. There is no notion of any downtime that a company can use to install a new release of its Web system.

Most companies (other than pure Internet companies that only came into existence when the Internet economy took off) have legacy systems that they need to maintain in parallel with the Web system. For instance, the Web system could simply be a "Webification" (add a browser inter-face) of the legacy application, or it could be a complete redesign of the legacy application, or it could be a partial one. I have found that the vol-ume and frequency of change on the Web system drive the volume and frequency of changes to the legacy systems. This is because companies like to keep updates to their Web systems and legacy systems synchro-nized. You see, these systems typically share code, and it is much easier to keep all the pieces synchronized and at the same version. When you have a system made up of thousands of pieces and a significant percentage of those pieces are shared, it is wise to upgrade pieces in parallel.

Changes to a Web system are driven by:

- Bugs (show stopper, high-, medium-, or low-priority ones);
- Enhancements and upgrades to shared code/data/libraries;
- Site redesign (either the content and/or the site layout templates);
- Site merges, such as when companies are acquired;
- Product expansion, when new sites are added;
- Rollback of sites in case of a crash;
- Performance or scalability problems;
- Business strategy shifts in response to competition;
- New technology or retooling (servers, security, dynamic content, languages, tools);
- Globalization: multilanguage requirements.

In Chapter 3, I present a typical scenario of a start-up company over 4 years of its life and show how the change complexity easily and quickly builds such that it overwhelms even a very successful company. In fact, success typically breeds more change complexity because there are more variants of products. Much of the maintenance work then evolves around knowing how to propagate the right version of the right fix to the right version of the variant, and when.

The mindset in fixing a Web bug is typically this: "I see a problem and can, or need to, fix it immediately because it is globally visible." Many companies feel that because of this urgency to make a fix, they cannot follow any good software engineering principles such as recording the change request, doing impact analysis, using a review team (such as a change control board, which is discussed in the next chapter), authorizing change, and testing. Because the change can be done so easily, process is often bypassed. This means that the company loses track completely of its changes. *It has then lost most of the business value in doing the changes.* For instance, management cannot glean any crucial corporate information such as how many changes were made last month, why, by whom, how long did it take, what percentage of changes failed and why? This information is crucial to companies in their planning and estimating of release dates for upgrades.

Repeatability will be a difficult benefit to achieve. Rollback of a site may be the only option for companies. The company is just reacting. It is not being proactive, nor is it taking advantage of or learning about the work it does. *An opportunity to capture corporate knowledge as it goes about doing its business is wasted.* Such knowledge would help the company do its business more easily, optimize the way it does business, and hence grow—which is what the Internet economy is all about. The company is simply surviving, which is not enough in this new economy. A configuration management solution could help a company achieve all of these benefits in an efficient manner.

Variant explosion challenge

As described in Figure 2.1, it is clear that Web systems inevitably face a variant explosion problem. This problem means that a company could end up with a nightmarish number of parallel versions that it must maintain. Any time a bug fix or an enhancement needs to be made, it has a snowball effect on all versions of the Web system (i.e., variant) in the sense that a decision has to be made for each variant as to whether that fix or enhancement pertains to that variant and whether that fix or enhancement can be applied directly or be fiddled with (i.e., customized to that variant).

Consider a very simple example. A company has one Web product. The product connects with five different devices. That is, its content can be displayed on five different devices (such as a PDA or smart phone). The company will only support the last two versions of each device's micro-browser. Similarly, the product will work with two PC browsers, but only the last three versions of each. Hence, so far, the company has to maintain $(5 \times 2) + (2 \times 3) = 16$ variants. But then, being a global product, it has to support four different speaking languages (English, French, German, Spanish). Now, the variant equation is

$(5 \times 2 \times 4) + (2 \times 3 \times 4) = 64$ variants. Then if we add in site redesign variants $(5 \times 2 \times 4 \times 2) + (2 \times 3 \times 4 \times 2) = 128$, add in six customer special additions, we could get the number of variants to $(5 \times 2 \times 4 \times 2 \times 6) + (2 \times 3 \times 4 \times 2 \times 6) = 768!$ So, it is easy to see how the number can escalate and why. And this is just a simple example that does not take into account multiple Web sites/products, and different technologies, legacy applications, and more connected resources.

The explosion comes from various avenues:

‣ The multiple resources (shown in Figure 2.1 such as ERP systems, mainframes, and data warehouses) that can make up a Web system, and all versions of those;

‣ The need to display content across many different kinds of devices (with micro-browsers) as well as PC browsers, and all versions of those;

‣ Multiple product lines, where typically one Web site represents a particular product or e-commerce/e-business package;

‣ Customer specials that are tailored forms of the Web system that suits particular clients;

‣ New development, such as site redesign or new products, which must be developed in parallel with the live Web systems;

‣ Different platforms, middleware, protocols, and customer needs;

‣ Internationalization, which caters to different speaking languages and cultures. For instance, what might be acceptable content to one county/culture may not be acceptable to another so different Web sites are generated to support this.

To support variants, companies have to set up multiple teams working on each. Without variant tool support, teams can easily make mistakes, such as overwriting each other's code changes. Their communication is limited, they cannot reuse each other's changes, and they have considerable difficulty propagating changes across the right variants at the right time. They have trouble building the right configuration of pieces to make up a particular variant version. They lose track of all the versions of files used in each variant baseline. But configuration management tools can come to the rescue because they provide superb parallel development team support along with variant and concurrent baseline support.

Dynamic content challenge

Web content can be dynamic if it is created on the fly from a user's or agent's (device, robot program) request. It is active because programs are executed in response to the request and based on the user's environment, which takes into account the version of the browser and plug-ins on the client side. HTML is a static language, but when combined with active controls (such as ActiveX), it becomes dynamic. This can change the entire nature of a Web site. For example, when entering input to a Web site, the users can be given feedback on the type of data they are supposed to enter. Content (such as tables, forms, database queries, documents, and code) can be generated and changed in real time.

The challenge for Web systems is how to keep track of all the dynamic content and all the pieces (tools, options, variables, who, when) that generated it. Companies need to know what they are producing, and how to recreate it for testing or audit purposes. For instance, company A could be sued if it generated data that was inaccurate and company B made million-dollar decisions based on that inaccurate data. The court would require company A to show all the details of that data's creation. Maybe there was in actuality no mistake by company A. Maybe in transmission, data got garbled—and so on. In short, companies need to protect themselves from many different perspectives: legally and technically.

Types of content in Web systems

Web content can be static or dynamic. It can consist of data objects and code and component libraries that are compiled or interpreted or transformed. Examples of data objects are data files, tables, documents, images, and streaming video. Code can be active controls and scripts. Scripts, or behaviors, can be attached to Web objects allowing, for instance, the user to alter attributes, such as color, positioning, and font size, of objects or execute applications. Scripts or active controls can be written in ActiveX, C++, VisualBasic, HTML, DHTML, XML, VRML, OLE controls, Active Server Pages (ASP), Java applets, VBScript, JavaScript, and ISAPI, CGI, and Perl scripts.

Component libraries are reusable code that can be quickly used to develop applications. Examples are JavaBeans, Microsoft Foundation

Classes, and Lotus's eSuite of business applets. An applet, or an active control, is a compiled binary file that HTML could reference, for instance. A script is source code that can be embedded directly in the HTML tag. With the easy availability of component libraries, Web development is becoming more and more container based, or component bundled.

Companies need to track all of these components, their versions, how they are compiled or interpreted, and any intermediate forms that are used to create the content. Some code may require a series of steps before it can be executed. For example, a Java file is compiled into platform-independent bytecodes, which are then processed by a JIT (just-in-time) compiler to yield fast native instructions for a particular platform. An .asp file (Active Server Page, which is a combination of static HTML and VBScript) generates a Web page. Its VBScript is interpreted along with the appropriate database being accessed and then the server creates the full HTML on the fly generating the displayed Web page.

In addition to the objects in Web content just discussed, hyperlinks exist. Hyperlinks can point to any other object within or across Web pages anywhere in the world.

Not only do the objects in Web content create a management challenge, metadata also needs to be tracked by a company. Metadata is the knowledge about all the content; for instance, knowledge that only certain hyperlinks are valid for a particular version of a Web site, or only particular versions of content can be published against certain corporate templates for the Web site. Templates enable separation of content and its format or presentation style. (Again, configuration management perfectly supports metadata management.) Other types of metadata also need to be managed:

- External structure such as the hierarchy of Web pages;

- Internal structure such as embedded objects;

- Transaction indicator, indicating that, for example, these data are involved in carrying out an atomic e-commerce activity;

- Security information associated with each object;

- Audit logs related to the activity on each object;

- Tool compatibility details such as the version of the browser and plug-ins for which this object is valid;

> ‣ The bill of materials, which includes the make files and the artifacts used to create the object (its tools, tool options, data, files, person, machine, date of build);

> ‣ Intermediate forms such as a Word document that needs to be converted into HTML;

> ‣ Validation rules such as a form that requires input validation for each field;

> ‣ Handler rules such as a database access request that requires certain tools and operations;

> ‣ Relationships between objects, such as what pieces go with each other.

Metadata need to be tracked so that Web teams know how to do the right kind of maintenance on them, such as which pieces go together or not, which pieces must be updated together, and how to build valid sets of items. Configuration management tools provide excellent metadata support because the metadata is managed in the CM repository. Depending on the tool, it can be automatically generated. Chapter 3 will explain further.

Process support challenge
Making changes to Web content is typically done in a dangerous "code–publish–code–publish" cycle. Programmers are under considerable pressure to do this. Most of the Web tools (like HTML editors and Web content management tools) encourage this approach. Scripting languages (such as JavaScript, JScript, Tcl, VBScript) obviously have an effect on the way that applications are developed too. Most of these are interpretive languages or require JIT compilers. This leads to a style of "change on the fly" with little emphasis on a well-engineered release cycle. Such a cycle breeds mistakes as I discussed earlier because there are no checks and balances in place. The Web industry needs Web engineering techniques [49, 50] so that we can improve the quality of our Web systems and maintain them more efficiently.

We know from my discussion in Chapter 1 and from others [23, 24] that Web development is different from traditional development so we expect different techniques. But still, all the good practices of software engineering such as documenting requirements and design, doing

Table 2.4
Key Phases of Web Development

Major Activity in Web System	Who Typically Does the Work
Design and creation	Web team or IT Department or outsourced
Infrastructure support: servers, network connections, databases	Outsourced to network management company, or hosted by IT Department
Testing, e.g., compatibility of content, link accuracy, viewable by all kinds of browsers	Web team or IT Department
Publishing of content	Business units or Web team or IT Department
Registering of sites on search engines	Web team or IT Department
Security checking: access control, hacker analysis, virus detection	Web team or IT Department or security consultant
Monitoring: traffic performance; intelligent load balancing and Web page redesign; replication; Web accelerators/caching; traffic shaping; capacity planning	Web team or IT Department
Maintenance: content evolution via changes, enhancements, deletions, redesign	Content experts or Web team or IT Department

Source: From [26].

different kinds of testing (unit, integration, stress, human factors, customer, performance, usability), having reviews, and doing quality assurance and configuration management all apply to Web systems. Table 2.4 highlights specific Web development steps. To accomplish these steps, we need to embed all the traditional software engineering techniques but make them adaptable to the needs of Web development and maintenance.

To support the engineering practices, Web environments need to provide process automation. Such automation ensures that code goes through all the necessary steps before being published and does not pass onto the next stage of the cycle until the proper review or authorization or sign-offs have been done. A typical question I get at this point is "But won't the process slow things down?" My answer is always "No." Of course, if the processes are too restrictive or dogmatic, they will get in the way of the maintenance activities. So the key is to design flexible processes that suit all situations. For instance, a low-priority fix should not use the same process as a show-stopper bug. Configuration management tools all have some form of process support that is designed to get code safely and efficiently through its change cycles. This is discussed further in the next chapter.

Performance effect challenge

As discussed earlier in this chapter, expectations have changed. Users expect results immediately, in real time. If not, they go to the competitor's site. Hence, your users' satisfaction with their "Web experience" at your Web site is very important. A new breed of industry has arisen—traffic monitoring. Some businesses' sole purpose is to measure and analyze all the traffic to your Web site—who visits, how long they stay on each page, what they did, how many links they traversed, what bottlenecks users had to navigate (such as too many pages to get to the right content), and so on.

Traffic monitoring is very important because it gives companies some kind of indication about customer satisfaction as well as tracking customer hits. They can use the information for technical and business value. For instance, technically the company can see where to improve its Web system in terms of usability and response time. Business-wise, the company can use the hit statistics to garner more advertising revenue.

High-performance Web systems use continuous traffic monitoring. Users must have immediate access to quickly changing content under any load situations. When a company finds there is a performance problem with its Web system, it has several options: Add in some performance patches, redesign the site, add more servers, or add Web server accelerators (dynamic caching schemes), as IBM did with the Olympics site [40]. The Web site was redesigned on the fly to make access much easier and speedier along with adding caches. Performance improvers, like the accelerators, do create a dependency, though between the version of the Web system, the server, and the accelerator. Such dependencies have to be tracked so that when any upgrades or changes are made, the appropriate changes are made to the accelerator.

Web accelerators, or caches, are beginning to play bigger roles in performance enhancement with content being designed to take into account caching techniques for accelerators. As a contingency, companies develop server crash plans, which generally entail replicated content across servers, which, in turn, means synchronization and distribution of real-time updates. Configuration management tools provide the capabilities to manage dependencies, replicate and synchronize content, and assist propagation, as will be further discussed in Chapter 3.

Scalability challenge

The scalability challenge for Web systems is voiced as "How can huge Web systems continue to evolve?" The Olympic [40] and Nasdaq [43] sites are examples of huge Web systems in terms of number of pages (millions), amount of traffic (millions of hits per day), and number of databases and Web servers. Newspapers [41] are also good examples of scaling, because each day they need to add thousands of pages of Web content. This addition needs to be done in a controlled, structured manner and the hyperlinks arranged carefully. Scaling up of content inevitably raises questions: Where should we add the content—vertically or horizontally in the tree structure? Also, what pieces do we delete or replace? To be able to answer these questions providing the most options, companies need to be able to safely add or remove collections of pieces (that is, know what are valid configuration items), plug-and-play with them to test out different structures, and relate pieces.

Millions of pages cannot be efficiently stored in a flat file system, and we know that databases scale up well. Database vendors are redesigning their products so that Web applications can be stored directly in the database, such as Oracle's WebDB. This helps with scalability, reliability, and administration. I anticipate that first-generation Web systems will be redesigned to use Web-enabled databases. A CM system will help manage the evolution of the Web system's architecture.

Outsourcing challenge

A major trend in the software industry is to *outsource*, or contract to a third party, to do certain work. Creating the initial Web system is very often outsourced and many companies outsource their maintenance too. Outsourcing provides these benefits: Reduces operating costs, shares risks with others, accesses leading-edge technology without having to purchase the infrastructure for it, uses expertise not found in-house, gets things done more quickly, and does not distract from the company's core business so that it can focus more on its own core competencies.

Although outsourcing provides many benefits, it also requires thorough management oversight and good testing and quality assurance practices to verify the integrity of the Web system. It also requires good background checks on the outsourcing companies to verify that they really know how to do Web maintenance well. I know many companies that just hire anyone who knows how to use an HTML editor. Just because someone can create a Web site with a tool does not mean he or she knows how to maintain it in an efficient and cost-effective manner.

Configuration management solutions are very familiar with outsourcing, commonly called subcontract management, where all parties find a mutually agreeable set of processes and checks and balances.

Politics challenge

One big phenomenon of the Web is how it is changing the political environment within companies. The first question that arises is that of "Who controls the Web system?" Does Marketing, the Web team, the IT manager, or the product manager control it? Who owns the Web system; who authorizes changes; who pays for changes; who gets the credit when everything goes well; and who owns the gatekeeper (or Webmaster) that is the last bastion to publishing to the live site? How are the corporate structure and its roles and responsibilities affected by the Web system? What is the best corporate hierarchy to support Web systems? Figure 2.3 shows why the answers may not be readily apparent for companies.

Consider who provides and changes the content for the Web system: everybody, potentially, from financial people, through marketing people, to software developers. Who decides what can be published to the live site? In large companies, groups publish independently of each other. If they are not synchronized and coordinated, companies keep making mistakes of publishing inconsistent content. Also, they cannot guarantee that corporate standards (such as testing, using the right version of templates,

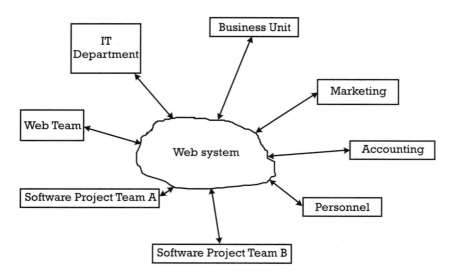

Figure 2.3 Anyone in a company can be a Web content creator and maintainer.

quality assurance checks) are followed before publishing. Who assumes responsibility for the accuracy of the information on the Web site? Who ensures that quality control processes have been followed before information is published to the site? Who is responsible for making changes? Who assumes the cost of change? Some companies decide that the IT Department is in charge; others pick the Marketing Department.

Whatever the choice, the role of the IT Department is a crucial strategic decision for a company. The effectiveness of that role often determines how good the support environment—the tools, installation, training, hot-line services—will be. The role of IT is changing from that of an infrastructure provider to that of a strategic adviser and standards producer, with many of its traditional functions (such as network administration) being outsourced.

Politically, companies face the delicate balancing act of controlling Web system development and maintenance while still leaving employees freedom to meet their deadlines. Companies are struggling to find the best corporate infrastructure and team boundaries. While the beauty of the Web is that it acts as a solvent to any entry barriers, it also provides more choices for companies as to how to manage their Web systems, which can be perplexing. Configuration management helps with this challenge by providing the safety net for the company. Everything is version controlled so that nothing gets lost. An audit trail is kept of all that happened so there is a record of what happened, why, when, how, and who did it. CM ensures that corporate processes are followed in the publishing cycle, regardless of the corporate structure. That is, whatever the political machinations, the right processes are followed.

Immaturity challenge

The immaturity challenge refers to how everything related to Web systems is in its infancy. This includes tools, engineering techniques, skill sets, languages, standards, middleware, toolkits for building Web systems, browsers, Internet devices, our understanding of what are best practices, and the best skill sets for Web systems. The challenge is how to continue developing and maintaining Web systems when nothing is stable and at some point, you have to upgrade to the new version of the tool, language, browser, and so on.

As I discussed earlier, many Web systems as part of their evolution go through a retooling, or a rewrite, using a more modern language. Many decisions have to be made by Web developers and architects as to which programming technologies to use. For the client side of the Web system, do we use HTML, cascading style sheets (CSS), plug-ins, helper applications, ActiveX controls, Java applets, JavaScript, VBScript, Perl, or Dynamic HTML? For the server side, will we have CGI scripts, Java servlets, ISAPI/NSAPI programs, Active Server Pages, server-side JavaScript, or database middleware? In Chapter 7 of [49], the intricacies of these technologies are discussed. All present decision tradeoffs imply maintenance complexities.

What companies need is a way to track the version of every artifact, configurations of related artifacts, all the tools, and all versions of the environment used. Configuration management tools assist with all of this.

Summary of the nine challenges

Table 2.5 summarizes the Web crisis challenges and indicates the role of configuration management in the solution. The next chapter will discuss configuration management in detail.

Table 2.5

How Configuration Management Addresses the Web Crisis

Solution: Configuration Management	Challenges
Track all changes from "birth to death"; that is, from the moment a change request is suggested to the moment that the change is published and is itself replaced/upgraded	Speed of change
Parallel development, concurrent baselines, build management, distributed development	Variant explosion
Audit logs, build management, configuration items, snapshots	Dynamic content
Change and publishing cycle automation, notifications, authorizations, event triggers, state changes	Process support
Concurrent configuration items	Performance effect
Configuration items, relationships, baselines	Scalability
Process support, baselines, change propagation, status accounting, audit trails, query facilities	Outsourcing
Version control of everything, status accounting, audit trails, process automation	Politics
Version control of everything: tools, code, data, change requests, processes, query and reporting facilities	Immaturity

Signs of a crisis point

If a software company does not have any form of configuration management practices or tools, that is already a sign of a Web crisis. Of course, if a company does not have an awareness of CM (which is prevalent for Web teams), then it has to look at other certain signs. Typical signs include those given in Table 2.6.

The nature of Web programming

The key differences from traditional software development and maintenance compared to Web development and maintenance boil down to the items listed in Table 2.7. The speed of change of everything—bug fixes, enhancements, site redesigns, company spin-offs, mergers, languages—goes up dramatically. Developers are programming now for situations they did not have to concern themselves with before. For instance, they have to program for high user hit rates or a high volume of user requests along with programming around all the security firewalls. Web systems can be made up of many resources distributed around the world and usage must be programmed asynchronously. That is, the resource may not be available when requested. It could be down, broken, busy, picky, or choosing not to respond. The programmer must code around these eventualities. Also, programmers must be more aware of international or globalization issues. Their code or content must suit a particular speaking language or cultural mores.

Table 2.6
Signs That the Web System Is in Crisis

Site needs to be redesigned because it cannot evolve.
Site has become unusable; that is, users cannot find the information they need within a few pages. The navigation system has become too convoluted and the user gets lost.
Site does not support the necessary rate and number of changes.
Site does not support the volume of users needed.
Site cannot provide an appropriate response time.
Site has an unacceptable error rate in content.
Upgrades to servers often cause an outage.

Table 2.7
Key Differences Between Web World and Traditional Software World

Velocity and urgency of change
Business strategy and technical operation synergy
Higher volume of users and traffic
Security needs
Distribution of services
Asynchronous programming
Stateless programming
Globalization
Code conversion (retooling)
Component reuse
Browser and platform transparency
Nine Web crisis challenges

Programming languages used now are more object oriented so programmers make heavy reuse of source or binary objects. Of course, any source code from libraries that they changed must be tracked so that any upgrades are synchronized with those changes. Also, programmers must code for all possible platforms and browsers and all versions of browsers. This includes micro-browsers for all future devices (such as Internet-connected telephones or any device or agent that functions via the Internet).

As Web systems evolve and better technology and languages come about, companies must offer better performing Web systems. For instance, with Web server management, companies are fine-tuning performance via load balancing as well as by changing languages or scripting. Many companies are rewriting their applications in Java. Companies are converting their HTML code into more efficient code, such as XML, XSL, and VML.

Another difference with Web programming is that the programmer must write generic code, that is, code that has platform and browser transparency—it can run on any platform and browser (and versions thereof).

Web programming is asynchronous. That is, the programmer writes code assuming that system/Web resources may not be available when the code executes. Synchronicity may not exist between resources. A resource may be busy, or it may fail during execution, or it may hang, or it may not exist. The programmer must take all of these possibilities into account.

Web programming is stateless programming. A big difference between the client–server style of programming and that of the Web is the notion of state. Client–server retains state—that is, context information between calls to methods (procedures), whereas Web programming is typically built on a transportation protocol such as HTTP, which is stateless, so no internal information is retained between method calls. Any information would have to be passed as parameters to the methods. All requests and responses going back and forth between the Web server and the client browser are separate entities, "stand-alone pieces of conversation with no permanent relationship between them. In a nutshell, the page that issues the call and the page showing the results are two different pages, even though they have the same name" [51].

A consequence is that there is no way to synchronize the client's request and the server's response, hence the asynchrony. For the Web, the server generates a completely new page that the client displays, whereas for a client–server situation, the client waits for a stream of data that the server is preparing and when it is received, the client updates its own interface to reflect the results.

Globalization is also a new issue for the average programmer [52] where different languages and cultures need to be taken into account, along with the parallel maintenance of foreign sites. Techniques are available that enable foreign-language Web sites to be kept constantly up-to-date with the development version. It is not efficient to take the original site and then convert it to the foreign language since the original site is constantly evolving so fast that by the time the translation team finishes with a particular snapshot, the production team might already have a newer version.

Web tools and languages are different too, including compilers, JIT compilers, and interpreters. They are dynamic and thus require a slightly different kind of testing. The code must be tested in the exact environment as the Web site, otherwise the code interpretation may vary. Programmers now make use of component libraries (such as JavaBeans or Microsoft Foundation Classes). This means coding is done in a much more RAD (rapid application development) mode by reusing components. Some components may be in source form, meaning they can be customized by the programmer, or they may come in binary form and cannot be altered.

Programmers must be very cognizant now of security issues since, in theory, the world could try and hack into the Web system. Also, the programming must take into account very high volumes of users and dynamic page generation that has to include internationalization factors. They also have more pressures on them, working in a continual change mode and responding to higher rates of change requests.

Different skills are required too: more graphics design capability and more communication are needed along with human factors skills to be able to collaborate with nonsoftware people in creating content. Most of the Web content designers and creators tend to be graphic design artists or user interface experts. As I see it, the WWW is forcing an evolution in the capabilities of our software programmers.

Key messages from this chapter

This chapter has provided an overview of the nature of Web systems and the challenges companies must face in order to avoid a Web crisis. The key messages from this chapter are as follows:

1. The nature of Web development and maintenance breeds a complexity that cannot be managed manually, especially for large-scale, high-performance Web systems.

2. A Web crisis can be avoided, but it requires addressing nine key challenges.

3. Configuration management is the necessary core support system that will enable companies to wind their way through those nine challenges.

4. Make sure your Web team has an experienced software developer or manager who can pass on the lessons learned about software engineering practices, in particular, configuration management.

5. Internet companies typically go through four phases (excited, stimulated, stunned, grateful) toward acceptance of the Web challenges. Companies stuck in the stunned phase are in the middle of a Web crisis.

6. The potential growth rate of Internet business may not be reached if companies get bogged down by the Web crisis.

7. Web system creation is relatively easy. It is the maintenance that can be overwhelmingly complex.

8. The biggest challenge for the Web community is how to develop maintainable Web systems that are highly responsive to requests for immediate, high-volume changes.

9. We are starting to see that what is missing from the e-commerce/ e-business success equation are software engineering practices to make it work efficiently. Configuration management must become the core of the development and maintenance environment.

10. Web development and maintenance provide more challenges in terms of engineering techniques and management practices than traditional software development.

11. With the synergy required between executive decision-making and technical operations, a Web environment needs CM in order to achieve the flexibility, agility, speed, and integrity demanded of this synergy.

References

[1]   Krantz, M., "Nasdaq Tops 5000: Record Ushers in a Brave New World," *USA Today*, Mar. 10, 2000, p. 1B.

[2]   Geirland, J., and E. Sonesh-Kedar, *Digital Babylon: How the Geeks, the Suits, and the Ponytails Tried To Bring Hollywood to the Internet*, New York: Arcade Publishing, 1999.

[3]   Bank, D., et al., "Staying Alive? Forget About 'Saturday Night Fever.' Start-Up Fever May Soon Be Coming to a Living Room Near You," *The Wall Street Journal*, Nov. 4, 1999, p. B6.

[4]   Waldman, P., "Silicon Valley, Where the Conversation Comes With a Caveat," *The Wall Street Journal*, Nov. 3, 1999, p. 1.

[5]   Schwartz, P., P. Leyden, and J. Hyatt, *The Long Boom*, New York: Perseus Books, 1999.

[6]   Editorial, *Business Week*, Nov. 15, 1999.

[7]   Smith, B., and A. Bebak, *Creating Web Pages for Dummies,* Foster City, CA: IDG Books Worldwide, 1998.

[8]   Rosenfeld, L., and P. Morville, *Information Architecture for the World Wide Web: Designing Large-Scale Web Sites,* Sebastopol, CA: O'Reilly and Associates, 1998.

[9]   Siegel, D., *Secrets of Successful Web Sites: Project Management on the World Wide Web,* Indianapolis, IN: Haydn Books, 1997.

[10] Lynch, P. J., and S. Horton, *Web Style Guide: Basic Design Principles for Creating Web Sites,* New Haven, CT: Yale University Press, 1999.

[11] Spool, J., et al., *Web Site Usability: A Designer's Guide,* San Francisco, CA: Morgan Kaufmann Publishers, 1999.

[12] Stein, L. D., *How To Set Up and Maintain a Web Site,* Reading, MA: Addison-Wesley, 1997.

[13] Lowery, J. W., *Dreamweaver 2 Bible,* Foster City, CA: IDG Books Worldwide, 1999.

[14] Korper, S., and J. Ellis, *The E-Commerce Book: Building the E-Empire,* Orlando, FL: Academic Press, 2000.

[15] Seybold, P. B., *Customers.com: How to Create a Profitable Business Strategy for the Internet and Beyond,* New York: Times Books, 1998.

[16] Easton, J., *Striking It Rich.com: Profiles of 23 Incredibly Successful Websites You've Probably Never Heard Of,* New York: McGraw-Hill, 1999.

[17] Hartman, A., J. Sifonis, and J. Kador, *Net Ready: Strategies for Success in the E-conomy,* New York: McGraw-Hill, 2000.

[18] Siegel, D., *Futurize Your Enterprise: Business Strategy in the Age of the E-Customer,* New York: John Wiley & Sons, 1999.

[19] Modahl, M., *Now or Never: How Companies Must Change Today To Win the Battle for Internet Consumers,* New York: HarperCollins, 2000.

[20] Wallace, P., *The Psychology of the Internet,* Cambridge, UK: Cambridge University Press, 1999.

[21] Standing, C., *Internet Commerce Development,* Norwood, MA: Artech House, 2000.

[22] Madrona, E., *Global Distributed Applications With Windows DNA,* Norwood, MA: Artech House, 2000.

[23] Gellerson, H., and M. Gaedke, "Object-Oriented Web Application Development," *IEEE Internet Computing,* Jan./Feb. 1999, pp. 60–68.

[24] Lockwood, L., "Taming Web Development," *Software Development,* Apr. 1999.

[25] Dart, S., "Webcrisis.com: Inability To Maintain," *Software Magazine*, Sept. 1999, pp. 50–57.

[26] Dart, S., "Content Change Management: Problems for Web Systems," *Proc. International Symposium on SCM*, Berlin, Germany: Springer-Verlag, 1999.

[27] Schwartz, J., "Schwab Builds Redundancy," *Internetweek*, Mar. 13, 2000, p. 1.

[28] Bloomberg News, "eBay Restores Site After Saturday Outage," *Los Angeles Times*, July 12, 1999.

[29] Ohlson, K., "E-Billing Bug Hits 21 Banks," *Computerworld*, May 10, 1999, p. 38.

[30] Gasparino, C., "Merrill Faces a Challenge With Web," *The Wall Street Journal*, Nov. 4, 1999, p. C1.

[31] Schwab, C., with C. Fredman, "Success Through Failure" *Hemispheres* (United Airlines), Nov. 1999, pp. 54–56.

[32] Bank, D., et al., "The Day the Lights Went Out," *The Wall Street Journal*, Nov. 4, 1999, p. B6.

[33] Cahill, J. B., "Whirlpool Experiences Shipping Delays Over Computer Glitches in SAP Software," *The Wall Street Journal*, Nov. 3, 1999, p. A3.

[34] Boudette, N. E., "Europe's SAP Scrambles To Stem Big Glitches," *The Wall Street Journal*, Nov. 4, 1999, p. A25.

[35] Miller, G., "Yahoo! To Own GeoCities Content, Riling Members," *The Wall Street Journal*, June 30, 1999.

[36] Bulkeley, W., "Raytheon Employees Resign in Wake of Lawsuit Protesting Internet Postings," *The Wall Street Journal*, Apr. 5, 1999.

[37] Menn, J., "Prevention of On-Line Crashes Is No Easy Fix," *The Wall Street Journal*, Dec. 1999.

[38] Dart, S., "Containing the Web Crisis Using Configuration Management," *Proc. ICSE99 Workshop on Web Engineering, International Conference on Software Engineering*, Los Angeles, CA, May 1999, pp. 94–105.

[39] Wayt Gibbs, W., "Software's Chronic Crisis," *Scientific American*, Sept. 1994, pp. 86–95.

[40] Iyengar et al., "Techniques for Designing High-Performance Web Sites," *IBM Research Report*, Mar. 1999.

[41] Fan, X., and J. Chen, "Design for Maintenance: Experience of Developing an ICP Web Site," *Proc. ICSE99 Workshop on Web Engineering, International Conference on Software Engineering*, Los Angeles, CA, May 1999, pp. 57–64.

[42] Miller, M., "Technology Upends All Info Systems: The Proposal for a Free On-Line Ivy League-Scale University Is Revolutionary," *Los Angeles Times,* Mar. 23, 2000.

[43] Hutcheson, M., "The NT Application That Wouldn't Die (NASDAQ.com)," *Enterprise Development,* Vol. 1, No. 1, Dec. 1998.

[44] Sliwa, C., "Maverick Intranets: A Challenge for IT," *Computerworld,* Mar. 15, 1999.

[45] Gibson, M., "Pan European Fish Auction: Hauled Into the 21st Century by Electronic Intranet," *Financial Times,* Oct. 20, 1999, p. EB-1.

[46] Bennett, J., "Web Technology Opens Up a New Market," *The Wall Street Journal,* Nov. 4, 1999, p. B17.

[47] Nelson, E., et al., "Wal-Mart, AOL Marketing Pact Being Discussed," *The Wall Street Journal,* Dec. 13, 1999, p. B25.

[48] Guth, R., "Japan Is Bringing Miniaturization to the Internet," *The Wall Street Journal,* Mar. 29, 2000.

[49] Powell, T. A., *Web Site Engineering: Beyond Web Page Design,* Upper Saddle River, NJ: Prentice Hall, 1998.

[50] Murugasen, S., and Y. Deshpande (Eds.), *Proc. ICSE99 Workshop on Web Engineering, International Conference on Software Engineering,* Los Angeles, CA, May 1999.

[51] Esposito, D., "Remote Object Scripting," *Microsoft Internet Developer,* Vol. 5, No. 1, Jan. 2000, pp. 15–23.

[52] Vasilyev, K., "Multilingual Web Site Development," *Microsoft Internet Developer,* Vol. 5, No. 1, Jan. 2000, pp. 58–56.

Contents

Understanding the Many Views of Configuration Management

"When I'm hanging head-down in my web. That's when I do my thinking."
—E. B. White, *Charlotte's Web*

Configuration management (CM), at a high level, is a discipline. It is a bunch of techniques that can be applied to anything—hardware, software, firmware. It is very much like inventory control—you keep track of all products and all the pieces that go into each version of them. While the techniques of CM during the last 30 years have stayed the same, what changes and gets better constantly is the automation support for software CM, which is discussed in Chapter 4. In this chapter, I discuss the spectrum of operational techniques or aspects involved in software CM. Hardware and firmware CM are described elsewhere [1].

CM is going through a resurgence, a renaissance, so to speak, because Web teams are finding out that they need CM, which is creating a whole new marketplace for CM tools. As a result, the CM vendors are recreating themselves and their products for the Internet era, which is discussed further in the next chapter.

In this chapter I talk about the definition of CM and why people typically have differing definitions. I present a unified view of CM and describe the eight functional areas of CM along with their 35 operational elements. My goal is to present CM as simply as possible but still unveil the power of CM practices. CM cannot be discussed in detail without looking at the role it plays in the software development and maintenance engineering models. Then I focus on the value of CM to companies—the business and technical benefits of CM.

Companies typically think only about the technical benefits of CM, such as the merging of files in conflict. But the really important part of CM is the business value it offers, such as enabling companies to avoid the Web crisis (described in Chapter 2) or being able to recover quickly from a Web site crash, not to mention maintaining the integrity of their software assets. CM is the core of any software development and maintenance. Without CM, companies could survive, but not thrive—and particularly not in an optimal way. Lots of resources are wasted. Developers are overworked. Good software engineering practices are bypassed because there is no time for them. We are already seeing a shortage of Web developers, and those who are available are on call 24 hours a day, and are expected to perform 24 hours a day, 7 days a week. The Internet requires a business operational model of continuous change, continuous growth. Companies will *have* to learn to thrive or die; survival is not good enough.

After presenting the many benefits, I discuss the typical signals or signs that are company indicators of CM problems. Following that, I present the drivers, or the catalysts, that compel companies to implement a CM solution. One of the biggest drivers is success—growing at too fast a rate. I give an example of how a very successful start-up company achieved so much success with its product that it reached a breaking point where growth was no longer possible without automated CM. The chapter ends with a detailed description of the operational aspects of CM along with the two key mistakes that I see companies making in their approaches to CM.

Configuration management is configuration management regardless of object type

CM represents general techniques for controlling the creation and evolution of objects. We could be talking about CM for software, hardware, firmware, airplanes, toys, whatever. CM is CM regardless of the type of object under discussion. That is, the techniques or principles are the same. The essential differences would be in the terminology and the kinds of objects (e.g., software code versus engineering drawings or chip sets) and relationships (e.g., the relationship between code and its requirements document versus that between an engineering design drawing and the layout of its circuitry on the board). Note that CM techniques can be applied manually or via automation in any type of tool such as a CM tool or any IDE (interactive development environment) or CAD (computer-aided design) environment. That is, pieces of CM functionality can be distributed across tools.

At a high level, CM is a disciplined approach that manages the creation and evolution of a product along with the practices involved. For software, it is the disciplined approach to managing the evolution of the software's development and maintenance practices and their products and artifacts, that is, all the code, data, tests, results, Web content, and so on, and the processes involved in creating and changing them.

All CM standards (official or de facto) [2–5] and CM books [1, 6] define CM as follows:

1. Identification;

2. Control;

3. Status accounting;

4. Audit and review.

Identification refers to uniquely identifying every version of an item that makes up the software product. In the case of a Web system, this includes all files, data, tests, video/audio files, graphics, applets, components, and libraries. It also includes all the versions of tools that were used to create or change the objects such as the HTML editor, Java interpreter, and all pieces that make up the IDE. Then the product itself, the Web system, also has a version number. In fact, it is a configuration or grouping of all of the pieces we just mentioned.

Then there could be variants (variations) of the Web system, such as the live Web system that is running in the United States, along with the ones running in the United Kingdom, Spain, and Germany. So each variant has a unique identification too. The unique identification of objects and configurations of objects provides the entire foundation that makes

CM work because such identification forms the basis of the metadata kept in the CM repository (which I will discuss later in this chapter).

Control refers to controlling and tracking changes to any versions and configurations throughout their life cycles. This means that all the reasons for changes are tracked along with who changed what, when and how, and what impact it has on other files, libraries, configurations, and so on. For instance, if a show-stopper bug is found on the Web site, all the events and actions and notifications that take place to make that fix happen are tracked. Whether that change had to be propagated to the variant sites is also tracked. The change request itself is an object that has a unique version identification along with a life cycle that is tracked too.

Status accounting refers to recording and reporting the status of all versions of objects, including files, change requests, and configurations. For instance, at any point in time, the Web team manager could execute a query to find out how many bugs (change requests) are pending, how many are being worked on and by whom, what priority they are, at what point in the life cycle they are (such as being tested), or what bugs were fixed and hence published to the current U.K. Web site, for instance.

Audit and review refers to the process of keeping an audit trail of all actions, events, and notifications that happen to all the objects under CM control and ensuring that, at any point in time, a configuration item is a valid, consistent set of components and that CM activities are being carried out correctly. For instance, an audit log is automatically kept of all the development and maintenance activities carried out on the Web system. This log can be reviewed to prove that the right things were done or not done, such as: At no point in time could a new version of the Web site be published that had inconsistent parts (e.g., the version of the template has to match a compatible version of the content; version 4 of the Web content can only be published with version 2 of the templates at the site in Germany).

Many more aspects of CM are typically not captured in a standard definition of CM, since the definition originally came about before the existence of CM tools. Also, the definition is at a very high level rather than an operational one. CM tools enable the expansion of CM activities beyond what was envisioned as manual activities. Things like code building, process management, teamwork support, and the automation of events and communications are very powerful operational features of today's CM tools.

CM standards and books tend to be rather dull and "dry" reading at times. (I hope you don't find this book to be so.) CM has never been viewed as an exciting or "sexy" topic, except by me and some CM managers and CM researchers. I have always wondered why few have seen the magnificence of CM. One reason, I believe, is that CM is such a foundational issue, not a cutting-edge hot topic. As I said in Chapter 1, CM is analogous to the pylons of a bridge. CM techniques came out many decades ago without any tool support. It was all done manually so it was not in the hands of developers, but rather, CM librarians. And when CM is done manually, it is rather mundane. Nowadays though, the tools empower all developers and managers with CM facilities and put a wealth of information into their hands. Hence, to me, CM is definitely one of the most interesting and exciting practices in a software development environment and process, especially now with the Internet era and looming Web crisis. The Internet economy is definitely elevating the importance of CM, since it will help solve the many challenges I discussed in the previous chapter. Also, with the synergy required between business strategies and technical operations, a Web environment needs CM in order to achieve the flexibility, agility, speed, and integrity demanded of this synergy.

My goal in this chapter is to expose you to CM in as simple a way as possible, yet raise awareness about the power of a good CM solution. The low-level technical details about CM can easily be found elsewhere. You can read other CM books [1, 6, 7] to find details along with looking at consulting companies' CM reports such as Ovum's, or tracking down information on the Internet through the CM yellow pages or various CM e-mail lists. Also, at least nine international conferences [8] on CM have been held for which you can get a copy of the proceedings. The proceedings contain all papers, most of which are of an academic nature. Of course, you will get the best details out of a CM vendor, through their technical sales engineer and their services people. And you can always ask vendors to give you reference sites that allow you to ask their customers how they implemented their CM solution. What I have concentrated on in this book is highlighting the need for CM in the Web development world along with focusing on all the issues that I see companies struggle with in adopting a CM solution. Those issues tend to relate to CM strategy and CM deployment, which are discussed in Chapter 4. Here, I focus on the meaning of CM.

Some people just think of CM as version control: "Oh, I check out a file, then I check it back in." There is much, much more to CM than just version control, especially now with the advent of very sophisticated, mature CM tools. As mentioned, the tools themselves are discussed in the next chapter. Here, I focus on the operational side of CM, which each CM tool implements in its own way.

The essence of configuration management: Key notions and terms

Configuration management can be quite a complex subject, especially when dealing with very large software systems made up of millions of pieces. I will simplify CM to what I consider the minimal notions. If you understand what the terms *version, configuration item, baseline, variant,* and *change request* imply, then you can master the essence of CM. I will use an airplane as an everyday example.

A version is an instance of an object. A configuration item is a specific version of a group of objects. A baseline is a configuration item that is frozen in time to represent a specific state of a product, such as "This baseline has all the bug fixes in it and was released (shipped) to the customer" or "This is the test baseline that is undergoing QA (quality assurance) tests." A variant is a configuration item that slightly differs from another so it has a relationship with that other item. In effect, it is a variation on a theme. A change request is an on-line form that captures all the details regarding the request, or desire to make a change to a configuration item.

An everyday example

Imagine that Boeing, an airplane manufacturer, sold a specific version (release) of a 747 plane to United Airlines. Imagine controlling or keeping track of all the millions of pieces (nuts, bolts, electrical wiring, chairs, upholstery, toilet seats, and so on) that go into a huge Boeing 747 airplane. To make a seat, a grouping of parts is required, which is a specific baseline of pieces, including all nuts and bolts, and upholstery, electronic pieces, headrest, seat belt, seat control levers, flotation cushion, and other items. Each seat has specific versions of pieces to make up the seat configuration item. In addition, there are different types of seats: economy, business, and first class. Each seat is made of the same basic pieces just described but with some differences suited to that type.

A particular instance of a seat is a variant of the baseline. For instance, we have a basic seat that represents the baseline, and the variants would be a first class seat, a business class seat, and cattle class (ah, I mean, economy-class) seat. (Another way to think about this is that there is a meta-type called seat and each instantiation of that type is parameterized to create a variant type.) A first class seat will have all the fancy extras such as full reclining ability for sleeping, full electronic lumbar and footrest controls, built-in phone, TV, and computer power socket. A business class seat will have partial extras such as some reclining ability, manual footrest control, and the computer socket. An economy seat will have none of these "frills" and will be smaller in size with no built-in comfort factors.

Now, consider how complex all these issues can become. For instance, consider the different configurations for the seats. For example, some planes have seats abreast 2, 3, 2 or 3, 4, 3. Different fixtures or nuts and bolts are required depending on the seat layout. Then the situation gets more complex when we start to consider changes, scaling up, and evolution. For instance, consider an airplane during flight in which employees find that the bolts holding down the first class seats break away under certain conditions. The manufacturer has to fix this problem.

United Airlines, who bought the plane, files a change request demanding this to be fixed and, by the way, it is a high-priority fix that needs to be done as soon as possible. But first, Boeing has to find out in which planes and for which seats those bolts are used. It has thousands of planes all over the world that possibly use that version of bolt in its seat configurations. Then it has to decide what to replace the faulty bolts with, and then, how to do the replacement, given that planes are in flight most of the time and that there is no time to replace all the bolts between flights. Then it has to worry about whether the bolts on business class and first class seats have the same problem. Then it has to consider whether this fault applies to the different types of airplanes: the Boeing 727, 737, and 767, for example.

You can see that if Boeing could not access all that information about every single plane in existence, it could not address this faulty bolt problem. Now, imagine even further complexity because there may be 100 faulty objects on a plane—parts in the engine, the galley, and other places—that need fixing. Further, as new technology comes along (for instance, the airlines want to put DVD players into the first class seats), Boeing must cater to enhancements and improvements that can easily plug in and plug out of planes. Then again, what if United Airlines instead of Boeing made the fixes or enhancements? How would Boeing then keep track of any of these customizations that United Airlines made to its planes? How could it keep track of everything then if the maintenance and upgrades are done without Boeing's knowledge or involvement?

You can easily imagine how complex it can get over time. These same issues of different versions and configuration items and baselines, in large volumes, dealing with many changes at any point in time and scaling up as time evolves, are the same issues for software. All of these kinds of issues relating to the seats are exactly akin to CM issues that have their counterpart in software. You can substitute a "Web site" for "seat." For the nuts and bolts, substitute all files (such as HTML files and VisualBasic files) that make up a Web site. Then you add changes to the Web site along with evolution of the site into multiple sites. Then the same issues and principles apply.

A software company must track all pieces (code, documentation, audio and graphic files, dynamic pages)—everything that it creates—so it knows what exists, so it knows what and how to fix or upgrade, and so it knows how to make proper business decisions about its products. All that knowledge is needed for the company to survive and to thrive; survival in the sense of being responsive to customers and their change (bug, enhancement) requests, and thriving in the sense of knowing how easy and how long it will take to upgrade its software products. All of these issues are CM issues. Without CM, Boeing, for instance, could not be so successful.

The old view and the new view of configuration management

In all the companies that I have seen around the world, people (software developers and managers) always have different interpretations of CM. There is also what I call the *old view* and the *new view* of CM. The old view pertains to the manual way of doing CM, which essentially meant "tossing the code over the wall" to the CM librarian. The new view comes about because of the wonderful CM tools and capabilities that exist now, which means everyone involved in the software development and maintenance life cycle (chain of events) can be empowered to do their work in a CM-controlled environment and with independence and integrity.

The old view comes from the initial days of CM when CM was carried out manually by a specific set of people, typically called *CM librarians.* In essence, programmers wrote the code, tested it, and then "threw it over the wall" to the CM librarians whose job was to archive it into the library along with all the related pieces of documentation and related artifacts. Today, this approach to CM is no longer needed or followed because of CM automation.

Everyone in a company can now be empowered to automatically and easily do CM. Developers, for instance, can work in safe environments where their code is automatically CM controlled. Dependencies on others are controlled and safety of interaction and updating can be ensured. There is no longer the notion of "throwing code over the wall" to an anxious and ogre-like CM librarian. Yes, the old view of CM typically caused animosity between programmers and the CM group. It was an inevitable animosity: The programmers' concerns were on creating or fixing code; the CM librarian's concern was on control, precision, completeness, and timing.

Manual CM can only achieve a portion of the benefits that are described later in this chapter, especially for Web systems due to the speed and volume of changes, and the variant explosion problem described in Chapter 2. CM has been carried out for many decades, especially by companies with mission-critical software systems, such as the NASA space shuttle, most of the world's government applications such as warfare defense systems and government contractors, and telephony exchange systems around the world. Any business with mission-critical software demands its use. Now Web systems are definitely mission-critical systems, as described in Chapters 1 and 2. A failed Web site can cost millions of dollars, lose customers to the competition, and cause litigation proceedings.

Typical software development and maintenance life cycles

To completely understand the benefits of CM, we need to examine the role it plays in the software development and maintenance life cycle shown in Figure 3.1. Software typically goes through the following stages: requirements specification, functional design, coding, unit testing of code by the developer, integration and system testing by the team of developers, quality assurance testing by the QA or formal test team, which typically makes sure the builds are repeatable and the code passes through all the regression test suites as well as all human factors or Web site performance, traffic, and usability tests.

This is followed by the first customer test—the alpha release—of the product to a select group of customers who "volunteered" to be the first testers. For instance, the alpha test customers log into a particular URL, which is the alpha test version, or the alpha test version is distributed to the customer for installation on their machines. From their feedback, which usually consists of glaring bugs and performance, usability, and specific platform issues, the company can fine-tune the product.

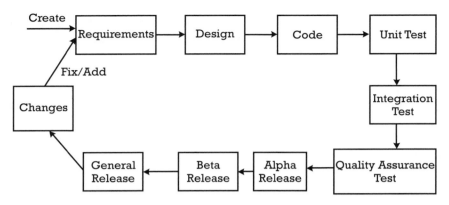

Figure 3.1   Typical software development life cycle.

After that, the second round of customer testing—the beta release—is carried out. From beta testing, the company gets more feedback, which should bring out more subtle bugs or performance and usability issues. With this feedback, the company can make further improvements, resulting in a very stable, ideally bug-free, reliable, well-tested final version of the product. Then it is ready for general release, which means it is ready for the general public or customer base. At this point software companies officially "cut the gold version," which is a phrase they use to indicate release of the final version (general release). Companies even release it on a gold-colored CD.

But, of course, nothing is ever final with software. "Final" in this sense means "we got a certain number of bug fixes and enhancements into this general release." Once a general release version exists, bugs, enhancements, and customizations will always be needed. This is a natural part of the evolution of software so the product now goes into maintenance. Change requests are generated in response to bugs, enhancements, and customizations. As changes are made, new versions of the product start to multiply, creating more variants of the product. The changes will typically go through the same life cycle described earlier. So the cycle repeats and the number of variants that go into maintenance mode escalates.

Software engineering models

Most companies follow these phases, whether or not they are recognized or articulated as official or formal phases. Small companies may not have separate testing teams, for instance. Instead, they have the developers conduct the different kinds of testing. In software engineering, various software life cycle models are recognized: waterfall model, spiral model, and the RAD (rapid application development) model. All of these models address essentially the same phases because software, in order to be reliable, has to go through all those phases. For instance, all software development goes through requirements gathering, design, coding, unit testing, integration testing, system testing, quality assurance testing (such as human factors or stress testing or traffic testing), alpha and beta releases, and, finally, general release or distribution. Then maintenance begins and essentially the same cycle continues. Where I believe the models really differ is in the timing or the length of time for each phase.

The waterfall model implies that development is not done until all the requirements are gathered. In the spiral model, only a portion of the requirements are gathered and then development begins, whereas in RAD, one requirement is gathered and code is immediately thrown together in the sense of creating a prototype and then testing it. Each model does some form of requirements definition but each results in a longer or shorter requirements phase. Whatever model is used in an organization, CM is needed. Yes, even for RAD [9].

In general, CM spans all phases because it controls all the software artifacts (the files, design documents, drawing, graphics, Web content) along with the processes involved in creating and maintaining them (from requirements gathering through to release). Some companies see CM as only needed at a certain phase, for example, just before release, and then archive everything into the CM library. This is the old-fashioned view again where the developers would "throw the code over the wall" to the CM librarian. With modern CM tools, CM participates in every step of the software/Web model as you will see from the eight functional areas of CM discussed later in this chapter. CM is a discipline that works with any kind of engineering model and is required in every kind of software engineering or Web engineering model. That is the beauty and the strength of CM.

The value and benefits of configuration management

CM offers many benefits to companies, not just technical benefits, which are what CM vendors and standards institutes have traditionally presented. Looking back at Figure 3.1, CM plays a role in all those boxes (phases) and in the arrows between those boxes (phase transitions). By that I mean that every artifact involved in a phase (such as requirements, designs, code), every action (edit, notify, compile), every person (developer, tester, manager), and every transition between phases (passing a test baseline onto the QA department) are a part of CM.

In short, CM is pervasive across the software development and maintenance life cycles. It is the core support system that enables safe and efficient development and maintenance. For companies that implement a full CM solution (rather than a partial one), they do achieve all the business and technical benefits shown in Table 3.1, whereas partial CM solutions obviously give partial benefits, as with everything in life.

Table 3.1
Business and Technical Benefits of Configuration Management

Business Benefits	Technical Benefits
Support of reactive or proactive business strategy	All objects versioned
	Metadata in repository
Insurance against the unknown	Failure recovery, rollback support
Resistance to faults and failure	Everything under version control; repeatability of all steps; rollback
Adaptable to changes in business strategy and processes	Customizable, multiprocess support
Very easy audits	Queries and audit log
More responsive to customers	Faster change cycles
Better forecasting and planning	Visibility into all work status; history
More independence	Less reliance on a single person
Foundation for process and quality improvement	Enable standards certification since all require CM
Eliminate avoidable mistakes	Process enforcement
Fewer bugs in released products and Web site	Only tested Web content is published or released
Automatic quality control	Automation of processes/workflow to give the effect of an assembly-line production
More product lines	Minimal change complexity; variant management; change propagation
Teamwork optimization	Parallel development; concurrent baselines; private workspaces
Enables survival and thriving	Control over everything

I already mentioned that CM is needed to pass through the nine challenges of the Web crisis discussed in Chapter 2. Now I dig deeper into CM itself. The business benefits shown in Table 3.1 are from the perspective of high-level management making decisions about what infrastructure, tools, and techniques to invest in to avoid the Web crisis. The technical benefits are more from the perspective of the Web team manager or software project leader figuring out how to improve the development and maintenance cycle times. The key message that I want to leave you with is that CM provides many, many benefits at all levels in a company.

Business and technical benefits

From the business perspective, there are many high-level benefits. CM supports any software engineering model as well as any kind of business strategy, whether it be a reactive style of management where teams react to events as they happen or whether it is a proactive style of management where visions and processes are defined and then deployed. CM provides an insurance policy. It protects against unknown or unpredictable events that could happen because with CM, every artifact and process is under CM control so you can back up to any point in time in case something goes wrong, such as a server crash or high employee turnover.

CM helps make your company resistant to faults and failure. For instance, if a serious problem is found on your Web site, you can quickly roll back or regenerate a new Web site. Or you can pull certain fixes or patches from the live system. CM is very adaptable to changes in business strategy and processes, especially if the processes are automated in the CM tool and even under CM control themselves. A manager can simply change processes through the user interface of the CM system and automatically; that process then becomes the way of doing business. Audits become very easy because the CM system keeps an audit trail, a log of every action that was carried out. So, passing an audit can be as simple as printing out the audit trail.

With CM, companies can be much more responsive to their customers. The customers want to know which bug fixes or enhancements have been made, or what happened to their change request, or when their fix will be released. All this information is readily available in the CM repository and can be accessed by simple queries and via a Web browser or even through other tools, such as help desks.

CM enables better forecasting and planning of releases because the development and maintenance activities are automated and so can be timed. Your company can track how long each step of work takes; in particular, how long is a typical release cycle. Based on that track record, managers can make more accurate decisions and predictions from that data.

With CM, companies have more independence in the sense that they no longer have to rely on one person, such as the CM librarian or the guru developer, to control the entire release cycle. Everyone involved in the development and maintenance activities is enabled by the CM system, which means everyone (who is permitted) has access to the right information at the right time. They do not have to track down people to get the information. Also, because all the software asset knowledge is in the CM system, if, for instance, an employee leaves, that knowledge is still with the company.

CM provides the solid foundation for process and quality improvement. All software standards or de facto standards, such as ISO 9000 or the Capability Maturity Model Integration, have CM as a core requirement to pass certification or assessment. Once CM is in place, then all the other aspects of the standards can be addressed. Also, CM is an essential part of any company's quality processes. When CM is fully automated, it means that every software asset along with every software process and role responsibility is automated. I have found that as soon as processes are automated, companies very quickly see the strengths and limitations in the process and can quickly fix any problems.

With CM, companies eliminate avoidable mistakes. The wrong version of a file does not get published and the right fix gets into the right baseline. "Rogue" files do not accidentally end up in builds. Everything gets tested before it is released. Fewer bugs are found in released products and Web sites because, typically, 50% of the bugs that customers find are bugs that could have been avoided had there been good CM in place.

Automated CM ensures automatic quality control. That is, the CM system ensures that the right processes are followed and the right code is released. It gives the effect of an assembly line for code development and maintenance. So, if you follow the right processes and do not introduce any problems along the way, you can be assured that the products coming out at the end of the line are of high quality (assuming the processes themselves are of high quality).

CM also enables a company to manage more product lines because it manages concurrent/variant development very well along with all the changes. Teamwork is optimized because CM systems provide safe working areas for each team member so that they coordinate, collaborate, and communicate without deleteriously affecting each other's work.

All software artifacts are under version control providing a history of everything. All the metadata, the knowledge or characteristics of the software artifacts, are in the repository and can be accessed as needed. CM enables Web systems to be regenerated in the face of a failure or a bug being found. All the steps used to create a software artifact, such as Web content, are repeatable.

Processes such as the release cycle for code (change, testing, QA, reviews) can be automated and changed as needed. The CM repository with all the metadata means that queries, metrics gathering, and reports can be quickly generated.

In short, CM helps a software/Web company to survive by protecting the integrity of all its software assets, and because it addresses all the Web challenges, CM plays a significant role in enabling a company to thrive.

Signs of a configuration management problem

When consulting with companies, I use the following questions as indicators of problems requiring a CM solution:

1. Can you keep track of all the variant baselines and Web sites that share code?

2. Can you handle the speed and high volume with which changes to your Web content occur?

3. Can you meet release deadlines?

4. Can you release multiple fixes simultaneously or does it have to be one fix at a time or all or none?

5. Do you know what went into a release that was distributed to a customer or all the pieces that are currently published to your live Web sites?

6. Were all the right versions of pieces shipped or published in the latest release?

7. Do you know how many bugs are outstanding?

8. With a simple query, can you find out how long it typically takes to complete different kinds of changes?

9. Are developers reusing bug fixes across releases rather than wasting time fixing the same bug that was fixed in a previous release or Web site?

10. Can a bug fix be propagated to all variants (e.g., across all Web sites) or do different teams fix the same bug for their own Web site?

11. Do you know for sure that everything that was released or published to the live Web sites went through the necessary testing?

12. Do you know why the upgrade to your Web server caused a crash?

13. Can you roll back your server or your Web site to recover from a bug in a short amount of time?

14. Do you know which developer or content author is editing code or content and in response to which change request?

15. Can you quantify the quality of the baseline that was last released or Web site that was most recently published?

16. Are enhancements for software projects or Web sites always done?

If the answer to any of these questions is no, I can guarantee that your company has a CM problem—either there is no CM in place, or the CM in place is inadequate and needs to be updated or automated.

What drives companies to a configuration management solution

Feeling pain—all those "no" responses to the preceding questions—is always a catalyst for companies to deploy a new or better CM solution. When there is a lot of pain, a company struggles to survive; in fact, it is so busy surviving that it cannot thrive. But there are also other reasons, beyond pain, as to why companies get forced into a CM solution. I discussed the many drivers in Chapter 2 and highlight some of them in Table 3.2.

Success is one of the biggest factors that force companies to a CM solution. Because if they do not use CM, they will reach a breaking point or "wall" at which they are busy surviving rather than thriving. For companies to thrive in the Internet economy, they have to continue their

Table 3.2
Configuration Management Drivers

Driver	Explanation
Pain	Breakdowns, mistakes, wasted time
Corporate mergers, acquisitions, spin-offs, and partnerships	Combining or splitting products (Web systems) along with all the business and engineering practices
New technology	New languages and technologies (Java, XML, VRML, DHTML), new tools (interpreters, just-in-time compilers), new IDEs, better CM tools
Failure to pass audits	Industry- or government-required audits
Cannot certify for de facto standards	SEI's Capability Maturity Model or ISO 9000 or SPICE
Competitive edge	Core competency in CM

amazing pace of growth, which means they have to be able to work through all the Web crisis challenges mentioned in the previous chapters. Let me walk you through a typical start-up company's success to show you how success, or hypergrowth, can drive a company insane.

How success drives companies to configuration management

Consider Figures 3.2 through 3.5, which depict 4 years in the life of a software start-up company. This company began pre-Internet. In year 1 (shown in Figure 3.2), the company developed and released its product for one platform, Unix. The development teams followed all the right software engineering practices, taking the product through test and production. The product baseline consisted of four pieces, each piece developed by a different team (working on their own team baseline).

In year 2 (shown in Figure 3.3), the product has been very successful with customers requesting ports to other platforms (Windows 95 and 98) along with bug fixes, patches, and enhancements to the baseline product. So now there are at least three development teams for three platforms supporting at least 10 variant baselines for all the platforms and customer specials. More staff was hired to do the additional development, testing, and QA work.

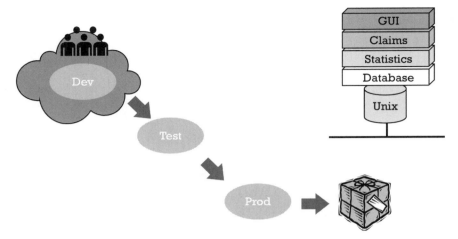

Figure 3.2   First year in the life of a start-up company.

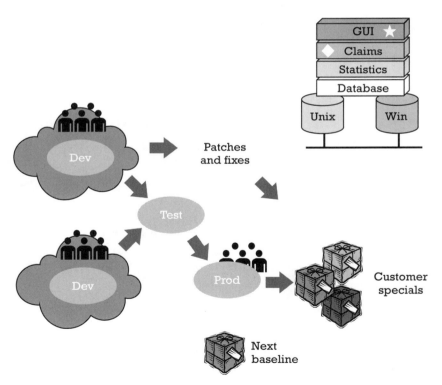

Figure 3.3   Second year in the life of a start-up company.

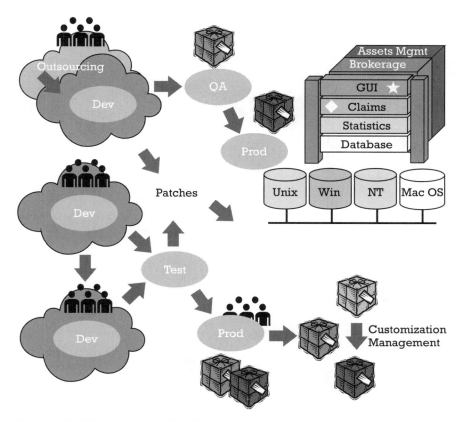

Figure 3.4 Third year in the life of a start-up company.

In year 3 (shown in Figure 3.4), the product continued to be very successful. Many more change requests flowed in demanding new ports to Windows NT and Mac OS platforms. The company did not have expertise with the NT or Mac OS platforms and could not hire all the necessary developers, so it had to outsource the work to third-party "boutique" software shops that had that expertise. As well as the new platforms, major enhancements were made to the product that added a couple more modules (consisting of 1,000 files) to the baseline.

With the continuing influx of bug reports, enhancements, platform specials, and customizations, the company is now managing more than 100 variants of the baseline product simultaneously for its marketplace along with managing the outsourced work and its contracts. You can

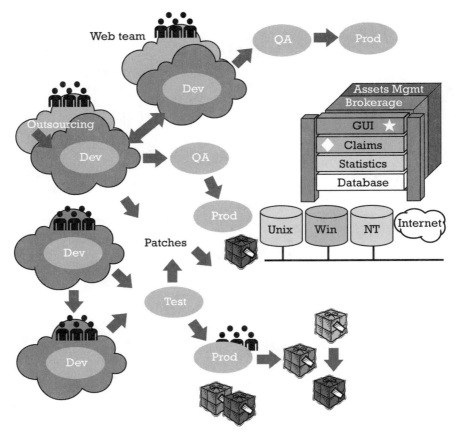

Figure 3.5   Fourth year in the life of a start-up company.

imagine how the company can very easily become overwhelmed by all the new management requirements along with the new technical demands and challenges.

Then, in year 4 (shown in Figure 3.5), the Internet era dawns. Now, the company has to jump on the bandwagon and "Webify" its products, that is, slap on a browser front end. Since it does not have the in-house expertise, again it has to outsource. The company gets its Web sites and "Webified" product on-line. After a short time, it realizes that the "Webified" product really isn't ideally designed for Web commerce. The company knows it will have to redesign the product and also redesign the Web sites every quarter to keep customers returning and to attract new clients. This requires hiring a Web team to do the redesign and a Web maintenance team to maintain the live sites and do any retooling, and keeping the outsource company on contract until the redesign of the product is complete and the company has hired all the staff it needs.

Something else the company notices is that the volume and frequency of change requests on the "Webified" system are much higher than it ever had on the legacy product. The ramifications are that the company has to respond to changes a lot more quickly than before to avoid losing customers. Also, since it needs to keep all product variants synchronized and up-to-date with the same fixes and enhancements, including the Web variant, the faster pace of change to the Web version means a faster pace of change to all the legacy (non-Web) product variants. So, everything has been escalated due to a "snowball" effect.

Hence, the company, its teams, and its products have been dramatically transformed during the 4 years. The company has been very successful but has reached a point where it could easily fall victim to the nine Web crisis challenges discussed in Chapter 2. To continue thriving, it has to continue to turn to CM to help manage its many business and technical challenges. If not, the company will struggle to survive.

Unified view of configuration management

I now present the aspects that I consider to be the operational elements of software CM. I call this a *unified view* of CM because it brings together all of the pieces. In the next chapter, I will show how the CM tool industry is evolving to a unified view too. In [10], I went into detail as to the spectrum of CM functional areas and operational aspects. Note that for this book, I have changed some of the terms and groupings of elements to make for easier reading. I chose the separation into eight functional areas because typically CM tools break down or are designed around those areas. The CM tools provide features to support one, some, or all of the functional areas. I feel this functional area breakdown makes it easier for companies to generate their initial, prioritized list of CM requirements. Also, some companies end up buying several tools and integrating them to achieve the same effect.

In all the companies I have worked with around the world, people view CM differently, as I mentioned earlier. One of the reasons is because there are so many operational elements to CM, and not all companies implement or need those elements—they want a subset of CM. And there are CM tools that support different subsets of CM aspects as you will see in the next chapter when I discuss the spectrum of CM tools (from evolutionary to full-process tools).

People have different mindsets about CM based on what tools they were initially exposed to, whether CM was done manually or with tools, and based on the nature of their business. For instance, any company doing government contracts is subjected to audits so auditing operations are vital, but other companies do not worry about such things so do not see the need. It is not in their CM requirements list. Let us look now at all the operational elements of CM—the unified view of CM.

Table 3.3 shows the eight functionality areas and associated operational aspects. The best way to use this table is to treat it as a spectrum of functionality. Then, a company can develop its initial set of CM requirements from this list. Keep in mind that tools will implement the functionality differently or not at all. This table presents an operational definition of CM and from it, companies can glean their initial, high-level set of CM requirements. Companies will need to add tool- or environment-specific requirements (such as must be accessible from the Web) as discussed further in Chapter 5. The rest of this chapter focuses on the operational meaning of CM.

The eight functional areas of software configuration management

My unified view of CM entails eight functional areas:

1. *Version and configuration control* is concerned with uniquely identifying every type of object from a version of a file to configurations of configuration items, and keeping track (e.g., history) of all the knowledge (metadata) about them. The metadata are vitally important because they enable the CM system to function. All the benefits accrue through the saving of the metadata in the CM repository since this provides the foundation to enable all the processes, notifications, queries, and analysis. In fact, one of the biggest lessons that corporate America learned from its Y2K

Table 3.3
Unified CM: Functional Areas and Operational Aspects

Functional Area	Operational Aspects
Version and configuration control	Version identification
	Configuration items
	Baselines, snapshots, releases, and variants
	Types of components
	History records
Configuration item structuring	System architecture
	Relationships and traceability
	Version selection
	Consistency management
	Project contexts
	Repository management (deltas, administration, metadata)
Construction of configurations	Build management
	Build optimization (partitioning, interfaces)
	Repeatability/regeneration of baselines
Change management	Change impact analysis
	Change requests and classification of change
	Change tracking and escalation
	Change sets
	Change propagation
	Release planning
Teamwork support	Workspace management
	Parallel development (merging, conflict resolution)
	Variant management
	Distributed and remote development
Process management	Notifications
	Event triggers
	Workflow and release management support
	Role support and access control
	Task and project management
Auditing	Logging
	Validation of integrity of CM activities
Status reporting	Queries on status of CM activities and artifacts
	Report generation
	Metrics gathering

preparation is about the incredible value of having all assets on-line. AT&T's Y2K vice president said that it finally had the best and most accurate inventory ever [11].

2. *Configuration item structuring* is concerned with capturing all the logical and structural knowledge about objects and storing them in an efficient manner and using the knowledge to ensure that configuration items are kept consistent within and between each other.

3. *Construction of configurations* is concerned with optimally building and regenerating configuration items.

4. *Change management* is concerned with controlling all aspects related to changes (such as bug fixes and enhancements).

5. *Teamwork support* is concerned with enabling teams of developers to work safely and in parallel on configuration items.

6. *Process management* is concerned with supporting all the workflow steps that files and configuration items go through in their lifetime and merges that with typical project management activities.

7. *Auditing* is concerned with keeping an audit trail of all CM activities and configuration transactions as well as providing their integrity.

8. *Status reporting* is concerned with providing visibility and generating management reports and metrics about the history, the status, and projection of all work and data.

Let us take each functional area separately and examine the operational aspects of each area as shown in Table 3.3. Note that I use the terms *CM system* and *CM tool* interchangeably.

Version and configuration control
Each version of every object is given a unique identification. An object can be a file or a configuration item (CI). CIs are a logical grouping of related items. For instance, all the objects that make up a Web page could be considered a CI. All the icons, text files, graphics, buttons, forms, template, links, and so on, together make up a specific version of a CI. Each object has a certain type—specific attributes or metadata about it that the

CM tool can use to know how to compile it, for instance, or to know with which valid objects it can be combined to make up a CI.

CIs have unique names too. The naming system is typically defined by the CM tool. For instance, a CI name may be a combination of names including the project name, customer name, version number, and date. Synonymous names for CIs are *baselines, snapshots,* and *releases.* Companies use these terms to suit their own needs. For instance, a *snapshot* may capture a CI in an intermediary state such as when a few changes have been added. The developer may want to test some ideas so she or he snapshots the CI. A *baseline* is often used in a generic sense to mean the main code-line from which each team is working. A *release* is typically the latest version of the CI that is released or published and subsequent changes are made relative to that baseline.

Variant CIs support concurrent or parallel development. For instance, each customer may get its own customized version of a product. That is, each gets a variant of the standard product.

Every version of an object, whether it be a file or a CI, has its history completely tracked. That is, metadata (such as how the object was changed, when, why, the makefile) are automatically kept about each object as it undergoes transformation.

Configuration item structuring

CIs have a structure, an architecture. That is, objects are related to each other in a certain manner. Such information enables the CM system to validate good CIs (yes, all these objects can be used together at the same time) or bad CIs (no, there is a conflict between this group of items). Groups of CIs can also have a structure. In essence, the CM repository contains all metadata associated with the entire architecture of a product that consists of versions of CIs.

Objects can have relationships. These could be physical such as in a hierarchy of files, or header files might be needed to compile a C program. The relationships could be logical, in which objects all go together to make up a particular product, such as specific requirements documents go with specific design documents that go with specific baselines of code that go with specific test suites that go with specific makefiles that go with specific release notes. Relationship metadata then enable the CM system to track valid combinations or CIs of objects, which enables companies to know, for instance, that whenever certain files are changed, the related test suites, requirements document, design document, and release notes must be updated as well.

A CI is put together by a version selection mechanism. Developers or testers or managers can specifically designate versions to be selected or the CM system may be smart enough to know how to generate specific versions of CIs. The important function the CM system serves is consistency management. That is, it validates and maintains the integrity of the CI by ensuring that all the objects that make up the CI are appropriate ones. Nothing stray enters the CI by accident or maliciously.

Some CM tools support the notion of project contexts. That is, developers can work in views or sandboxes or workspaces where all the work they do is under CM control. At no time is work done out of the CM system, which would denigrate the integrity of the code.

Each CM system has a repository that is typically a database for the more modern CM tools, or files for the simpler, older CM tools. Repository management is required. For instance, CM tools store optimized versions of files by using a delta mechanism [6, 12], or change-set-based CM systems [13] optimally store the actual changes to files. The CM repository does require administration such as backups, as any database would.

Construction of configurations

CIs are created or generated by a build management system, such as by makefiles or, for instance, by bringing together via version selection all the pieces that make up a Web page. Some CM systems do build optimization in the form of allowing developers to partition their CI in order to compile them in a load-sharing environment. Also, some CM systems have derived object pools that allow compilations to be avoided by reusing existing executables rather than having to rebuild, which could take a long time for large software products/systems.

With build management comes the bill of materials (such as a makefile), or the list of everything used in the building process, such as all the versions of files, tools, tool options, and so on, that went into a build. This build record or bill of materials enables the CM system to repeatedly regenerate a particular version of a CI at any point in time.

Change management

Managing changes is a very crucial support function of CM. An on-line change request (CR) form is used to track changes. All fields (such as severity, priority, state) in the form contain the metadata about a change. A change cycle is initiated with the submission of a CR. One of the first steps in the cycle is to conduct a change impact analysis. Because the CM system has all the metadata about files, it can determine, via the dependencies (relationships), what other files and CIs will be affected if a particular file and/or CI is changed. This impact analysis is used by the decision-makers to schedule changes.

So as not to get overwhelmed by the volume and frequency of changes, change classification (bug, enhancement, customization, and so on) is required. Different types of change request forms and cycles can be automated in the CM system. Every step that the change goes through (such as impact analysis, review board, task assignment, fixed, tested, and QA) can be tracked by the CM system, typically via the *state,* an attribute of the CR.

Companies typically set up change control boards (CCBs) to make decisions and monitor the progress (state) of every change. The CCB meets on a regular basis to decide what will happen to each CR. For instance, they must determine whether a particular CR will be deferred or be done, in which case they have to weigh many issues such as the cost of the change, the risk of doing it (or not), the time it will take, and how it will affect existing schedules. Changes that are deferred or low-priority ones that never seem to get done must have some kind of escalation method. Otherwise, they will be constantly ignored.

One of the very crucial business practices for a company is its release planning. That is, companies have to make important decisions about scheduling changes that determine when they schedule new releases. CM systems help companies make these crucial decisions, which could easily affect their ability to be competitive (another benefit of CM). In the traditional software world, companies would schedule, for instance, major releases every 6 months and minor or point releases every 2 months. This enabled them to release minor bug fixes every few months, whereas the major bug fixes and enhancements came out twice a year.

Companies that release many variants often have to deal with large volumes of changes to each variant. They need to manage their changes at a higher level than just the file level. In such cases, they use change sets. A *change set* is the collection of all the fixes to all the versions of files that make up a particular change. This enables companies to plug in and plug out a change set. That is, they work at the logical level of change rather than the physical level, which gives them many efficiencies and removes room for error. For further details about change sets, refer to [13]. One of the big benefits is that it enables very easy change propagation. For instance, a company has 20 variant Web sites and it has to propagate certain changes in each site. Using change sets, this could be done with a few commands to the CM system that would look something like this: Add change 10 to site A; pull change 9 from site B; and then add change 10.

Teamwork support

One of the real beauties of CM systems is its teamwork support. CM enables teams to work in parallel. Developers could be sharing the same files, or making different kinds of changes at the same time. In the meantime, the testers are busy testing the test baselines, which were the changes the developers made yesterday. Similarly, the QA group is doing their preproduction work on the frozen baselines from last week. Everyone functions optimally by working in parallel on their specific baselines. This is enabled by the separate baselines along with the workspaces that each can use. Some companies use separate staging areas on separate machines. Others use different CM workspaces to achieve the same result.

With parallel or concurrent development, conflicts can arise. Note that I use these terms interchangeably. Some people think of parallel development as relating to developers sharing files. Then concurrent development means developers creating variant (related) baselines at the same time. It is all a matter of perspective (file or baseline) and one goes with the terminology that suits the company. Back to the conflicts. When developers make changes to the same files at the same time, they create possible conflicts that have to be resolved. The CM system can detect conflicts and can assist developers to resolve them by merging the code. Sometimes the resolution can be done without intervention; at other times it requires the developer's guidance in order to be resolved.

The CM system helps companies manage their variant (parallel) baselines. Variants are typically related to each other in some manner. Essentially, they belong to a family of products. For instance, a company develops a product that needs to be customized for each customer. Then the CM system needs to track which changes are applied to which variant, when, how, and why.

Much software development in large companies is done by remote, distributed teams. In such cases, the CM system has to accommodate remote changes, which could mean that a portion of the code base is checked out to a remote site, changes are made, and then the updates have to be synchronized and reconciled back to the central repository for code as well as back out to any other remote sites using that code.

Process management

All the workflow (processes) required for development and maintenance activities can be automated in the CM system. All the states or phases that a file and CI (baseline, release) go through can be captured. As each object moves through its phase and the work is completed, it can be promoted to the next state. Promotion to a new state can be dependent on certain conditions (pre- and postconditions attached to states) such as, "The manager must review this before it is authorized to proceed." Many CM tools implement the workflow via e-mail notifications and event triggers on tools.

Many processes are involved in development and maintenance. The main process is release management, which entails all the steps involved from the time an object is changed to the time it is released to the customer base. That process entails all the coding, preproduction, and production work that is needed.

Associated with workflow are all the roles and responsibilities of people involved in a process. For instance, developers code, testers test, QA people do quality control, build managers build baselines, and release managers ensure product readiness. People have access to the information they need to fulfill their jobs.

Tasks can also be associated with roles and with changes, such as developer Darcy is assigned to make the change for adding the new feature to the main code-line as well as to the redesign code-line under development. Such tasks can be tracked by the CM system, including when the task is initiated, the progress that is being made, as well as when it is closed or completed. Further to that, the task information is relevant to project management activities, such as how long each task is taking. CM systems can provide project management facilities or integrate with an appropriate tool to support them.

Auditing

A key part of CM is auditing. A company needs to determine that CM activities are being carried out properly; that the integrity of the development and maintenance activities has not been compromised. An audit log provides an audit trail of every CM activity carried out, such as which files were checked out and by whom and at what time. Was testing done on the latest release? Companies can then very easily do their official audits by printing out the CM audit trail.

Status reporting

The CM repository contains valuable corporate and technical information. Managers want to collate relevant metrics such as how many show-stopper bugs were fixed in the last release and how many bugs went unfixed. They also want to generate reports about the status of development and maintenance. CM systems enable them to query the CM repository and generate metrics and reports and analyses.

This concludes my overview of the operational aspects of CM. Companies may have all or some of these CM requirements.

Key decisions companies must make, or mistakes I see too often

Most companies looking for a CM solution typically make two big mistakes:

1. In the definition of CM;

2. In picking a CM strategy.

By this I mean that companies can expend a lot of effort in selecting and deploying a CM solution that may not succeed because of these issues. For instance, companies may issue an edict: "We are committed to implementing a good CM solution." This sounds fabulous, but when everyone reads this, because they each have their own interpretations of CM, their expectations are all different. For instance, the seasoned software developers are thinking, "Hey, we're gonna get a great merging tool." The CM manager is thinking, "Wow, everything I've ever wanted will now be automated." The Web content authors are thinking, "Hmm, this doesn't have anything to do with me." The QA manager is thinking, "Yes! I will now have visibility into all the changes," and so on. If expectations are set incorrectly up front, unnecessary confusion is created that can lead to failure.

The second biggest mistake I see at companies is that they fail to pick a CM strategy. That is, they fail to say whether all eight functional areas of CM will be implemented up front in what I call the *full CM strategy*, or whether a subset of CM functional areas will be implemented up front or over time, which I call the *evolutionary CM strategy*. More about these in Chapter 5.

Key messages from this chapter

CM enables companies to change rapidly, whether it is their business processes, products, people, or technology. The key messages to be gleaned from this chapter are as follows:

1. CM has been around for a long time and has been applied to many different kinds of products including hardware, software, firmware, and non-computer-related products.

2. CM is a discipline and its techniques can be applied to anything.

3. If you understand the intentions of the terms *version, configuration item, baseline, variant,* and *change request,* then you have the gist of what CM is about.

4. The standard definition of CM is identification, control, status accounting, and auditing.

5. The unified view of CM brings together all operational elements of CM, which entail eight functional areas and its operational aspects.

6. CM is suitable for any kind of software and Web engineering model and is needed in all of them.

7. CM provides significant business and technical value to companies.

8. The bottom-line values are elimination of mistakes, cost-effective code building, quality automation, teamwork optimization, change complexity management, insurance against total failure, and survivability and growth.

9. CM is going through a renaissance due to the Internet era.

10. CM is invaluable for maintaining Web systems, so do it during development because you will most assuredly need it during maintenance.

11. One way or another, through pain, or from business growth, or due to success, a company is drawn to CM. Companies that get on the CM bandwagon as soon as possible can reap more benefits, more quickly than the competition.

12. If your company is seeking a CM solution, make sure there is a clear, universal definition of CM so that expectations are set correctly. For example, does CM include all eight functional areas or just some of them?

13. Also, make a strategic decision as to whether the CM solution will be evolutionary (that is, over a period of time all the functional areas of CM will be implemented) or full (that is, all eight functional areas will be implemented up front).

References

[1]   Buckley, F. J., *Implementing Configuration Management: Hardware, Software, and Firmware*, Los Alamitos, CA: IEEE Computer Society Press, 1996.

[2]   ISO 9000-3:1997, *Guidelines for the Application of ISO 9001:1994 to the Development, Supply, Installation, and Maintenance of Computer Software*, Geneva, Switzerland: ISO, 1997.

[3]   MIL-STD-973, *Configuration Management*, Washington, DC: U.S. Department of Defense, Apr. 1992.

[4]   SEI, *Capability Maturity Model, 2000*, http://www.sei.cmu.edu.

[5]   ANSI/IEEE Std-1042-1987—IEEE, *Guide to Software Configuration Management*, New York: IEEE, 1987.

[6]   Leon, A., *A Guide to Software Configuration Management*, Norwood, MA: Artech House, 2000.

[7]   Kelly, M., *Configuration Management: The Changing Image*, Berkshire, UK: McGraw-Hill, 1996.

[8]   Estublier, J. (Ed.), *Proc. 9th International Symp., SCM-9*, Toulouse, France, Sept. 1999, Berlin, Germany: Springer-Verlag.

[9]   Wiborg-Weber, D., "CM Strategies for RAD," *Proc. 9th International Symp., SCM-9*, J. Estublier (Ed.), Toulouse, France, Sept. 1999, Berlin, Germany: Springer-Verlag, pp. 204–216.

[10] Dart, S., "Concepts in Configuration Management Systems," *Proc. 3rd International Software Configuration Management Workshop*, Norway, Scandinavia, June 1991, New York: ACM Press, pp. 1–18. Also published as "Spectrum of Functionality in Configuration Management Systems," CMU/SEI-90-TR-11, Apr. 1991. On-line at http://www.sei.cmu.edu/tr.

[11] Starkman, D., and D. Stessa, "Debugging Yields Corporate American Unexpected Benefits," *The Wall Street Journal*, Dec. 27, 1999, p. A10.

[12] Feiler, P., "Configuration Management Models in Commercial Environments," Technical Report, Software Engineering Institute, Carnegie Mellon University, 1991.

[13] Dart, S., "To Change or Not To Change," *Application Development Trends,* June 1997, pp. 55–61.

The Automation of Configuration Management

"Nobody feeds me. I have to get my own living. I live by my wits. I have to think things out, catch what I can, take what comes. And it just so happens that what comes is flies and insects and bugs. And furthermore," said Charlotte, shaking one of her legs, *"do you realize that if I didn't catch bugs and eat them, bugs would increase and multiply and get so numerous that they'd destroy the earth, wipe out everything?"*
—E. B. White, *Charlotte's Web*

The 105 families of spiders in the world consist of more than 17,000 species. Just like spiders, there are species, or types, of configuration management (CM) tools (of course, not the same number of types as there are spiders). Each tool supports a few, many, or all of the functional areas of CM described in the previous chapter. In this chapter, I give you an overview of the spectrum of CM tools. But I don't talk about specific tools themselves because this book is really about principles of CM. So I talk about

107

concepts in CM tools and strategic decisions that you need to make when considering a particular CM tool.

You can easily find out about the specifics of tools by examining the CM vendors' Web sites (listed in Table 4.1), by using Internet search engines to locate the various Web sites with the meta-keyword "configuration management," by examining some of the books that do give specifics on CM tools [1, 2], or by buying expensive reports from industry analysts such as Ovum [3], Gartner Group [4], or IDC [5]. The CM tools are constantly evolving so any book that discusses the specifics of a CM tool (or any software tool) would probably be out of date by the time it was printed.

In this chapter, I present the important issues or principles about CM tools. First, I discuss the spectrum of commercial CM tools, which at one end consists of version control functionality, and at the other end, consists of everything imaginable in a CM tool—full process CM. I discuss the significance of the spectrum and why it is important for the Internet economy. Then I look at 10 aspects that need to be addressed by CM tools to meet the needs of Web development and maintenance. Following that, I give some insight into CM vendors who have some of the world's best experience in CM, and then I discuss the best tool. Following that, I present the many ramifications for companies in deciding the scope of their CM solution—enterprise-wide or group-specific? After that, I look at the relationship of CM to other software tools needed for development and maintenance. I end the chapter by discussing the demise of the CM industry as we know it along with the key messages of this chapter.

Table 4.1

The Leading Configuration Management Tools and Their Vendors

CM Tool	Vendor	Web Site
AllChange	Intasoft Limited	www.intasoft.co.uk
Continuus	Continuus	www.continuus.com
ClearCase	Rational	www.rational.com
Harvest	Platinum Technology	www.platinum.com
Perforce	Perforce Software	www.perforce.com
PVCS	Merant	www.merant.com
Source Integrity	MKS	www.mks.com
SourceSafe	Microsoft	www.microsoft.com
StarTeam	Starbase Corp.	www.starbase.com
TrueChange	True Software	www.truesoft.com

Automated, not manual, configuration management

The automation of CM enables all the benefits and values I described in Chapter 3. Without automation, companies get stuck in the old view of CM (discussed in the previous chapter). CM tools have turned a once very bureaucratic inefficient way of doing CM into an empowering, efficient means of eliminating chores and harnessing the creativity of developers, software engineers, testers, QA staff, and managers.

As I wrote in [6], not all CM tools are equal, meaning that, while there are many commercial CM tools, they are quite different: Different because they each implement features to support one, some, or all of the functional areas of CM that I mentioned in Chapter 3. Different because tools were not built to a single, universal model or definition of CM. Different because some tools are more mature than others. Different in the CM strategy they support, such as evolutionary CM or full-process CM (which is discussed later in this chapter).

Knowing that there are differences makes it easier for companies during tool selection time, as I will discuss in Chapter 5. It also avoids problems of comparing apples to oranges: For instance, Merant's PVCS Version Manager is an evolutionary CM tool, whereas Merant's PVCS Dimensions is a full-process CM tool. Thus, any comparisons would have to take into account that Version Manager will be a lot cheaper than Dimensions because they are quite different tools, although they both address CM requirements, but in different degrees.

Spectrum of configuration management tools

I view CM tools as belonging to a spectrum: at one end are the evolutionary tools; at the other end, the full-process tools. Figure 4.1 attempts to visualize this spectrum. Use it only as rough guide and keep in mind that the tools are all evolving into a unified view of CM, albeit via different implementations.

With the evolutionary type of tools, a company is buying a partial CM solution (pieces of the eight functional areas presented in Chapter 3). These tools enable a company, if it desires, to "grow" its CM solution. For instance, a company may start out with Perforce and at some point realize that it needs change management support. It then has the choice of either building its own into Perforce or buying an existing change

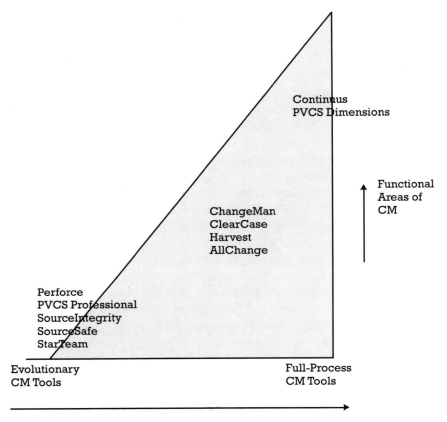

Figure 4.1   Spectrum of CM tools.

management (bug tracking) tool or completely replacing the tool. I always encourage buying ready-made solutions rather than building your own because the maintenance of the home-built tools will get in the way of building your own products. Similarly, a company might buy Clear-Case and then decide it needs to evolve into change management, in which case it would be encouraged (by Rational) to buy ClearQuest.

On the other hand, if a company wants to buy everything out of the box—all the CM functional areas of Chapter 3—then it would choose tools at the other end of the spectrum, typically Continuus or PVCS Dimensions.

Not all configuration management tools are the same

Most of the CM vendors claim that their tools provide complete CM. Although they do not, their terminology may indicate that they do, which can be confusing. For instance, a lot of evolutionary tools may have a variable or label or field or tag on their files called *state*. This state can indicate the different states in the workflow or process model. Now, you can implement a very simple form of workflow using that state variable, but it does not compare to the notion of state in the full-process tools like Continuus or Dimensions. The full-process tools have semantics or knowledge and metadata that are automatically associated with the notion of state, such as roles and actions or version binding rules (file selections). Hence, the notion of state in the full-process tools is much more powerful.

In the evolutionary tools, the users have to manually (specifically) do the things that are automatically done by the full-process tools. A simple example: In evolutionary tools, a user would have to tag every file saying it is part of a configuration item, or this configuration item has changed state, whereas with full-process tools, with one command, the user completes an action that automatically triggers a state change to a whole series of configuration items, which can trigger new workflows in change requests, which can trigger workflow movements in related data (as well as in other tools). Hence, everything is tightly, seamlessly integrated in full-process tools and the tool makes use of that knowledge to do "smart" things that, in evolutionary tools, users would have to keep track of or initiate themselves. With full-process tools, users are faced with fewer "chore-like" tasks and with less room for making mistakes.

Of course, there are obvious tradeoffs in choosing between an evolutionary tool and a full-process one, as shown in Table 4.2. The tools that are in between on the spectrum have different degrees of tradeoffs. It all boils down to which tool meets all of your requirements within the given constraints, or tradeoffs. In Chapter 6, in the case studies, you will see that some companies chose evolutionary tools because they were cheaper and easier to train their Web authors on.

Table 4.2
Tradeoffs in Configuration Management Tool Choices

Tradeoff	Evolutionary Type	Full-Process Type
Cost	Lower	Much higher
Ease of use	More intuitive	More complicated
Chore factor	Very high	Very low
Error potential	High	Low
Spectrum of functionality	Low; must add to	Very high
Training time	Low	High
Selection complexity	Low; buy by phone	High; relationship with vendor
Deployment	Theoretically quick	Longer
Variety of users/roles	Lightweight	Heavyweight (broad spectrum)

CM for Web teams

The traditional software CM tools are applicable to Web content, because Web content is software. The CM vendors are enhancing their tools to better support Web users. Table 4.3 shows specific Web requirements for CM tools:

1. Delta algorithms for efficient storage and retrieval of types of content, such as graphics, audio, and video, are being added. Traditional CM tools typically support source and binary code delta techniques.

2. Program interfaces are being included, including interfaces or APIs (application program interfaces) for Web IDEs and tools, such as for Java, XML, HTML editors, Web testing tools, traffic monitoring tools, and so on.

3. User interfaces vary, so lightweight and heavyweight interfaces are being provided to support the different kinds of content creators, ranging from content authors who are not software engineers right through to experienced software developers.

4. Browser access to CM functionality supports any kind of user, for instance, someone who has to change content, someone who

Table 4.3

Extra Web Requirements for Configuration Management Tools

Web Requirement	Explanation
Delta techniques	Algorithms for efficient storage of versions of all types of content
Program interfaces	Integration with or access to all types of tools
Lightweight and heavyweight interfaces	Multiple user interface types to suit type of user (author, developer, manager)
Browser access	Access to functionality via various browsers
Transparent access	No need to know physical address of a file to change it
Template access	Access to specific version of template
Dynamic content support	Capturing dynamic configurations
Multiple change life cycles	Different workflows depending on type of change
Transitory content	Dealing with incomplete configurations
Component library management	Managing run-time changes to libraries

needs to submit a change request even if they do not have a CM client license, and someone who needs to view specific CM information such as a supplier.

5. Access to Web content is transparent under CM control. That is, authors can access content on the live site or a development or staging area site without having to know the actual physical address of the files.

6. Access to the template for the Web site versus access to the content that gets published into the template is distinguished. Also, access rights to a template or to content are based on role. For instance, content authors can only change their own content and only for a specific version of the template, whereas a Web developer can change code or back-office applications associated with his or her group, and graphic design artists can only change icons in the latest version of the template.

7. Dynamic content support allows users to capture configurations of dynamic content. Not all companies need this but those that have stringent auditing requirements or litigation risks will require it.

8. Being able to support different types of change requests and their life cycles is important. For instance, show-stopper bugs will most likely follow a different path than enhancements or low-priority bugs.

9. CM tools will have to be able to function with incomplete configuration items because parts of them could be transitory, making it impossible to put under CM control.

10. CM tools are able to manage the run-time (dynamic) updating of reusable components and libraries that make up the Web system.

A few of these issues require further discussion.

Lightweight versus heavyweight tools

Everyone who creates or changes code or content must do CM. This means that anyone who is accessing, adding, or changing content needs to be using the CM tool in some form or other. Now, if all the users were experienced software developers, then it would be a simple matter to merely train them on the tool. As illustrated in Figure 4.2, however, a company's Web content may be manipulated by many new types of users—users who are not software developers but rather content specialists (such as insurance adjusters, marketing personnel, and salespeople), technical writers, graphic design artists, and so on. Such people have no clue about CM, nor do they want to, or should they need to. They are specialists in their own fields. At the same time, the software developers, such as those in the Information Technology (IT) Department, need full CM facilities.

This means, then, that CM must be presented to each of the different types of users in a palatable manner, which implies that their training (if any) needs to be adjusted to suit their backgrounds, and then the CM tool's user interface, or usage model, needs to suit them. Hence, the content specialists need a very "lightweight" user interface, whereas the software developers need access to all of the functionality offered by CM and, hence, need the "heavyweight" user interface. Thus, the CM tool needs to have different interfaces or usage models to suit the particular user.

Some vendors have taken different approaches to this requirement. For instance, Starbase hides CM from content authors simply by tagging a file that they change, which in turn flags the CM person that new

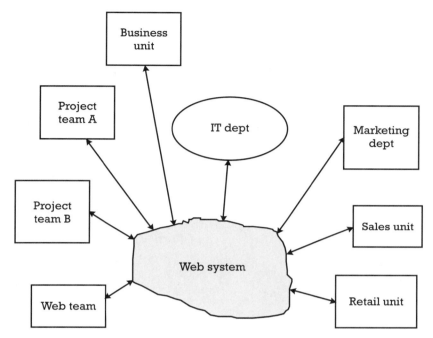

Figure 4.2   Different departments in a company change the Web site.

versions of files exist. On the other hand, Continuus's WebSynergy CM tool presents interfaces and commands specific to the role of the user.

Dynamic content

Some companies must provide a means to track their dynamic content—content that is created on-the-fly based on a user's Web request, for instance. Companies that have stringent auditing requirements or may face litigation risks if they publish or generate incorrect information on which their clients act (such as stock trades), or Web systems that must run nonstop and be fault-tolerant need to track their sites' dynamic content.

One way of achieving this would be to make the CM tool become part of the Web's execution environment. In effect, the CM tool automatically captures (records) dynamic configurations as they are created. The other, simpler way is to make use of existing CM facilities and basically snapshot the state of the content before the dynamic stuff is created, and then snapshot the state after it has been created. This gives a before-and-after effect.

Component library management

Web systems and Web content can be built out of reusable components, such as Microsoft Foundation Classes or JavaBeans. During the execution or running of the Web system, the components and dynamic link libraries can be upgraded or new ones added. This obviously changes the state of the complete configuration or release of that Web system. Anytime an update is made, or a new component added, huge compatibility issues arise. For instance, incompatible components or libraries can cause a server to crash or create other dangerous situations: A new component version might work for one Web site or server, but not another; moving the Web system to another machine or platform can cause a crash or different behavior; or any automatically generated code could be incompatible with the new component or library, causing a crash. Such problems and solutions are described very well in [7].

What the configuration management vendors are doing

Vendors are taking different approaches to CM for the Web. All have added Web functions to their tools by offering access to some or all CM functionality through a browser. They continue to work to provide all the Web requirements listed earlier. Some have chosen brand new products for the Web, such as Continuus's WebSynergy or MKS's WebIntegrity. Each vendor has their marketing strategy for the Web, such as Merant's "Egility."

Some vendors are positioning their tools differently for the Web. For example, Merant's PVCS is being positioned as the core foundation for any environment. All vendors have renamed *configuration management* to *change management*. I feel this renaming is limiting and perhaps a mistake by the vendors, because Web teams still need CM regardless of what it is called. I see change management as just one of the eight functional areas of CM (as mentioned already in Chapter 3). But this renaming is not a serious problem. It just boils down to the same issue mentioned in Chapter 3: Make sure your company knows exactly what the term *change management*, or CM, means.

Also, changing the term puts the CM tools directly in competition now with a new breed of Internet tools, called *Web content management tools* [8]. Table 4.4 shows some of the well-known Web content management tools. Some of these tools, such as StoryServer or TeamSite, are high-priced tools designed to support all aspects of Web content. They had very little CM in their initial few versions, but that has to change because CM support is needed. Hence, they are now direct competitors to CM tools.

Apart from repositioning their products for the Internet, vendors will have to focus more energy on CM services. As you will see in Chapter 5, CM solution deployment (like any other software tool) has its challenges and requires strategic decision-making on the part of companies, especially with full-process CM solutions. Many companies that buy CM tools fail to implement or deploy a CM solution because they fail in their technology adoption practices. They do not do the necessary strategic decision-making, or training, or setting expectations correctly, and so on. Tool selection and deployment issues will be discussed further in the next chapter.

CM vendors will eventually provide an out-of-the-box solution, rather than giving the client a "skeleton" and saying, "Hey, go build your own solution. You can do anything with this tool." Companies can ill afford to expend a lot of effort creating their own CM solution from a skeleton. Vendors will provide better parameterization of their tools so

Table 4.4
Some Web Content Management Tools

Content Tool	Vendor	Web Site
ArticleBase	Running Start	www.runningstart.com
ColdFusion	Allaire	www.allaire.com
DreamWeaver	Macromedia	www.dreamweaver.com
DynaBase	Inso	www.inso.com
Frontier	Userland	www.userland.com
FrontPage	Microsoft	www.microsoft.com
Fusion	NetObjects	www.netobjects.com
Raveler	Platinum Technologies	www.raveler.com
StoryServer	Vignette Corp.	www.vignette.com
TeamSite	Interwoven	www.interwoven.com

that their customers can more easily tailor the tools to their processes. Also, vendors will eventually provide industry-specific process templates out of the box rather than just one approach, which will speed up start-up time.

What is the best configuration management tool?

This book does not tell you which CM tool or vendor is the best because there is no such thing. A tool is good when it suits the needs of users, and there are so many different kinds of users and needs in the world that every tool has its value. Also, I do not want to focus on specific tools because they evolve, vendors merge or get bought out, and eventually, the CM industry will "die" as I discuss at the end of the chapter. By this I mean that eventually IDEs will all have embedded CM capabilities so CM, integrated with a full suite of tools (requirements, testing, traffic monitoring, site administration, help desks, software distribution tools, and so on), will be an automatic capability in IDEs.

People often ask me: "What is the best CM tool?" Because none of the tools is "equal" [6], answering such a question is like trying to compare apples to oranges: Today I need more vitamin C, so I prefer oranges, but tomorrow, I prefer apples. Also, although some of the fabulous CM tools are based on at least a decade of solid CM automation, I do not believe there is such a thing as "the best" CM tool because a tool is only as good as how well the company uses it. For instance, at a high level, I judge a CM tool by three key factors:

1. The user interface must perfectly suit each kind of user.

2. The tool's concepts or features (such as the commands and the CM process indicators) must be intuitively obvious to the user.

3. All features of the tool must be usable.

Now, these factors are all subjective. For instance, one developer may prefer Dimensions over Continuus because of the user interface. Another may prefer ClearCase, regardless of its features because it does not appear to change the user's existing interface. Hence, to me, the best CM tool is the tool that a company can easily deploy, as well as make use of all the potential it offers.

I certainly have tremendous admiration for the full-process-oriented tools because they have the most powerful CM features and can solve many problems. But such tools serve no purpose if the users cannot understand them or use them. So, it boils down to this: What functionality needs to be supported? What value is to be gained? Is this tool easily used? Does it provide the performance needed?

Enterprise-wide solution or project-specific solution?

In Chapter 3 I mentioned several key strategic decisions that a company must make. Another one to add to the list is the scope of the CM solution. That is, will the CM solution be enterprise-wide or group-specific? This has ramifications on the tool chosen as well as the selection and deployment approach. The enterprise-wide solution means that all groups use the same CM tool. A group-specific solution refers to the situation in which each group decides what is best for itself. Either decision has its own ramifications, as shown in Table 4.5. As usual, every decision has its "pros and cons," its positive and negative sides. It all depends on the goals and vision your company has as to which approach it adopts.

Companies that follow a decentralized approach to their management techniques and infrastructure typically decide on a group-specific CM solution because each group is responsible for its own tools and processes. Small, medium, and large companies that practice centralized management typically choose the enterprise-wide solution because they want to have a uniform tool set across groups, that is, the same CM tool (and other tools) for everyone.

Table 4.5 shows all the good and bad ramifications of the CM scope decision. With an enterprise-wide CM solution, a company ensures that each group will be using the same tool. That way, the company can more easily budget for its tool support and maintenance activities. It can also centralize and have all tool support and help-desk facilities in one spot, rather than in each group. There will be a group (maybe the Tools Group or the CM Group) that acquires all the CM knowledge by helping each group deploy and maintain its CM solution. Of course, selecting and deploying the uniform CM solution require much more effort to be put into selecting the right tool since everyone has to agree on the CM requirements and the tool.

An enterprise-wide CM solution also means a company can get a much bigger price cut because it is buying a lot of tool licenses,

Table 4.5
Ramifications of an Enterprise-Wide or Group-Specific CM Decision

Decision	Good Ramification	Bad Ramification
Enterprise-wide CM solution	Uniform tool and process support	Longer tool selection and deployment
	Tool administration and help desk located in one place	Each group becomes dependent on the one location of tool support
	Disseminate CM knowledge through company and leverage other teams' experiences	More resource outlay for selection and deployment
	Bigger price cut on tool licenses and after-sales consulting and support	Bigger commitment to single vendor
	Sets foundation for corporate-wide process improvement activities	Could get stuck in process analysis paralysis
	Teams can share code and use same components, resulting in efficiencies	Business model may not suit sharing
Group-specific CM solution	Quicker CM tool selection and deployment	Company ends up supporting multiple tools and disjointed processes that eventually must be integrated
	Only pay for CM functionality that particular group needs, so pay less	Intergroup communication and workflow are limited by ability to integrate disparate tools
	Group can fine-tune or optimize its activities	Limits company's ability to do process improvement since there is no global knowledge

consulting, and maintenance from the vendor. But it also means the company has committed to a single vendor and has to spend more money up front. The enterprise-wide CM solution greatly aids a company in its corporate process improvement efforts (such as the Capability Maturity Model Integration, or SPICE, or ISO 9000). Because all groups use the same tool, they participate in similar or related processes (workflow), which means that a tremendous amount of corporate knowledge (meta-data) is stored in the tool's repository. The company can tap into that knowledge and easily make process improvements from that. But companies can sometimes overdo the improvements, taking away from the practicality of the CM solution.

With the choice of a group-specific CM solution, this means that the group can much more quickly select a tool and deploy it, as it only has to worry about itself, and no other group or decision-makers. But the end result of this is that, over time, the company ends up having to support many different CM tools and live with many unrelated processes and practices. On the other hand, the group only has to pay for the CM functionality that it needs rather than possibly a bigger, more expensive tool with features it would not use. But it also limits the ability for intergroup communication depending on how well the tools can be integrated. On the good side, though, the group can fine-tune and optimize its CM activities. But because each group has its own tools, processes, and practices, it makes it much more difficult for the company as a whole to pursue major process-improvement or standardization efforts. All the knowledge is resident in each group's tools. That is, it is distributed and not centrally located for easy access, and the quality or amount of knowledge retained is uneven.

Companies that want to achieve an enterprise-wide solution like to "hedge their bets," or mitigate their risk to committing to a single tool and vendor, by starting out with a group-specific solution. They use that as the pilot, the "proof of concept" project, so to speak, to give them confidence in picking that tool. In effect, they cut their risk up front, work with an enterprise-wide solution in mind, but start out by implementing a group-specific solution. Deployment decisions and strategies are discussed in Chapter 5.

As with everything in life, there are good and bad aspects to all decisions. The key is to find the right balance for your company while understanding the ramifications of the decisions. The bad ramifications can be nullified or mitigated by basic risk management techniques, as I will discuss further in the next chapter. Anything is possible.

Relationship to other disciplines and tools

Where does CM fit in relationship to other practices in a company regarding software development and maintenance? As shown previously in Figure 3.1, CM plays a support role in all phases of the software development and maintenance life cycle. Figure 4.3 shows the process more from

Figure 4.3   The bigger picture for configuration management.

the business perspective. The intention is to show that CM information is pertinent in all business areas: from sales, to support (such as help desks or hot lines), development, testing, building, change managers (such as quality assurance), software distribution, and, finally, the users.

People in all of these areas need CM information or access. For instance, salespeople need to know what the latest release of the software product is and which bug fixes it has. The support personnel need to know if there is a work-around for the current bug notification. Developers need to know which bug fix or enhancement to work on today. Testers need to know when a new version of a release is ready for testing. Build managers need to know when they can do a final integration build. Change managers need to know when to package all of the fixes and give them the final regression test or traffic monitoring tests. The distribution people need to know when to notify customers that a new version of the release can be downloaded. Users want to know if all the fixes and enhancements they requested actually went into the new version. These are just some of the issues. What companies typically do, then, is to buy a range of tools, as shown in Figure 4.4.

CM tools are often combined with other tools to meet the needs of all areas of business. Help-desk tools assist the hot-line or support staff to track and respond to all customer requests and queries and bug/enhancement reports. Salespeople use their customer relationship management

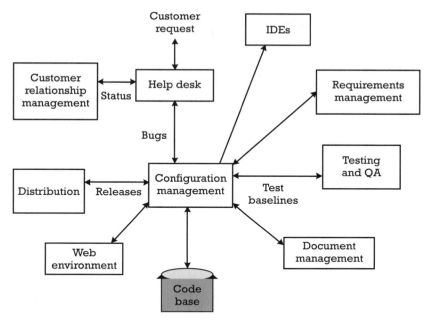

Figure 4.4 Configuration management tool integrated with other tools.

(CRM) tools to track the sales and issues related to their clients and prospects. Designers use a requirements management tool to track all the requirements and then associate versions of requirements with versions of code or Web content. Testers and QA staff use the testing tools to regression test code or content, while using the CM tool to determine which test baselines to use. Customer service people use the document management tool to access all the appropriate forms and use the CM tool to determine which are the latest versions of the forms. Build or release managers use the distribution tools to download upgrades to the field or notify customers that the new version is on the Web site. Those managers use the CM tool to determine when there is a new release and what pieces are involved.

The Web development environment (IDE) is integrated with the CM tool so that all the CM benefits described in Chapter 3 can be attained. Companies integrate these types of tools to get the best possible software and Web production, delivery, and service solution. Now let us examine in detail the concepts that are found in CM tools to support all the functionality areas discussed in Chapter 3.

Concepts, or architectural elements, in configuration management tools

Three key papers [9–11] have addressed the concepts, or architectural elements, of CM tools. Each took a different approach, "slicing and dicing" up the tools. In [11], I presented the 15 key concepts that existed across commercial and academic CM tools to support all the functional areas shown in Chapter 3. For this book, I have simplified the concepts I wrote about earlier in [11] to 12, in order to suit commercial CM systems. Excellent research CM tools [12–20] have come from industry and academia, but because of business reasons, or because the concepts were too complex, they did not enjoy a long life as a commercial CM tool.

I present 12 concepts: versions, repository, system models, workspaces, builds, relationships, change requests, change life cycles, change sets, processes, tasks, and audit trail. By "concepts," I mean the fundamental implementation notions in the CM tools. In Table 4.6, the concepts are related to the operational elements of CM (which I discussed in Chapter 3). You can use this list of concepts as a way of further understanding, and articulating objectively (that is, *independent of a vendor's terminology*), what would be important to you in a CM tool.

Many innovative CM tools—NSE [12], Jasmine [13], SMS [14], Adele [15], CMA [16], shape [20], Rational [19] (I'm speaking here of the original Rational CMVC system that was built into the hardware, not the purchase of ClearCase by Rational), and Aide-de-Camp [17]—had either short life spans or were used mostly in research situation. All of these, and others, have greatly contributed to improving the quality and nature of automated CM.

Versions

A *version* is an instance of a component and is given a unique identification. It is typically created when a file is checked out or checked into the CM repository (see below). A component can be any type: data file, document file, HTML file, ASP page, JavaScript, C code, library of code, a single requirement, a Word file, an audio or video file—basically any kind of software file or portion thereof. For storage efficiency, algorithms are developed (generically called *delta techniques*) to minimize space and maximize version extraction time.

Version control then is a generic term covering many aspects, which include tracking the component's lifetime; that is, keeping knowledge

Table 4.6
Concepts in Commercial Configuration Management Tools

Tool Concept	Chapter 3 CM Operational Aspects	Chapter 3 Functional Area
Versions	Version identification	Version and configuration control
Versions	Configuration items	
Versions	Baselines and variants	
Repository	Types of components	
Versions	History records	
System models	System architecture	Configuration item structuring
System models	Relationships and traceability	
System models	Version selection	
System models	Consistency management	
Workspaces	Project contexts	
Repository	Repository management	
Builds	Build management	Construction of configurations
Builds	Build optimization	
Builds	Repeatability	
Relationships	Change impact analysis	Change management
Change requests	Change requests and classification	
Change life cycles	Change tracking and escalation	
Change sets	Change sets	
Change sets	Change propagation	
Change requests	Release planning	
Workspaces	Workspace management	Teamwork support
Workspaces	Parallel development	
Versions	Variant management	
Repository	Distributed and remote development	
Processes	Role support and access control	Process management
Tasks	Notifications	
Processes	Event triggers	
Processes	Life cycle and workflow support	
Tasks	Task and project management	
Audit trail	Logging	Auditing
Repository	Validation of integrity of CM activities	
Repository	Queries	Status reporting
Repository	Report generation	
Repository	Metrics gathering	

(metadata) about the component. This knowledge includes who created this version, why, when, how, its predecessors, its successors, any relationships it has with other components, and so on. Thus, at any point in time, a user of the tool can query the history of that version.

Associated with versions are structural elements: means for relating versions of components to each other. A generic term is *configuration item,* or some people prefer the term *baseline, snapshot,* or *release.* Meaning can be assigned to the terms. For instance, a release can be a group of components that are built together, or compiled, or belong on the same Web page.

All of the versions of components that make up the configuration item have a logical relationship, such as they belong in the same build (compilation) or to the same Web page.

Further, configuration items can be related to each other. These are called *variants* because they are a "variation on a theme." For instance, configuration item A could be the Web site variant for the United Kingdom, while configuration item B could be the variant for Spain. With variants come the ability to do version comparison, at the component (file) or the configuration item level, and detection of differences.

To support multiple developers and teams working on the same version of a component or configuration item, the notion of branching exists. A branch is created and uniquely identified. The person or team can work on that branch.

A branch can have many logical meanings to the user, such as "I'm branching off to test a certain fix," or "The team has to branch off this release to create a variant Web site for Germany," or "The new development team is branching off the latest release of the U.S. Web site in order to begin the site's redesign." The CM tool provides facilities to support the user's interpretation of branching and its method of teamwork.

In general, a branch represents a logically separate piece of work. At some point, the branch may be merged back into the original line of development or it may keep evolving as a separate configuration item. The gap between the branch point and the merge point needs to be filled. That is, all the changes that happened during that gap must be added or merged in at the merge point. As you can see, branching creates lots of complexity but serves many purposes. Companies get themselves into lots of trouble by not merging frequently enough. Conflict detection and resolution can be a lot of work and some tools can automatically merge on certain types of differences.

Repository

The *repository*, or CM database or library, is the most fundamental notion in a CM tool. The repository gathers all the metadata, or knowledge, about everything that is under CM—all the attributes or information about each version of component or configuration item, branches, audit trail, relationships, process descriptions, change requests, build information, and the bill of materials (everything that went into the build). Knowledge is gathered at every CM action, such as check-in or check-out. The repository is typically implemented via a commercial database system so it requires the usual database administration and provides fault tolerance and scalability benefits. Hence, typical database query systems (such as SQL) are supported, and data can be analyzed and reports generated.

For remote, distributed development, CM tools support some kind of replication and synchronization facility. This enables a user to replicate a branch, for instance, or a complete copy of the code, to a remote site or onto a different machine and continue working there. At some point, all the remote user's changes can be reconciled back to the main code base and CM repository. Similarly, the remote user can synchronize his or her code base and CM repository with any changes made at the main site or to his or her remote or replicated site. Replication, reconciliation, and synchronization are all implemented as atomic transactions to ensure the integrity of data in the repository.

Workspaces

A *workspace* is a working environment or context that provides safety from another developer's or another team's work on the same, or different, versions of files or configuration items. All work done in the workspace is under CM. A workspace can insulate one developer from another so that they cannot overwrite each other's work, for instance, when writing a bug fix to the same file. On the other hand, a developer can merge changes to his or her workspace in order to keep up-to-date with all the changes to the main code-line. Each tool provides different semantics for workspaces, but the main idea is to support teamwork with parallel development activities (variant construction and evolution).

A workspace can also represent a project context so that all the tools and the versions of files brought into the workspace are specific to that project.

System models

System model is a generic term for all the knowledge about a buildable or constructable configuration item. For instance, all files that went into compiling the COBOL-coded insurance system, or all the HTML and ASP and text files and template that went into the latest release of the U.S. Web site would be in the system model. The system model captures the relationships between the files, the versions of files used, the rules about how the files were compiled or put together or generated (a makefile, for instance), and verification rules (such as "C header files do not get compiled with Pascal code," or "Only one template file can be used in constructing a Web site").

Builds

Builds are all about generating or compiling configuration items. Think of a build as being all the rules to create, such as executing a makefile that contains all the information about what to build and how to do it, and then all the results of executing that makefile (typically called *bill-of-materials*) such as the versions of files used in that build, the tools, the options on the tools, the libraries, the data sets, the template, the version of operating system and machine, and person responsible.

Some tools have the added notion of an object pool where all derived components are tracked so that they can be reused in builds, which can save a considerable amount of compilation time. Each build is given a unique identification so that the resultant configuration item (release, baseline) can be regenerated at any point in time given the bill-of-materials.

Relationships

Versions of components are *related* to each other. For instance, files are predecessors or successors of each other so they have a chronological relationship. All components in a configuration item belong together to make up that version. Variants are related to each other in that they may share code and changes. Files can be related to each other such as C header files and C code files. The makefiles are related to configuration items.

All relationships are tracked by the CM tool and some tools have specific relationship types that define certain semantics or rules between those related items. For instance, when analyzing the impact of changing a file, the CM tool will find all the related files and determine the effect on making that change. Changing a name on the Web site may affect all 1,000 pages and maybe 50% of the back-office application code.

Change requests

A *change request* appears to the user as a form with fields. The change request represents all the information about a change, from the time it is created until it is completed or closed. A change request is generic enough to capture any type or class of change such as a show-stopper bug, a patch, an enhancement, or a low-priority fix. Some tools allow users to assign many fields to a change request.

Change request reports can be generated to be used by change planning or release planning teams (such as a change control board). Change requests are kept in a database (for full-process tools in the CM repository, or for evolutionary tools, typically in a separate database).

Change life cycles

Change requests (or simply, changes) go through their own *life cycle* (as discussed in Chapter 3 and in [21]). Some tools provide active workflow or process support such that during each phase of the change cycle, such as the arrival of a new change request, completion of impact analysis, or task assignment, a particular person is notified by e-mail. The help desk, for instance, might be notified that the change request has been deferred until a later date. Or the Web coordinator might be notified that testing has been completed on the change so it can now move onto the publish stage.

Change escalation is supported. That is, at some point, changes that were deferred or had low priority have to find their way "up the priority level" in order to be done. Some tools enable users to be notified when certain classes of changes have been "sitting" in the database biding their time. The priority level or urgency level can be altered.

Change sets

A *change set* is implemented in various ways, although no tool implements "pure" change sets—pure in the sense that the underlying technology is change based rather than file based (as are all commercial CM systems). The TrueChange tool did, but no longer appears as a commercial tool at the time of this writing. Details of change sets are discussed in [22], but briefly, a change set (called a *change folder* in the manual view of CM) is a logical change. That is, it is the knowledge that for any given change, all those files were adjusted. For instance, a "fix the copyright name" change set might entail the updating of 1,000 files.

Users can work with configuration items at the logical change level rather than the file level. For instance, users can ask the CM tool to tell them which changes went into the latest Web site. The response will be the "fix the copyright name" change set. They do not need to know the names of the 1,000 files (although that information would be available, too).

Change sets are perfectly suited to variant management. For instance, in the case of variants, the user wants the "fix the copyright name" change set to be applied across all variants—to the Web sites in Spain, Germany, and the United Kingdom. So it can tell the CM tool to generate new variant versions with that change set applied. Files are automatically merged if possible, or else the user is notified to do the merge.

Processes

Some CM tools have the notion of process. A *process* is the workflow, or sequence of events or states, that a component (such as a configuration item) goes through, as described in Chapter 3. A process is implemented in different ways. A simple process (often called a promotion model in evolutionary tools) is one in which a state variable is attached to a component; in a more complex process (such as for full-process tools), a process object captures all the knowledge (metadata) for the workflow, including all the roles involved and events, and conditions that must be triggered before the component can move forward to the next state, along with automatic notifications to affected parties.

Tasks

Some CM tools have the notion of a *task.* That is, there is an assignment of work associated with a developer (or tester, QA manager, and so on) to a configuration item. A task can be assigned to a developer when a change request is authorized. That task notion can be integrated with project management tools to track, for instance, how long it took to make the change or how much it cost.

Audit trail

The CM tool logs all commands and data changes so that a trail or report can be generated that shows all the actions, events, and changes that took place, when, how, and by whom.

As you can imagine with all the concepts, and the complexity involved in their implementation (such as scaling it up to millions of components), developing a great CM tool is not an easy job. It takes about a decade for a commercial CM tool (especially a full-process one) to mature (along with the business side of the vendor). The really mature CM tools have typically gone through several prototypes or have been completely redone.

I have tremendous respect for CM tool developers and architects. Not many software tools can offer all the benefits I discussed in Chapter 3 along with helping the world avoid a Web crisis. The only comparable tools in complexity would be distributed operating systems and possibly enterprise resource planning tools. So, when you pay a lot for a good CM tool, you recoup that outlay very quickly (assuming the tool is properly deployed, of course).

The death and resurrection of the configuration management industry

The Internet economy is offering the CM tools industry a chance to resurrect itself, to reposition itself. The pre-Internet CM tools industry will die or, rather, change form. CM vendors will redefine themselves and their products in the wake of the Internet economy. CM will be transformed into a core or foundational element of any Web IDE or tool suite because the Web crisis will force it and the software industry to this point. Looking back at Figure 4.4, you can see that many tools are typically integrated with the CM tool. Eventually, CM functionality will either be embedded in those other tools (because those tools have the metadata about the data it manages), or else those other tools will have to open up their repositories so that CM tools can access the necessary metadata. CM tools (or services) will be sold as an embedded solution, as a partner to other tools. For all of this to happen, efforts at standardization and publicizing of application interfaces are required.

CM vendors will become much more involved in the services side of the CM solution. CM customers will start consolidating their tools back into a more centralized approach. CM vendors then will need to make sure that their tools interact with other CM vendors' tools.

As CM tools approach the unified model of CM discussed in Chapter 3, albeit via their own implementation methods, we will see a CM services industry develop; "services" in the sense of "plug and play" where companies and vendors of non-CM tools will want a CM service plug-in for their IDE, or to integrate with their tool set. They might want to rent that service over the Internet, thereby avoiding the need for client software.

The Internet economy also brings more competition to the CM vendors with their content management tools, as shown in Table 4.4. CM vendors will need to merge their technology with that. It will take a long time for the Web content management tools to catch up to the same CM technology. As part of this competition, the CM vendors now call CM *change management,* which I feel is a misnomer because their tools provide much more than just change management.

Key messages from this chapter

1. There are many wonderful, commercial CM tools. There is no need for a company to build its own. If it cannot afford to buy one, it can get free ones off the WWW. (But of course, you get what you pay for. Free tools can create more problems for a company than they solve.)

2. Web content is software. Traditional CM tools work well with Web content.

3. CM tools are either evolutionary ones or full-process ones. You either create a complete CM solution by plugging together several tools over time, or you can buy everything out of the box at one time that interacts seamlessly.

4. A strategic decision that a company must make is whether the CM solution will be enterprise-wide or group-specific. This has ramifications on the tool chosen as well as the selection and deployment approach.

5. CM tools are often combined with other tools to meet the needs of all areas of business. Obvious tools to have include the help desk, requirements management, distribution, and testing tools.

6. Commercial CM tools can be viewed as consisting of 12 concepts or architectural elements: versions, repository, system models, workspaces, builds, relationships, change requests, change life cycles, change sets, processes, tasks, and an audit trail.

7. The Internet economy enables the CM industry to transform itself.

8. CM tools are fabulous. Use one today!

References

[1]   Whitgift, D., *Methods and Tools for Software Configuration Management,* Chichester, England: John Wiley & Sons, 1991.

[2]   Leon, A., *A Guide to Software Configuration Management,* Norwood, MA: Artech House, 2000.

[3]   Ovum, on-line at http://www.ovum.com.

[4]   Gartner Group, on-line at http://www.gartner.com.

[5]   IDC, on-line at http://www.idc.com.

[6]   Dart, S., "Not All Tools Are Created Equal," *Application Development Trends,* Oct. 1996, pp. 39–50.

[7]   Larsson, M., and I. Crnkovic, "New Challenges for Configuration Management," *Proc. 9th Int. Symp. on System Configuration Management,* Toulouse, France, Sept. 5–7, 1999, pp. 232–243.

[8]   Dart, S., "WebCrisis.Com: Inability To Maintain," *Software Magazine,* Sept. 1999, pp. 50–57.

[9]   Feiler, P., "Configuration Management Models in Commercial Environments," SEI Technical Report SEI-90-TR-7, 1990, on-line at http://www.sei.cmu.edu/tr.

[10] Cagan, M., "Configuration Management for Team Engineering," Continuus Software Corp. White Paper, 1994, on-line at http://www.continuus.com.

[11] Dart, S., "Concepts in Configuration Management Systems," *Proc. 3rd Int. Software Configuration Management Workshop,* Norway, Scandinavia, June 1991, ACM Press, pp. 1–18; also published as "Spectrum of Functionality in Configuration Management Systems," CMU/SEI-90-TR-11, Apr. 1991, on-line at http://sei.cmu.edu/tr.

[12] Feiler, P., and G. Downey, "Transaction-Oriented Configuration Management," *SEI Report SEI-90-TR-23,* Software Engineering Institute, Nov. 1990, on-line at http://www.sei.cmu.edu/tr.

[13] Marzullo, K., and D. Wiebe, "Jasmine: A Software System Modelling Facility," *Proc. ACM SIGSOFT/SIGPLAN Software Engineering Symposium on Practical Software Development Environments*, Dec. 1986, pp. 121–130.

[14] Cohen, E., et al., "Version Management in Gypsy," *Proc. ACM SIGSOFT/SIGPLAN Software Engineering Symposium on Practical Software Development Environments*, Dec. 1988, pp. 210–215.

[15] Estublier, J., "A Configuration Manager: The Adele Data Base of Programs," *Proc. Workshop on Software Engineering Environments for Programming-in-the-Large*, June 1985, pp. 140–147.

[16] Ploedereder, E., and A. Fergany, "A Configuration Management Assistant," *Proc. 2nd Int. Workshop on Software Version and Configuration Control*, Oct. 1989, New York: ACM Press, pp. 5–14.

[17] TrueChange, on-line at http://www.true.com.

[18] Graham, M., and D. Miller, "ISTAR Evaluation," *Tech. Report SEI-88-TR-3*, Software Engineering Institute, July 1988, on-line at http://sei.cmu.edu/tr.

[19] Feiler, P., S. Dart, and G. Downey, "Evaluation of the Rational Environment," *Tech. Report SEI-88-TR-15*, Software Engineering Institute, July 1988, online at http://sei.cmu.edu/tr.

[20] Mahler, A., and A. Lampen, "shape—A Software Configuration Management Tool," *Proc. Int. Workshop on Software Version and Configuration Control*, Germany, Jan. 1988, pp. 228–243.

[21] Dart, S., and B. Harris, "Managing Web Changes With Egility: Implementing an E-Business Web Content and Application Change Management Solution," Merant White Paper, on-line at http://www.merant.com, Nov. 1999.

[22] Dart, S., "To Change or Not To Change," *Application Development Trends*, June 1997, pp. 55–61.

CHAPTER

5

Contents

Configuration Management Tool Selection and Deployment

"... it is a common sight to see by the roadside in Southeast Asia women selling satays of large, hairy, barbecued spiders on a stick. And in parts of China, where spiders are also eaten, they are especially savored because of their association with long life—owing to the permanence of undisturbed cobwebs. Apparently, ten years is added to the life of a person who eats spiders."

P. Hillyard, *The Book of the Spider: A Compendium of Arachno-Facts and Eight-Legged Lore* (New York: Avon Books, 1994)

Anyone who has been responsible for selecting and deploying a configuration management (CM) solution, especially in a large software company, has probably aged 10 years prematurely and could well do with the spider rejuvenation technique! Such premature aging happens because technology adoption, or tool selection and

135

deployment, as most companies call it, is typically done poorly, even with the best of intentions. As a result, many companies completely or partially fail in technology adoption. The tool becomes "shelfware"—it sits on the shelf gathering dust with no one using it. Or, they use the tool but not to its full potential, which in itself can create problems. *A tool is only as good as how well it is deployed.*

This chapter is not really about CM per se; it is about technology adoption. The techniques and processes could very well be applied to other kinds of tools that affect corporate product and processes, such as enterprise resource planning (ERP) tools. What differs obviously are the kinds of requirements and the specifics of the risks.

In this chapter I discuss why a CM solution typically "opens up a can of worms." I present, in gruesome detail, technology adoption—tool selection and deployment. I look at the good, the bad, and the ugly versions of it and give my thoughts on why companies fail at good technology adoption. Then I present all 22 steps involved in CM adoption, including setting up a deployment team, defining the CM requirements, doing risk management, planning the pilot project, and ending with the many lessons learned.

Following that, I answer some commonly asked questions about adoption time, return on investment, metrics, and how to recover from adoption failures. I give my thoughts about the CM tools vendors and how to make good use of them and discuss the big gap between standards and tools. The chapter ends with a summary of the key messages.

Throughout this chapter I will use the term *CM solution* instead of *CM tool* because the selection and deployment of the tool is part of the overall CM solution. The CM solution encompasses all aspects related to CM: the *people, process,* and *technology*; that is, all cultural issues surrounding the manner in which people view CM, all the process issues regarding how people do CM (some manual steps, some automated ones), and the technology, which includes the development environment (IDE) plus all the hardware and software support systems in which the CM tool will operate.

A reading of this chapter might suggest that a CM solution involves a lot of work. Certainly it does for an enterprise-wide solution that uses a full-process CM tool. But a small company that wants a simple version control tool will not have to go through the same amount of work. All the steps could easily be performed in a week, for instance. But bigger CM solutions obviously require much more effort. As a result, the rewards are much bigger. Do not be overwhelmed by all the issues I raise.

Many of the things I describe might boil down to be simplistic and have a quick resolution for your company.

Configuration management opens up a can of worms

The first thing I always notice in a company is that adopting a CM solution typically "opens up a can of worms." That is, CM "touches" or is involved in so many aspects across the company. It forces many work issues out into the open that may have been kept dormant or been ignored. For instance, a client of mine, a nameless, large hardware-software company, which had a decentralized (distributed) approach to management and development, had a company policy that mandated that each group could decide what practices it would follow and enforce regarding quality assurance (QA). This worked satisfactorily since it was a compromise that resolved political issues within the company. But when the corporate decision was made to improve the company's automated CM with a full-process CM tool, it meant all processes had to be defined so that they could be automated and tailored. Process automation then forced the company to open up this whole issue about QA and come to a real resolution rather than a compromise.

Size matters, but it does not change how adoption is done

Whether your company is small (one development group), medium (a couple of development groups), or large (many groups), it does not change *how* adoption is done. That is, the same steps are involved. But three factors do differ:

1. *Timing:* how long it takes each step to be done;

2. *Degree of formality:* the amount of communication and decision-making involved;

3. *Number of resources:* how many people are involved in the tool selection committee and deployment teams.

Regarding timing, small companies (or groups) can probably get most of the adoption steps done in a matter of days, whereas bigger companies take longer for obvious reasons: More people and teams are involved; bigger decisions need to be made; and there are more CM requirements because there are more teams. More people are involved as change agents—people who champion the cause and who act as the "stewards" of the CM solution.

The amount of formality and number of people involved differs across companies. For instance, a small company may designate one person—perhaps an IT tools engineer—to be responsible for the CM tool selection and adoption. He or she may be responsible for making all the decisions. He or she can keep all the information in his or her head and there is no need to document everything. He or she is familiar with everyone's requirements for CM. Then again, a larger company has many people involved in the selection and deployment teams. Lots of groups have to come to an agreement on decisions; maybe certain levels of management have to review and sign off on decisions. Group decisions take time and coordination. Bigger tool purchases take time to negotiate. Coming to agreement on the list of requirements, which tool to buy, and so on all take time and effort.

The tool selection and adoption process can be easier depending on the nature of the tool. For instance, an evolutionary type of CM tool (which was discussed in Chapter 4) requires a lot less effort for the selection and deployment process than does a full-process one (discussed in Chapter 4). It is the difference between addressing one of the CM functional areas (of Chapter 3) versus addressing all functional areas of CM.

Quick and dirty adoption or methodical adoption?

Table 5.1 identifies the key steps involved in tool selection and deployment. I spend the rest of this chapter discussing these steps in detail. But before I do that, I have to point out that some companies choose to do CM tool adoption in a "quick and dirty" manner, as I call it. It is quick because they come to the realization that they have a CM problem and they decide to buy the market-leader tool. It is dirty because they are setting themselves up for a blind tool choice—that is, when they sign the check to buy the tool, they have very little confidence that that particular tool is the right one for them.

Table 5.1
Key Steps in Configuration Management Tool Selection and Deployment

Step	Explanation	Iterative?
01. Select teams	Pick selection committee and deployment team	No
02. Sponsorship strategy	Determine how sponsorship and commitment will be maintained	Yes
03. Status of CM	How is CM done now? What are the problems?	No
04. Vision statement	Envision the solution and benefits and value	No
05. Benefits statement	List benefits and value expected	No
06. Readiness assessment	Is company ready to embark on change?	No
07. Requirements definition	List all requirements	Yes, very
08. Risk management	Plan for risk mitigation	Yes
09. Selection process	Define selection criteria and rating system	Yes
10. Strategizing	Make strategic decisions	No
11. RFP submission	Submit RFP to candidate tool vendors	No
12. Candidate tool demonstrations	View detailed exhibitions of tools	Yes
13. Finalist(s) choice	Pick the best tool(s)	No
14. CM plan and/or process description	Define CM plan and/or processes	Yes
15. Proof-of-concept piloting	Roll out tool(s) to pilot project team(s)	No
16. Pick tool	Choose tool and communicate choice	Can be
17. Complete risk mitigation	Address remaining concerns	Yes
18. Schedule roll-out	Plan for cutovers to each group	No
19. Train everyone	Prepare everyone for the roll-out	Yes
20. Prepare CM tool	Migrate data, customize tool, integrate tools	No
21. Monitor resistance	Manage resistance to change	Yes
22. Gather lessons learned	Capture knowledge about technology adoption	No

Companies make such decisions in haste for various reasons: Their pain level hit an unacceptable threshold and so they had to respond immediately; there was a window of opportunity in which funds became available so they were able to buy a CM tool; the political environment changed, paving the way for improvements in the company; and so on. For whatever reason, the period of time in which a decision has to be made is short. This is sometimes the only way that companies get to buy new tools. So be it. It is not the ideal way. Of course, this way of choosing is more risky, but it can work out in the end. In fact, any CM tool, in my opinion, is better than none. Of course, if it is not deployed successfully, then you have shelfware, which is useless.

The good, the bad, and the ugly about adoption

Failed technology adoption restrains a company from achieving its pace of business change or improvements and optimizations. This can be devastating for Internet companies because they have to maintain their rate of growth in order to keep their stock prices high. Thomas J. Watson Jr., founder of IBM, said that if an organization is to meet the challenge of a changing world, it must be prepared to change everything about itself except its core principles and beliefs as it moves through corporate life.

A company cannot afford to fail in adopting a CM solution or any other solution. There really is no reason why a company should fail. CM tools are used very successfully all over the world. Some of the CM tools are very mature, having undergone a decade or more of evolution.

Technology adoption is ". . . a decision to make full use of an innovation. . ." [1]. Adoption is a wonderful opportunity but it is also a responsibility. It is an opportunity to improve all aspects of product development and maintenance along with the quality of the products and Web sites. Yet it is a major responsibility because there are many ramifications associated with change. Chapters 2 and 3 focused on the opportunity—that is, all the benefits and value of change, of improving your company's CM solution. This chapter focuses on the ramifications of change—on all the technology adoption issues that frequently arise in companies, such as resistance to change and sponsorship issues. Technology adoption (that is, deploying a CM solution) generally involves:

- Preparing and planning for adoption (for change);
- Acquiring the appropriate resources to enable change, such as people, time, equipment, and budget;
- Performing risk management to navigate through all difficulties;
- Implementing the adoption strategy;

‣ Monitoring that implementation and making improvements along the way;

‣ Leveraging from the lessons learned during that experience to make adoption easier and quicker the next time around.

Good adoption to me means introducing a CM solution *successfully, effectively,* and *optimally.* It is successful if the success criteria are met. For instance, the quality of the resultant products improves and the number of bugs found in field releases or on the Web site are reduced. It is effective if all the designated people can use the solution. For instance, developers can edit the code safely and quickly and do their builds in a timely fashion. Testers know when to test changes and where to find them. The adoption is optimal when there is minimal change pain. For instance, the adoption happens as quickly as possible without seriously impacting the production group and release schedules.

Bad adoption to me means introducing a CM solution unsuccessfully, ineffectively, and not optimally. It is unsuccessful if the status quo remains or there has been no improvement in product quality. It is ineffective if users are not happy or satisfied using the tool, or no one uses the tool, or only parts of the features of the tool are used. The CM solution is not optimal if there was a lot of "change pain," a high degree of unchecked resistance, adoption took much too long, or time was wasted.

Ugly adoption to me means nothing positive resulted from the effort other than wasted time, wasted money, frustrated people, and negativity associated with CM. The tool is shelfware.

The "quick and dirty" approach to bringing in a CM solution most often ends up as a bad adoption experience. The solution is put into place, but at a higher cost than perhaps necessary. Of course, you always find companies with exceptional people who intuitively know how to do the right thing without reading a book about it or going to a training class. Such people are gems and should be treasured and rewarded handsomely!

Why companies fail at adopting a configuration management solution

A long time ago I wrote down 50 reasons why companies fail at adopting a CM solution. They can be summarized in the following list:

1. Lack of sponsorship and commitment for the solution, for example, no real backing or support from upper management;

2. Lack of responsibility and ownership for the solution, for example, no deployment team assigned;

3. Lack of understanding about all the issues involved in the solution, for example, ignoring people and process issues;

4. Failure to provide the necessary resources, for example, time, money, staff, equipment, decision-making, monitoring;

5. Underestimating the effort involved, for example, pick a tool, buy the tool, install the tool (the "silver bullet" mindset);

6. Not managing the adoption of the solution as a project in itself, for example, relying on the vendor to do all the work;

7. Not doing risk management, for example, ignoring the barriers to success;

8. Not involving everyone, for example, having one person make all the decisions without involvement from developers and managers;

9. Setting the wrong expectations, for example, expecting to roll out (or switch over) every group on the same day;

10. Not doing a pilot project, for example, rolling out the new tool to the production team without testing it first;

11. Picking the wrong criteria for a pilot project, for example, trying to break the tool.

In theory, technology adoption is straightforward. In practice, adoption, especially across an enterprise with lots of process automation, is challenging because it brings together all the complexities that companies have to face in making a significant change. For instance, many companies end up doing bad or ugly adoption because they think that all they need to do is address the technical issues related to the tool. They do not realize that there are other, more powerful or influential issues in adopting a solution as shown in Figure 5.1.

Configuration Management Solution

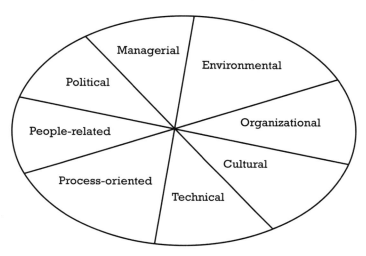

Figure 5.1 Types of issues involved in a configuration management solution.

The model of the configuration management solution

Figure 5.1 shows the myriad issues involved in a CM solution: managerial, process-oriented, organizational, cultural, political, people-oriented, environment-related, and technical issues.

Managerial issues relate to the management of change. For instance:

- Resource allocation;
- Planning and scheduling for change;
- Monitoring of staff in terms of their adjustment to the new solution;
- Supporting and empowering change agents;
- Managing the ramifications of change;
- Readjusting the organizational structure, if necessary;
- Funding the change;

- Working with resistance;

- Updating corporate standards, policies, and procedures.

Process-oriented issues relate to defining the way tasks are done. For instance:

- Corporate versus group-specific process models;

- Merging dependent processes;

- Automating processes;

- Improving processes;

- Certifying to standards;

- Avoiding process analysis paralysis;

- Knowing how to define and describe processes;

- Having process experts in-house.

Organizational issues concern infrastructure. For instance:

- Number of people on the deployment team;

- Ramifications of change on the existing organizational structure;

- New responsibilities of CM group and other groups;

- Automatic notifications;

- Dependencies between groups that may affect order of roll-out.

Cultural issues are concerned with the socially accepted customs and behavior of the company. For instance:

- Knowing what the culture is;

- Deploying a new solution in harmony with that culture;

- Working within the social customs;

- Finding the "power" people, the decision-makers;

- Knowing the best way to support growth.

Political issues are concerned with conflict resolution. For instance:

- The politics of change, that is, "whose toes are being stepped on" and "whose empire is being affected";

- Altering organizational responsibility, accountability, and boundaries;

- Reward system;

- Who will do the maintenance and provide "hot line" support;

- Sponsorship and commitment level.

People-oriented issues are concerned with personal aspects. For instance:

- Dealing with fears;

- Coping with resistance;

- Training people;

- Updating skill sets;

- Comfort level with new tool;

- Stability of groups;

- Time allocation.

Environment-related issues are concerned with the installation and maintenance of the tools. For instance:

- Hardware upgrades;

- New hardware;

- Network connections and types (LAN, WAN, intranets, extranets, VPNs, the Internet);

- All software (code, data, content, libraries) and their dependencies;

- Tool upgrades;

- Server downtime;

- Security;

- Fault tolerance;

- Performance of tools;

- Help desks;

- Space availability and allocation;

- Cost.

Technical issues are concerned with the technicalities of the CM tool and its positioning in the environment. For instance:

- Installation over the network;

- Database systems administration;

- Software clients for all platforms;

- Customization and integration;

- Build management and distribution;

- Shared code model;

- Change propagation.

As you can see, a spectrum of issues come into play in the CM solution.

Sequence of steps in the configuration management solution

Companies typically start at the wrong spot when approaching their CM solution. They make a common mistake of throwing together a list of CM requirements, then calling the vendors in to demonstrate their products and expecting to be told which tool is the best for them. But what typically happens is that each vendor tells them their tool is the best for the company. As a result, the company is unable to make a decision as to which tool is the best for it because every tool looks good. This often happens, which means that work that should have been done up front was not done. Most companies view a list of requirements as simply a list. In reality, the requirements list is really a process, which is why I marked that step as "iterative" in Table 5.1. The requirements list is basically a living entity, an evolving list that gets refined at each step until it gets to the point at which it is so finely tuned that it forces the tool decision as to which one is the best. That is, the requirements list drives the tool decision because it becomes so obvious that only a particular tool meets those requirements. Hence, in order to generate a finely tuned requirements list, several other things need to be done beforehand, as shown in Table 5.1.

In [2], I presented a short version of the rest of this chapter. What follows in this chapter is the long version about how to adopt a CM solution. Table 5.1 shows you all the steps involved in selecting and deploying a CM solution and gives a brief description of each step. The column labeled "Iterative" refers to the fact that the step ends up being a collection of incremental steps. That is, the actions involved may be done over and over again as part of refining the result, kind of like a spiral model approach to achieving the end result. In some cases, such as for sponsorship, actions must be carried out constantly throughout deployment. Sponsorship needs to be monitored constantly. Other steps such as creating a requirements list involve several steps because the requirements have to be refined based on new information gleaned from other steps. Similarly, risk management, the selection process, defining the CM processes (or plan), picking the tool, training people, and customizing and integrating the CM tool all involve multiple, incremental steps. The message of this column is not to expect these steps to be completed the first time around. Multiple passes are usually required in order to refine the data and make improvements.

I now discuss each step. Note that steps can be done in parallel, or in slightly different sequences, or as presented.

Step 1: Select teams

Someone or some group has to be responsible for owning, managing, and leading the CM solution. For a small company, it is typically one person; otherwise, it is a team. I generically call this team the *deployment team*. Some companies use a separate tool selection team and tool deployment team. I recommend that they be the same team because it saves time, money, and effort by not having to disseminate all the knowledge to new people.

The deployment team should be made up of representatives from each group who will be using or involved with the CM solution. That representative I generically call the *change agent*. This person acts as the champion for the cause—the cause being advocacy of the CM solution.

Such a person needs to be very positive, a good communicator, and respected by his or her own group.

The *sponsor* needs to be identified. The sponsor is the manager who is responsible for the deployment effort, who is not actively involved in the deployment unless called upon for help, and who pays the bills for the resources. The sponsor is a high-level manager who fosters the deployment effort, oversees it, and supports the needs of the deployment team.

The responsibilities of the deployment team are as follows:

- Lead and manage the CM solution deployment.

- Guide all required decision-making.

- Ensure all the deployment activities move forward.

- Monitor all the deployment activities.

- Maintain sponsorship.

- Act as the focal point of expertise for CM deployment.

- Coordinate all activities and personnel needed.

- Encourage the deployment.

- Educate and train their teams about the CM solution.

- Set the correct expectations.

- Be available when needed.

On the deployment team, there needs to be a *leader* who takes charge of managing the team as a project manager. This typically needs to be a full-time, very active position throughout the lifetime of selection and deployment.

Ideally, I like to see a person from each group in the company that will be affected by the CM solution on the deployment team. Ideally some will be *champions* and the others will be *user group representatives*. I distinguish between these only because of people availability limitations. I view champions as experts on the CM tool and in deployment who are full time and take a very active role in the deployment. The user group representatives, on the other hand, are part time in the group and consequently assume a lower level of activity in the deployment team. But they are important because they are acquiring a lot of knowledge and will eventually act as champions for their own teams when it is their turn to roll out the new CM solution.

Someone on the team needs to be a *boundary spanner*—one who can act as a go-between for management and developers. Someone needs to speak both "languages." This is someone who is in a technical leadership position, perhaps a senior software developer.

The skill sets of the deployment team need to include the following:

- Project management;

- Good communication (written, oral, aural);

- Delegation;

- Negotiation;

- Meeting facilitation;

- Group consensus building;

- Thick-skinned;

- Analytical;

- Detailed knowledge of CM;

- Ability to learn new tools;

- Technical expertise;

- Common sense;

- Respected;

- Leadership abilities;

- Active personalities (that is, they are doers).

The deployment team must be a respected team. That is, the technical community (developers, testers, content experts) must respect the team or they will not listen to them. Management must respect the team as being capable change agents. Respect by all parties is important; otherwise, the deployment will happen very slowly or not at all.

Some companies decide to put their weakest people on such teams. This is a big mistake because it slows everything down, sometimes even to a halt. The deployment team must show constant progress; otherwise, the sponsorship and commitment die down and eventually the deployment effort stops. On the other hand, companies also make a mistake by assigning their smartest technical person the leader of the team. Sometimes this works out, but only if that person is an excellent communicator—a good boundary spanner.

Once the team is put together, then it is time to look at sponsorship and commitment issues.

Step 2: Create the sponsorship strategy

If you do not have sponsorship, commitment, or backing for the CM solution from upper and middle management, then there is little hope of deploying a solution. Because this is the most crucial aspect, you need to take care of this up front as soon as possible. Think about whether you have sponsorship, make sure that you have it, and decide how you will maintain it. Yes, it is something that has to be maintained and monitored. For instance, if deployment is taking too long (even if it is not your team's fault), you need to know that someone higher up and lower down in the company hierarchy knows that and is willing to work with you and support you when times get tough. If things look bleak, someone has to be there in times of trouble. You need an ally.

You need to know whether you have real sponsorship and commitment, or whether it is just "lip service"—words that were said without substance, without backing and support. For instance, upper management can say things like, "Yes, we are committed to achieving SEI Level 2 of the CMMI, which requires us to implement a CM solution." But, many times, management may not understand the operational consequences of that statement, which are all the issues discussed in Table 5.1. They may be thinking, "Well, we buy a tool, sign the check, get it installed, and we've addressed our CM needs." This "silver bullet" attitude rarely works. With this attitude, management will not commit the necessary resources (time, people, money, equipment, schedule adjustments) to actually carry out all the work. Hence, they are not committed to the solution (often this happens purely out of ignorance).

Do you have sponsorship? Well, when you need something, such as more people or hardware, does the sponsor ensure that you get it as quickly as possible? Or, when you hit a problem such as one person on your deployment team is being dragged off to work on some other project, does your sponsor help you solve that problem? If the answers are yes to these questions, then you do have sponsorship. If either answer is no, then you do not have effective sponsorship and you need to realize that this greatly lowers your chance of adoption success. Get the hair dye—gray hairs or hair loss starts at this point!

If you have commitment and sponsorship, then work out a plan of how to maintain sponsorship. That involves essentially communicating with management at all levels about what is happening and why. It also involves setting their expectations correctly. With this knowledge, and with constant progress reports, and with visible results, sponsorship and commitment can be easily maintained.

If you do not have commitment and sponsorship, then you need to go about finding it, or live with the risk that deployment has a high probability of failing. You create sponsorship and commitment by:

▸ Educating management about what is actually involved in the CM solution;

▸ Making sure that the benefits and value of the solution are clearly defined;

▸ Setting correct expectations;

▸ Giving status reports and showing progress;

▸ Ensuring that the CM problems are understood;

▸ Talking to management.

Once the team has sorted out sponsorship and commitment, it starts to examine the status of CM in the company.

Step 3: Capture the status of configuration management today

Before a company can improve on any practice or set of tools, it needs to know exactly where it stands today. That is, how does the company do CM now? Surprisingly, especially in large companies, very few people, if any, have the complete picture. Hence, it is often necessary to track down all the information. I recommend doing this via a series of interviews. I interview all the key players: developers, testers, QA people, build managers, release managers, Web coordinators, Web gatekeeper (person who is responsible for publishing to the live site), project managers, hot-line support staff, users—in other words, everyone who is affected by CM in some manner or other. I use a standard questionnaire as shown in the Appendix, Section A.1. Then I collate all this information into a CM status report, for which a template is shown in the Appendix, Section A.7. Now that we know the current status of CM, the problems that people have identified, and their requirements, we can focus on the vision of the future.

Step 4: Define the configuration management vision

The CM vision presents the big picture view of the CM solution. It helps set the right expectations about the solution. A vision is a high-level perspective about the solution. It provides the direction for the solution. It is akin to a company's mission statement. Some visions are grand; some are simple. For instance, one grand vision has been: "We want to automate all the CM practices throughout the entire company worldwide so that we can improve upon our current rate of product delivery." A simpler vision has been: "Our group needs to get control over the fast pace of change of our Web site and ensure that nothing is published unless it has been through testing."

I prefer a vision statement to be one sentence because that makes it easier for people to remember. As we say among CM salespeople, we want a "three-minute elevator message." That is, it is an idea that can be pitched to someone in a short amount of time; a complete idea that can be conveyed while, say, riding in an elevator. Once the vision is sorted out, a direction has been defined so we begin to have a feeling for the scope of the solution. We also want to get a feeling for what we will have at the end of the deployment of the solution.

Step 5: Specify the configuration management benefits

We want to have a clear image of the end result or the goals and, hence, the benefits and the value we hope to achieve with the CM solution. Also, we want to be able to judge our success. Success is determined by evaluating success criteria, which are essentially questions about how well we achieved the benefits and value we intended. In Table 3.1 of Chapter 3, I listed the typical business and technical benefits that companies seek. Once we have the benefits and have completed the four steps listed earlier, we have a pretty good idea as to where we are going (albeit not yet how). Then it is time to give serious consideration to whether the company is really ready to embark on a change.

Step 6: Assess readiness to change

As we know from our life experiences, some people do not like change, whereas others relish it. A company is typically a mixture of both, leaning toward one end of that spectrum or the other. So, when a team of people wants to lead a company in deploying a new solution (whether it is CM or otherwise), that team needs to consider whether the company is ready for it. This may seem like a trivial, obvious issue, but companies have failed in technology adoption simply because they were not ready to embark on such an adventure and were not aware of what was involved in such an adventure. The readiness criteria that I typically use are shown in Table 5.2. A company is very ready to change if the answers to all questions in Table 5.2 are "yes." If most of the answers are "no" or "maybe," then the company is not ready. In that case, either be patient and wait another 6 months, or change the vision into a simpler one and approach the solution in a more incremental manner. Once we know a company is ready to change, then we start defining exactly what it wants—the requirements. If there are a lot of "maybes," then the issues must be examined in more detail before proceeding.

Table 5.2
Readiness Criteria for a Configuration Management Solution

Criteria	Yes?	No?	Maybe?
Recognition of CM problems?			
Desire for something better?			
Resources available for deployment?			
Is there time to change?			
Can risk be assumed?			
Is there money for the tool?			
Is there a real sponsor?			
Is there experience in deployment?			

Step 7: Define configuration management requirements

Getting the requirements right will take several iterations. No one ever gets the list of requirements right the first time unless they have done many CM deployments, in which case they know how to hone in on the right issues and are familiar with all the CM tools. To get the requirements "right" means to refine them in such a manner that it becomes very obvious from looking at them, and then looking at the tools, that a particular tool suits that list of requirements better than any other. Ideally, that is what the right requirements list will do for you.

Unfortunately, what a lot of companies typically do is write down a list of generic CM things, then ask all the vendors to visit and do demonstrations of their products. After those demos, companies find they cannot make a tool choice because all the vendors said that their tools meet all the requirements. So, no progress has really been made. The company has been exposed to the CM tools, but they are not any closer to being able to make a decision.

When this happens, it means the requirements list needs to be fine-tuned. The list will become more detailed and prioritized as the deployment team learns more about what is important and what is possible with the CM tools. That is, they get new ideas that they hadn't thought about before or were not aware of and they plug those ideas back into the requirements list. Each time they find something new from some experience, it can alter the requirements list.

A requirements list can evolve as follows:

1. An initial set of requirements is put together by the deployment team. Let's call this version 1.

2. It is distributed to all technical people for review. This results in changes to the list, hence version 2 is created.

3. It is distributed to the managers for review. Changes are made. This results in version 3.

4. The list is restructured by category or functionality area. Hence, version 4.

5. The list gets prioritized. Hence, version 5 indicates the "must have" list versus the "should have, but optional" list versus "wish" list.

6. The list is reviewed by an outside consultant who thought of extra issues. Hence, version 6.

7. The team saw several tool demonstrations and ended up adding some new requirements, changing the wording on others, and changing priorities. Now we have version 7.

8. Two candidate tools are chosen and pilot tests are run. The team likes both tools and has to make a tradeoff. For instance, the developers prefer one tool because of the interface while managers prefer another tool because of the easy process customization. The team has to find how to make a decision. Both tools meet version 7 of the requirements. The team thinks about it. They now have had a month's worth of experience with each tool. They decide to take another look at the requirements and readjust priorities now that they have had the hands-on tool experience. They come out with a new set of priorities based on that experience. Hence, version 8 of the requirements is formed. This version now enables them to make their tool decision.

As you can see, each iteration brought new or more detailed information to the team, which allowed them to refine the requirements list, which guided them closer to the tool decision. This is good. This is why the requirements list is so valuable and why it constantly needs to be refined. Hence, creating the requirements list is a process in itself. It is an evolving entity.

The requirements list serves many important purposes:

1. Captures everything the company wants.

2. Prioritizes, or puts in order of importance, what the company needs.

3. Provides a yardstick for comparing candidate tools.

4. Enables the creation of test cases for the tools.

5. Drives you to making an obvious tool choice.

6. Evolves in response to the environment (such as a change in budget or goals).

One issue that always arises is the wording of a requirement, or the level of detail. Should it be a generic thing, or should the requirement be very specific in its detail? Well, in the requirements evolution example given above, the requirements started out as generic phrases and evolved into a more detailed, feature-oriented list, which is fine because the purpose of the list is to enable you to make a tool decision. I would not start out with feature-driven requirements, though. Stay at as high a level as possible, and at each refinement of the requirements provide more detail as it becomes relevant. Be as specific as possible in the wording but do not be too prescriptive. Keep in mind that different tools achieve the same functionality but in different ways, through different implementation notions. So be careful not to rule out a tool by having a requirement that is too implementation dependent. And do not use vague terms. For instance, "handles large files" is too vague. Be more specific, such as "handles files of over 3 MB of data."

Do not forget to capture issues beyond functionality in the requirements list; issues concerning scalability, performance, usability, the vendor, security, network, hardware, fault-tolerance, support, and administration. These are described further in the Appendix, Section A.2.

Refining the requirements list continues up until the tool choice can be made. In parallel with this, the deployment team is working on risk management.

Step 8: Do risk management
As I wrote in [2–4], risk management is the essence of successful CM adoption. It enables all the correct strategic decisions to be made. This is important as most companies struggle in their technology adoption efforts because they are not certain of what to do next or what decisions have to be made. Also, risk management brings out all the constraints, challenges, and potential surprises. It has the surprising benefit of bringing together two often opposing forces: management and developers. Risk management achieves this by presenting a list of all the risks that a company faces in adopting the new technology or new solution. When confronted with lists of issues, it is very difficult for a company to ignore them. (Yes, the cynics will say that companies live in denial, but if that is the case, then it lowers the probability of success for the company.) Managers and developers end up united in the sense of dealing with the list of risks. They have a common focal point to rally around. So many resistance issues automatically fall out or are addressed by virtue of doing risk management.

Risk management is fundamentally easy to do. For instance, the simplest way of doing it is to talk to the managers—ask them what their concerns are or what barriers to success they see. Then ask the developers the same question. Voila! You have your list. Typically, for a medium-sized or large company, 30 items end up on the initial list. (Risk management, like requirements gathering, is an iterative process.)

Then you take the list, decide what attributes or properties you want to associate with risks (such as probability of happening or seriousness of risk), document the risks in a risk management plan along their attributes, and then decide how you will resolve or mitigate the risk. For the serious risks, you develop contingency plans. Then, you go about resolving or mitigating the risks. It is really that simple.

Some companies have actually automated risk management (RM), as I describe in [3] since it is rather methodical. Small companies that have a handful of risks typically do not need to go through all the documentation and analysis implied in the risk management plan given in the Appendix, Section A.8. They can typically do it all in their heads very quickly. But when a company reaches more than 10 risks, it is a good idea to write the plan.

Eliminating as much risk as possible or finding an acceptable level of risk is the goal of RM. Risk needs to be eliminated so that when users switch over to the new tool, their work is not negatively affected. Production teams cannot afford new risks in their daily practices. It is the responsibility of the deployment team to remove as much risk as possible before teams are cut over to the new tool.

In Section A.8 of the Appendix, I provide a template for a risk management plan. It gives further insight into how to do risk management along with all the attributes (or characteristics of a risk) involved in risk analysis. More formal views of risk management are available elsewhere [5]. In Section A.3 of the Appendix, I list the typical categories and examples of risks that I see at companies. These range from technical, to people-related, to organizational, to political, to CM skills, and through to resources.

Risk management is an ongoing, iterative task. Once it is under way, the next step is to determine the way in which the tool will be selected.

Step 9: Define the selection method

The deployment team needs to find a way of evaluating a tool. They can use the requirements list to design a rating system. For instance, with each requirement assign a rating from 0 to 5, where 0 means the requirement is not met at all by the tool, 5 means it meets it perfectly, and 1–4 means it somewhat meets the requirement at increasing degrees of satisfaction. Some companies get much more sophisticated in their rating systems by adding a priority weighting to the value. If all tools end up with the same rating, then it is time to go back and refine the requirements, as I described earlier in the requirements step. Once the team has settled on a selection method, then it has to make some tough, strategic decisions.

Step 10: Make the strategic decisions

I have already described in Chapters 3 and 4 some of the strategic decisions that a company has to make. I summarize them in this list:

1. Define your company's view of CM; that is, what functional areas of CM will be addressed in your solution. Chapter 3 lists the eight areas.

2. Decide whether an *evolutionary* or *full-process* CM solution will be implemented. Again, Chapter 3 offers guidance on this.

3. Decide how the risks will be resolved. I discussed this earlier in step 8.

4. Decide whether the CM solution will be *enterprise-wide* or just *group-specific*, as discussed in Chapter 4.

5. Decide if you will do multiple pilot projects, especially if you cannot decide between two tools.

6. If the company already has a CM tool, a legacy tool, how will it cut over to the new tool? Will it run the old tool in parallel with the new tool? Will it migrate all the data from the old tool to the new one? Will it just let new project teams use the new tool and existing teams stay with the old one?

Once the decisions are made or at least under way, it is time to start working with the tool vendors. The first thing to do is to simply ask them how they can help you.

Step 11: Submit the request for proposal to the vendors

Once you know what your requirements and risks are, you can submit a Request for Proposal (RFP) to the vendors. You basically document requirements and constraints, and you ask them how their tools and services can address these. The more detailed the requirements, the more detailed their response can be. Ask them to respond quickly.

When you have all the responses, you can start using those to rate the tools. The response gives you a starting point and a feel for the vendor. You may be able to filter out certain tools from these results and hence save yourself a lot of time. Then the next step is to invite the candidate tool vendors to visit and give detailed demonstrations of their products, based on your list of requirements and risks.

Step 12: Conduct candidate tool demonstrations

You should set the agenda for the vendor's visit and recommend that certain people from the vendor come along. For instance, you want a technical person to attend as well as a senior management type since your vice president will be at the demonstrations. If you do not set the agenda and inform the vendor of it, the vendor will go by his or her own agenda, which may not match yours. Give the vendor as much information as possible and he or she will do a better job for you. For instance, share your CM vision with the salesperson. The vendor does not want to waste the vendor's time or yours, so the more information you can impart to the vendor, the quicker and easier he or she can help you. From the vendor's perspective, he or she wants to qualify or disqualify you as a suitable prospect as quickly as possible.

Make sure that everyone on the evaluation team attends all the vendor meetings. Team members who miss particular meetings end up with different tool ratings. You want to ensure a fair and consistent evaluation.

Many people look down on vendors and their sales force, which is a shame. There are many free things that you can gain from vendors (as I describe later in this chapter). Remember that vendors are exposed to lots of CM solutions and have access to valuable information, such as customer reference sites.

Every deployment team member should have their tool rating sheets with them during the vendor's visit. They can fill in the values as the demo proceeds. Then, at the end of the meeting, all the sheets can be tallied to see the final value. But never make a decision after the first vendor's visit. Typically, the first vendor has a very positive impact on people. The reason being that it is often the first time the group has seen a real CM tool, so they get rather excited and are astounded at the abilities of the tool. Vendors often compete to be the first to demo their tool for this very reason. So, the first tool generally always ends up getting the highest rating initially. As other demos are done and the deployment team is exposed to other tools, their ratings start to even out and become more objective. The team gets closer to picking the final tool.

Step 13: Pick the finalist tool(s)

What typically happens is that, after all the demos, the deployment team rules out a couple of tools and maybe two or three candidates remain. The team has the vendors come back in and do more detailed demos and they rerate the tools (especially after refining the requirements as a result of the demos). If the rating system and requirements refinement lead to two tools rather than one, then the team often ends up doing two pilot projects.

As part of the preparation for the pilot project, the CM plan or the CM process definition is begun.

Step 14: Develop a CM plan or describe CM processes

To some people, process is a dirty word. It conjures up lots of boring paperwork, unnecessary controls, and too much management over-sight—and that is actually how it was prior to automation. But now, with process automation, the chores of CM (such as documenting and logging events) are done automatically, and the tool ensures all necessary steps are performed. Process is no longer to be feared [6]. A well-designed CM process, implemented in a CM tool, enables the many benefits of CM that I discussed in Chapter 3. Also, once a process is automated, any ineffi-ciencies or opportunities for improvement are made very visible. And process improvement can easily be done by tweaking its automation, most often via the graphical user interface.

Before CM automation, companies had to write CM plans. Such plans contained all the CM practices, procedures, roles, and responsibili-ties. With CM automation, especially full-process tools, CM plans often become redundant because all the information that would have been in the plans now resides in the tool. So, a CM plan is often not needed.

You can find an outline for a CM plan in [7]. Large companies that outsource a lot tend to need to do CM plans as well as CM process defini-tions. They need plans to help kick-start new project teams as well as to monitor the outsourcing efforts.

What is needed mostly these days is a CM process description—docu-mentation of the CM process. The CM tool may implement a process, but the tool has its own implementation notions, which are not intuitively understandable to the many potential users of the tool. That is, there is a difference between your company's document that defines the *process* and between the tool's *implementation* of that process. The difference is mainly in terminology and concepts. This is a subtle but tricky point to grasp and to explain. We need both, and what the vendor is good at is mapping or implementing your company's process description into their tool. But your company must define the process (perhaps even with the help of the vendor).

I raise this point because one of the problems companies hit is in describing their CM processes to the vendor's installation consultant. That consultant knows the tool very well. He or she speaks the vendor's language, though not the company's language. And typically, installation consultants are "techie" types. They are not hired to be adoption experts or change agents or great communicators. Often, there is a disconnection between the language that the consultant speaks and the client (your company) speaks. The consultant rarely has all the skills required to guide the client through adoption. (This is why the CM vendors are now tending toward hiring higher level consultants—people with more project management skills and communication skills who can offer adoption expertise, such as helping clients define their processes.)

Hence, a company needs a process description document. The CM process is described in terms that are meaningful to the company. Then the installation consultant, or even the deployment team, can map, translate, or implement that process description into the CM tool using its concepts and features.

A mistake that tool vendors and companies often make is that they let the tool vendor define the process using the terminology of the tool. This needs to be done at some point, but should not be the initial process description. You really need two process descriptions:

1. *High-level company process description* that shows, in the terminology of your company, all the steps involved in doing CM from the perspective of your own people;

2. An *implementation-level process description* that is the vendor's interpretation of your company's process documented (and/or automated) using the tool's terminology and concepts. This is the mapping of the company's model into a tool.

A *process description* is a model, an abstraction of the flow of all CM activities, roles, and responsibilities. I have found that using simple state transition diagrams and tables are effective ways of describing processes.

Circles show the states and arrows show the transitions and conditions. You can use formal modeling languages, but I have found the simplistic notions described in the Appendix, Section A.4, to be most effective. Keep in mind that many people with differing skill sets and backgrounds will need to view the process descriptions in order to validate them, so you want to keep the modeling language as simple as possible. The basic notions you want to capture in a process description are the *phases (states), transitions, actions, trigger conditions, roles,* and *assumptions.* I give an example of a process model in the Appendix, Section A.6.

Then the next question that arises is "What process?" That is, different levels of process can be described: object life cycles, personal processes, group processes, the CM process, the release cycle, and the corporate product process or life cycle. In the Appendix, Section A.5, the types of process descriptions are highlighted. The key thing to keep in mind is that all of those processes interrelate. They all need to be defined. For the CM tool, what essentially gets implemented is the process that details all the steps that a baseline must go through, which includes the time it is created (such as by the selection of versions of different types of files), through all the changes applied to it, and through to the release and distribution stages. A complete book could be written about the topic of process description for CM automation.

Once you have sorted out what kinds of process descriptions will be done, the next step is to sort out how to collect or define the processes. A method for capturing a process that I have found to be most successful is to do what we did when I worked at Continuus Software Corp. I would conduct process roundtable meetings where we gathered everyone together (such as the deployment team, project leaders, developers, testers, QA staff, build managers, release managers; that is, anyone involved in the life cycle of a change or baseline) and developed the description. I used a white board and drew up the process flow (as described in the Appendix, Section A.4) by asking everyone a series of questions about how a product is developed and how changes are handled. Then I went away and wrote everything up, as described in the example shown in the Section A.6 of the Appendix.

Developing the processes is an iterative approach. Once process definition has gotten under way, then it is time to plan the pilot project(s).

Step 15: Do proof-of-concept pilot(s)

Pilot projects provide the opportunity to resolve risks and to gain complete confidence in the tool. It is proof-of-concept because the goals are as follows:

- Prove that the tool works in your environment.

- Gain experience in using the tool.

- Get an early success by doing the first roll-out of the tool.

- Uncover any new risks.

- Find out what extra training or documentation will be required for your users.

- Become experts in the tool.

- Test your requirements with hands-on use of the tool using your own data.

- Be able to objectively rate the tool using your selection rating system.

A big question is always that of who will do the pilot project—which team? Sometimes it is the deployment team that basically does a simple pilot. It is treated as a "throw-away" project. Not many companies can afford to do this, though. More effective then, the pilot project should be a real project team who is willing to bear the burden of the extra risk in being the first to roll out, or cut over to, the new solution. The deployment team needs to work closely with them to actively participate in it since they have to acquire expertise in its use.

The pilot project needs to be planned. In the Appendix (Section A.9), I provide a template for a typical pilot project plan. A pilot plan needs to document:

- Goal and success criteria for the pilot;

- The ramifications of using this project team as the pilot;

- Schedule details;

- Scope of the pilot: data, code, content, integrations, process, customizations, people, activities;

- Risks;

- Training materials;

- Key steps or activities to be tested;

▸ Lessons learned and findings.

From the experience, the deployment team must gain certain knowledge in order to proceed with deployment:

1. Is this the right tool? Do we now have complete confidence in it?

2. What extra training is needed for our staff beyond what the vendor provides?

3. Were our success criteria met? Why or why not?

4. Is the process sufficient?

5. Are all the risks mitigated?

6. Did new risks arise and why?

7. How does this pilot change the rating values for this tool?

Some companies make mistakes with their pilots, which can stop a deployment completely. Common mistakes include these:

▸ Using the pilot as an opportunity to break the tool and stress test it. This is almost pointless. It is good to know the limitations of tools, but mature CM tools do not easily break. Some tools are badly designed but they tend to be the simple, cheap ones. The purpose of the pilot should be to see how well the tool operates under your normal working conditions. Good CM tools don't break and will scale up.

▸ Choosing a pilot group that is not typical of the company's project teams. You should design the pilot to test the most common activities of all your teams, not the least common (unless, of course, the least common is the most mission-critical).

▸ Not testing typical work scenarios and IDE tools with the CM tool.

▸ Not defining the scope of the pilot. Some pilots go on forever, never finishing. This happens because the pilot team gets overenthusiastic about the tool. They see its potential and want to dive in and do everything. You need to define a stopping point because the bigger picture is to deploy to the company.

▸ Not defining success criteria. It is very important to define success criteria because the pilot will act as the vanguard, the cheerleader, so to speak, to the rest of the company that the CM solution is fabulous. It helps reset expectations so that the next team to roll out the tool will know what to expect and there will be no unpleasant surprises.

Once the pilot(s) is/are done, then the tool decision should be obvious.

Step 16: Pick the CM tool

A pilot project confirms whether the CM tool is the right one or not. The tool meets the requirements and performs appropriately on the company's data, code, and content. This tool decision and the success of the pilot should be announced with flair and much aplomb to the company because a major milestone has been achieved. Some PR (public relations) work has to be done now to pave the way for the rest of the deployment. Excitement should build. It is akin to a marketing launch of a new product. This helps generate lots of positive "press" around the company or talk about the new CM solution. The easy part of deployment begins now because many of the difficult decisions have already been made and the deployment team now has objective knowledge that this tool is the right one for the company. It remains to tidy up any risks and schedule the rest of the roll-out.

Step 17: Complete risk mitigation

At this point, the tool decision has been made and success seen with the pilot project. It is time to review the risk management plan to make sure that all the risks are resolved or mitigated. Some new risks may have arisen from the pilot, so those have to be addressed too. The deployment team may decide that some risks will go unaddressed. They will not be resolved or mitigated. That is fine. Companies all live with some sense or degree of risk. The important thing is that the risk is documented along with knowledge about it so that a contingency plan can be put in place if need be. So, the company is "safe" and can move forward with the roll-out.

Step 18: Schedule roll-out

Some companies make a big mistake by scheduling all teams to roll over to the new CM tool at the same time. This is taking a huge risk. It can work if the tool is a very simple one, the groups are small, and the right training and procedures are in place. But it is tricky. It is much safer and more sensible to roll out groups in an incremental fashion. A schedule needs to be developed with the consent of the project managers and upper management. I say this because I have seen some interesting things happen regarding schedules.

For instance, at one software company I was leading the Lotus Notes deployment effort. (No, Notes is not a CM tool, but I used the same adoption steps documented in this chapter.) The CEO wanted all the teams to roll out Notes, but starting with the engineering group followed by others in a certain order. When I approached the vice president of engineering, he preferred to roll out last since he knew his developers would be the most resistant in the company. But I knew the CEO had a different plan. I approached the other managers. At the end of the day, I had two schedules. One that the CEO wanted, and one that all the other managers preferred. I went back to the CEO and presented both and recommended the latter. Once I explained why, he concurred. So, the lesson learned is to always communicate, especially with the CEO, and be well prepared.

Step 19: Train users

All users or participants in the new CM solution must be trained. The vendor offers standard training classes typically for novices and for system administrators. They also offer "train the trainer" classes where the vendor trains the person that will train the company in-house. The deployment team needs to evaluate these classes to see if they are appropriate for their own people. Large companies typically end up developing their own classes, with the help of the vendor. That is because the standard training classes use vendor terminology rather than company terminology. A training team typically needs to translate the classes and training materials into more meaningful jargon for their people. Thus, training becomes more effective.

Timing of training is always important too. The best way seems to be "just-in-time" training. That is, do the training just before the roll-out so that it is still fresh in the person's mind when the cut over to the new tool is made.

Vendors offer documentation and sometimes on-line tutorials to help novices. Again, the deployment team needs to evaluate the suitability of these for their people. Sometimes a "cheat sheet" is created by the team, again in terminology that is meaningful for their people. While people are being trained in the new tool, their environment needs to be prepared.

Step 20: Prepare the CM tool

Before rolling out a new user to the new tool, it is a good idea to make sure the tool itself is ready. For instance, any integrations, customizations, data migrations, new hardware, documentation, help-desk support, and network connections should all be set up and tested.

Step 21: Manage resistance

One big issue that always comes up is how to manage resistance given the kind of culture at the company. My advice regarding resistance is as follows:

1. First of all, resistance is natural in any situation regarding change. Do not be alarmed or frightened by it.

2. Expect it and expect different types of resistance. Figure 5.2 shows the different types of resisters that a company can expect. Have a strategy for each type of resister. (Figure 5.2 is discussed below in more detail.)

3. Understand that adoption gets more complicated as the number of people involved increases along with the complexity of the tool, as shown in Figure 5.3.

4. Realize that most resistance is based on fear. The solution then is to find ways of alleviating or calming that fear. Typical fears include these: I will lose my job; my current knowledge is useless; and I'll have to learn everything anew.

5. Monitor resistance by listening to people and finding out what they are saying. Any negative talk needs to be countered. Use the nonresisters to encourage positive talk.

6. Keep in mind the kind of culture at the company and work within that culture rather than outside it.

7. Do not push people until they are ready. Give people time to adjust.

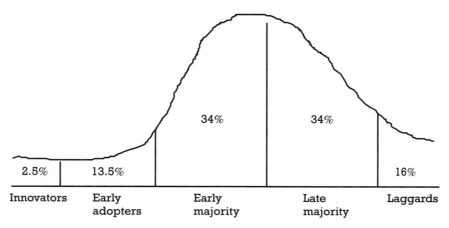

Figure 5.2   Types of resisters during adoption.

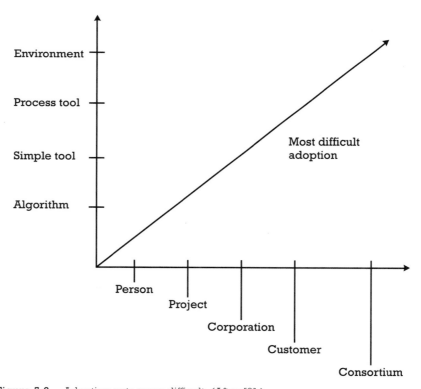

Figure 5.3   Adoption gets more difficult. (After [8].)

8. Have courage, patience, and persistence.

9. Be willing to rethink your approach if necessary when it doesn't seem to be getting results. There are many ways to achieve the same thing.

Figure 5.2 shows the different types of resisters—people with different acceptance levels for switching to a new tool—that a company can expect. I am extrapolating from the work of Geoffrey Moore, who published a similar bell curve that showed "the market penetration of any new technology products in terms of a progression in the types of consumers it attracts throughout its useful life" [9].

My experience in technology adoption of CM tools yields a bell curve very similar to that of Figure 5.2. This figure essentially shows that you can classify people in a company based on their willingness and ability to change to a new tool. The percentage values are quantitative measures showing the typical percentage of people within a company of that type. I do not remember exactly where I originally got the percentages because it was long ago, but I believe it was from the good work of Priscilla Fowler on technology adoption from my days at the Software Engineering Institute. The types of resisters include the following:

- The innovators who eagerly pursue a new tool because it is new (they are really nonresisters);

- The early adopters who see the vision and benefits of adopting the new tool (they are typically very low-level resisters);

- The early majority who see that it is practical and realistic to change to the new tool but only after the kinks or "teething problems" are sorted out;

- The late majority are those who eventually switch over because it is mandated;

- The laggards who do not want to change but have it forced upon them (these are the most resistant).

Hence, the implications are that in any technology adoption effort, such as deploying a new CM tool, you will find these five types of people in your company. You need to recognize them and realize that each category will switch over to the new tool at different points in time and for different reasons. You then need to structure your deployment strategy around those resisters. For instance, you would never use a group consisting of late majority and laggard types on your first roll-out effort or for your pilot project team. It would be like "shooting yourself in the foot."

Knowing your company's culture is important. *Culture* is "the totality of socially transmitted behavior patterns, arts, beliefs, institutions, and all other products of human work and thought characteristic of a community" [10]. Formal research [11] has been done concerning cultures within American organizations. There seem to be three types of cultures:

1. *Formalistic:* Control is via rules and laws; tend to be large corporations.

2. *Collegial:* Control is via group consensus; tend to be groups that are focused on the same product.

3. *Personalistic:* Control via self-concept; tend to be small, entrepreneurial companies.

When I talk to companies and ask about their culture, they always come up with much more cute names such as "macho cowboy" or "firefighter" culture as well as unmentionable names. The idea though is that each culture acts differently regarding:

• Decision-making;

• Where the power source is;

• Achieving a desired result;

• Focus time (short or long term);

• Interpersonal communication;

• Reactive or proactive style;

• The way the culture grows;

• The manner in which change is accepted.

Hence, when deploying a new tool (solution), change slows down and must be steered through the sometimes murky waters of the culture. The advice then is to "go with the flow" and not get trapped in a vicious cycle where everything must happen the way you planned it. Be aware, adaptable, tactful, and flexible at all times.

Step 22: Gather lessons learned

A company always learns lessons from a technology adoption effort. It is valuable to record and acknowledge those lessons since the company will always be doing technology adoption as new and better tools come along. I have learned many lessons from participating in and leading many CM adoption efforts. Those lessons are captured in everything that I have said about the 22 steps outlined here. But I do want to emphasize some issues:

1. Technology adoption is really about people handling change. So, do not ignore the people issues. And most people operate out of fear.

2. Adoption can be as simple or as complex as you want or need to make it.

3. Without sponsorship, adoption has little chance of succeeding.

4. Treat adoption as you would manage a project.

5. Adoption happens much more quickly if people with the right skills are on the deployment team.

6. Proper skills include facilitation, communication, enthusiasm, project management, analytical, and technical skills.

7. You need a deployment team—a group of people who lead and own the solution.

8. Resistance is normal. Do not fear it.

9. Risk management is the key to adoption success.

10. Do not forget to focus on all aspects of change: managerial, process, organizational, cultural, political, people related, and technical.

11. Set users' expectations accurately. Do not try to fool them.

12. A positive/negative force exists during adoption: Positive forces are the goals and vision and the negative forces are risks and resistance. Get a comfortable balance going.

13. Adoption can be good, bad, or ugly. Make your choice and deal with the consequences.

14. Make sure everyone gets meaningful, just-in-time training.

15. Do not cheat by expecting the vendor to handle all the adoption difficulties. Your company has the responsibility. The vendor is there to help you with the tool. Clarify the roles and responsibilities with the vendor.

16. Carefully select and define the scope of the pilot project.

17. A lot of adoption is public relations work.

18. Management sponsorship and commitment are ongoing, constant activities, not one-event things. They must be maintained.

19. Change can only be initiated and led in harmony with the kind of culture at the company.

20. A tool itself cannot be a "silver bullet"—a magical solution to everything. Work is needed beyond the tool, as shown in the 22 steps discussed in this chapter.

One question that always comes up concerns how long the process will take.

How long are the tool selection and adoption going to take?

There is no simple answer. It all depends on how long it takes to know the right answers for the strategic questions, along with knowing how easily the people in your company will adopt the new tool/solution. The factors that determine the time it will take include these:

▸ The complexity of the CM solution such as the kind of tool—evolutionary or full-process;

▸ The scope of the CM solution such as enterprise-wide or group deployment;

▸ The number of risks and their probability of happening;

▸ Dependencies between groups and the products;

▸ Skill set of the change agents and the user population;

▸ How quickly the culture adapts to change;

▸ The number of legacy product challenges;

▸ The resources available to support adoption.

It can range from a few weeks for simple solutions to a couple of years for very large, global companies. There is no particular yardstick, guideline, or formulas for one to use. You could always ask the vendor—they may have some useful data available. Even better, ask for a reference site from the vendor and then ask that site how long it took them. Hopefully, their situation is similar to yours.

Another question that always pops up concerns ROI and metrics.

ROI and useful metrics

Return on investment (ROI) consists of many parts beyond recouping money outlay:

1. Eliminating all the pains;

2. Gaining all the benefits and value;

3. Having the insurance to steer clear of the nine Web crisis challenges;

4. Getting a return on, and value for, your money;

5. Improving management metrics;

6. Improving development metrics.

That is, ROI is a combination of ridding a company of all the problems and pains (described in Chapter 3), gaining all the business and technical benefits and values (described in Chapter 3) of CM, steering clear of all the Web problems such as variant explosion (described in Chapter 2), and getting better results for important management and technical metrics. Of course, one can never quantify the "insurance factor"; that is, the insurance a company gets by protecting itself from big disasters as a result of having CM in the first place.

Regarding ROI values, one approach is to ask the CM vendors for their formulas for determining ROI. The vendors often have very valuable data and formulas gleaned from their customers that you can use. Go to their Web sites and track that down, typically in one of their white papers. Or, approach them directly. This is a typical, free service they can give you on request.

You can also create some values. I recommend that a company capture two metrics: one that is pertinent to management and one that is pertinent to development. For instance, how long does it take to get a change out the door (that is, how long is a typical release cycle), and how many bugs were found during development compared to those found in the field (once the code has been released to the customer or published to the Web site)? Capture the data for these two metrics before the CM tool is deployed and then after successful deployment, and see the difference. Typically, companies see early on that their release cycle time is cut dramatically (maybe from 2 months to 2 weeks), and that 50% fewer bugs are found in released products. As a rough guide, a company should definitely see an ROI after 12 months, if not much earlier, or even immediately. For instance, in some large companies, it costs them $1 million for every week they are late in releasing a new version of software. If they buy a $100,000 CM tool, and it takes them 4 months to complete its rollout to the company, at which time they release the next version of their product earlier than expected due to the release cycle automation, they have immediately achieved ROI.

Typical metrics that I have seen companies capture include these:

- Number of defects found after each release;

- Number and type of changes (bugs, enhancements, customizations, emergency patches, show stoppers);

- Number of defects found during development;

- Time to identify and correct defects;

- Amount of code delivered or content published;

- Number of reused lines of code or content;

- Number of bugs that still need to be fixed at each release;

- Percentage of code and content impacted by each type of change;

‣ Difference between estimated versus actual time taken on each task.

Metrics are important to help improve the productivity and quality of a company's products. They can also be used to help sell upper management on the need for a new CM solution. For instance, if management can be shown that automating the release cycle can cut it from 2 months to 2 weeks, then tremendous savings to the company are implied.

Metrics can also help a company isolate the source of problems. If it sees that more bugs are found after release rather than in development, then that implies not enough testing is being done before release.

Metrics need to be captured that have meaning to someone. For instance, the CEO wants a metric that tells him or her the break-even point for ROI. Managers want metrics that help improve the quality of the product while reducing the work effort to achieve such. Developers are concerned with productivity metrics such as build time or check-out time. Customers are concerned with the turnaround time to get a bug fixed or to get their customization done. Hence, whatever metrics your company picks, they must have meaning. In many cases, no metrics are available before a CM tool is installed. In such cases, I recommend that companies just pick two metrics to start with: one that is pertinent to management and one for developers, as described earlier. There should be no major overhead associated with collecting and analyzing the data. But as the CM solution evolves, the metrics get better (which is an indicator of good CM deployment). Well-chosen metrics can add substance to the adoption strategy and help maintain sponsorship of the adoption. For companies that want to embark on more detailed metrics, various books, including [12], offer help.

When I think of a metrics strategy, I consider five categories and create metrics around those:

1. Productivity metrics;

2. Process-oriented metrics;

3. Quality metrics;

4. Performance metrics;

5. Data-related metrics.

Productivity metrics are concerned with the rate of effective work; for instance, the release cycle time (how long it takes a change to go through the complete fix–test–release cycle), and the number of steps involved in delivering or publishing the next release.

Process-oriented metrics are concerned with the amount of effort in doing particular tasks; for instance, the number of people involved with each step in the release cycle.

Quality metrics are concerned with the measurement of goodness, for instance, the number of bugs found in each build or each publish step; the number of bad fixes (the changes that have to be redone because they were not right); and the number of leaky bugs (bugs introduced during development but found later during the integration test rather than during, say, unit tests).

Performance metrics relate to the time to complete tasks such as check-out time for files, build times for baselines, and publish times.

Data-related metrics are concerned with volume of data, for instance, the number of lines of code in files and baselines, amount of disk space consumed, and number of lines of source code versus binary code versus text in content versus static code versus dynamic code.

For Web content, the whole notion of those five categories of metrics is still a research topic. Some good research work has been done [13] and further work will be needed. Right now, companies are still focused on traffic monitoring statistics and on server uptime. Once companies get beyond their network infrastructure focus, they will need to focus more on these five areas for their content.

Another question I always get concerns failed adoption efforts.

How can we recover from tool adoption failure, or turn "shelfware" into "UseWare"?

I often get approached by people in companies that have failed in their attempts to adopt a CM solution. They want to know if recovery is possible. That is, can the "shelfware" tool that they invested a lot of money in become a viable and used solution? Also, can a tool that is not being used to its potential be resurrected into its full potential? For instance, many full-process tools sometimes end up being wasted as simple version control tools and companies want to know how to change this. Whatever the situation is for the tool, the following steps can help resurrect or recover from it:

1. Know that anything is possible and there is a 90% chance of fixing the situation.

2. Find out why the situation led to CM shelfware or a stalemate.

3. Find out if any of the 22 steps in Table 5.1 were followed, and why or why not.

4. Understand that CM, or the tool itself, or both, now have a bad reputation in your company. Lots of negativity probably surround the idea of an automated CM solution, which needs to be countered.

5. Typically, adoption has failed because few, if any, of the 22 steps in Table 5.1 were followed. Recovery means backtracking and doing the work of those steps that was never done. Basically, you start from scratch, and one of the risks is the negativity related to the previous failure of the shelfware. You just methodically work through the steps. Either the tool was the wrong choice, or it was the right choice but was not deployed properly. So find out which is the case and do the 22 steps of work.

Another question that always arises concerns how to properly use the CM vendors.

The value of configuration management vendors

Vendors are often misused by companies. Some people view tool vendors as rather low on the totem pole of living entities. Having been a sales and services consultant with various CM vendors, I have experienced a range of reactions. I am here to say that you can glean a lot of free support and valuable information from vendors that will help you significantly during your deployment effort. For instance, you can request the following from CM vendors:

> On-site demonstrations of their tools;

> Visits to the vendor's site to see how they use their own tool in-house;

> Responses to your RFP;

▸ References to users of their CM tool; you can interview these people and get a wealth of information;

▸ Sample plans such as the ones I mention in the 22 steps;

▸ Competitive analysis information; that is, why their tool is better than the competition and why the competitor's tool is bad;

▸ Examples of processes and scripts;

▸ Discounts on licensing, consulting, and maintenance fees;

▸ Access to experienced people at the vendor's site;

▸ ROI formulas;

▸ Success stories.

Vendors are the most knowledgeable source of information about CM. They implement very powerful solutions at Fortune 1000 companies around the world. They have seen a lot and that knowledge can be tapped into, free of charge.

One reason why people view vendors with caution is because they do not believe them. Sure, there are some incompetent people who will say anything to appease you. But 99% of the time, their sales and services people are just trying to do their best. Most often, especially with process CM tools, the sales force has not had the necessary training, nor do they have all the collateral (selling materials) to help them do a better sales job. A lot of this has to do with inadequate marketing. Traditionally, CM vendors have placed very little emphasis, even none, on marketing CM and the tools. This is a shame because marketing is needed to help educate the world about CM. The stock markets also need to be made aware of the value of CM.

There is typically a high turnover in a CM sales forces because, for instance, full-process CM is more difficult to sell than evolutionary CM. Evolutionary CM tools (such as simple version control ones) are easy to sell; they are a black-box sell, whereas a full-process CM tool sell is a much longer-term, strategic sell—a solution sell rather than a point sale.

When working with vendors, it is always a good idea to find out how long the person (salesperson, sales engineering support, technical consultant) has been doing that job. If it is under 1 year, chances are their knowledge is limited, so you may need extra help. I also recommend that the more you keep the vendor informed of your progress, the more they can help you. Salespeople want to build relationships with their clients and they want to keep their clients happy. But they need to know what is happening. They do not operate solely in sales mode—they operate in support or assistance mode too. They are motivated by making more sales and by using a client as a reference site—that is, having a happy and successful customer. When I work with a vendor, I see it as a relationship where each of us has certain responsibilities, as shown in Figure 5.4.

All the vendors have realized that they need to focus much more on services to support all the process needs of their clients along with supporting the adoption work described throughout this chapter. The vendors have to help their companies be successful with adoption. No tool vendor—for CM or other tools—really wants to tackle a company's technology adoption issues. I mean, who wants to get embroiled in the politics of a company? Certainly not the vendor. They really want to be in the business of selling a tool and supporting it. But because companies struggle with adoption in general, and because a CM solution can be a complex, enterprise-wide one that "opens up a can of worms," the vendor has to become a participant, whether it wants to or not.

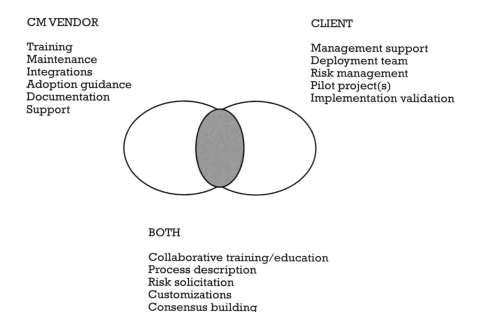

CM VENDOR

Training
Maintenance
Integrations
Adoption guidance
Documentation
Support

CLIENT

Management support
Deployment team
Risk management
Pilot project(s)
Implementation validation

BOTH

Collaborative training/education
Process description
Risk solicitation
Customizations
Consensus building

Figure 5.4   Relationship between CM tool vendor and client.

The customer relationship is being revised by CM vendors as part of the Internet era. Vendors know that they need to provide more adoption consulting for their clients as well as process consulting. In their sales model or techniques, vendors are trying different approaches regarding services. For instance, some companies (such as Serena) make a very clear demarcation between product and services where the salespeople sell the tool and special services people sell services. Most of the CM vendors, though, have their sales force sell services along with the tool. Many vendors (such as Continuus) originally had their own services group, whereas other vendors (such as Rational) outsource a major part of their services.

It is interesting to examine how vendors sell. Traditionally, they have sold reactively. That is, they sell in reaction to a company's pain level. They use a technique called *solution selling* in which they identify the user's pains and show how their tool addresses the pains. Eventually the CM vendors will learn how to sell proactively; that is, how to sell a CM solution into a company before it reaches its pain threshold. I realize most companies have reactive rather than proactive styles of management, but that has to change with the Internet economy. As CM tools approach the unified model of CM functionality presented in Chapter 3, they will have little to differentiate themselves apart from their services, and their ability to sell proactively.

To me, a vendor today could sell proactively by pointing out the nine challenges of the Web crisis that I presented in Chapter 2. They could simply ask their prospect two questions:

1. How will you manage the variant explosion problem?

2. How can you manage the fast pace of change?

Any company that has no answer to these questions is ripe pickings for a CM solution. Any vendor can become market leader if they work out how to sell proactively, rather than reactively.

Another question I get asked a lot concerns standards and CM.

The big gap regarding standards

One area of confusion surrounds the terms *process* and *standards*. As CM vendors start pushing process more, people can become confused about "what process." That is, there is the CM process itself, which is what many of the CM tools automate to some degree or other. Then there are all the processes that must be supported by a company in order to be certified to a standard. For instance, the SEI Capability Maturity Model Integration (CMMI) identifies many processes that must be supported, one of them being a CM process, another being a testing process. So when CM vendors say they support process, it is a good idea to have them explain that statement further.

There is a gap between processes defined in standards and what tool vendors do. For instance, many companies have jumped on the process improvement bandwagon, such as with the SEI CMMI certification efforts, ISO 9000 standardization, Bootstrap, and SPICE. Any industry de facto standard or international standard requires CM and process definition and implementation. Hence, vendors have to fill a big gap. The *gap* is between the requirements or goals in the standard versus the capabilities of the tool. For instance, level 2 of the CMMI has goals related to CM. The CMMI does not say how those goals are to be achieved; it just says what the goals are. The "how" has to be provided by the CM vendors.

Ideally, they have to provide the mapping from the goals to their implementation. Also, the standards are written with the presumption that all the goals can be achieved manually, that is, without tools. They do not preclude tools, but do not include any notion of them either. Hence, vendors have to provide the mapping to close the gap, and on top of that, they have to support the CM processes, along with the related process improvement activities.

The CM goals defined in the standards are very basic, such that any CM tool, by virtue of its proper deployment, easily meets those goals.

Another question that arises fairly often concerns process versus tools.

Should the tool follow the process or should the process follow the tool?

The question is whether companies should completely define their processes before they buy the tool, or buy the tool and then fit their processes to match the tool. My answer is *either approach works,* and it depends on the level of awareness and culture of the company, along with the amount of resources, that is, money, that a company can afford.

I know that pure process gurus firmly believe that you define your processes completely before you buy the tool. Well, this is a sensible idea, but I have worked with many companies who are incapable of defining their own processes or have no time to step back and define their processes. They are not sure what processes to actually define and no one person knows exactly what the processes are since much of the work is done manually, that is, without tools. Many companies will ask for a CM process template. I present them with the kinds of information in this book but they still need to tailor it to their situation, business goals, and strengths and limitations. These types of companies need a kick-start. They need help, and often buying a good CM tool that has process automated straight out of the box gives these companies the kick-start they need to get them functioning. Such tools also help educate them about process. So, sometimes, tool before process works well.

Of course, companies that understand process can step back, take their time, and define the processes and then go select the tool. But sometimes they can make mistakes. For instance, sometimes process-intensive companies can end up stuck in the process definition phase so no progress is made. They are stuck in the "analysis paralysis."

A good balance has to be found between process definition and selecting an appropriate tool. Yes, ideally you want to know all your processes before you buy the tool. On the other hand, companies have found process efficiencies in tools that they never expected. Sometimes certain processes cannot be implemented efficiently, which is why the tool vendor implemented its own version process. In general, CM vendors have tuned their tools to support basic out-of-the-box CM processes. The tools need to be given a degree of trust that they do the right thing, especially the mature, full-process CM tools.

Regarding process customization, a company does not want to end up customizing the CM tool too much. It creates the problem of having to merge those customizations with the eventual upgrades of the CM tool. So you had better keep your CM tool under CM control itself along with all your customizations.

Key messages from this chapter

1.   Technology adoption, or tool deployment, as most companies call it, is typically done poorly. A tool can only be as good as the success of its deployment.

2. For a quick and simple ROI case, capture two metrics: one for management, the other for development. Capture data before and after tool deployment and see the big difference. But ROI is really about the business value, not just technical value. Consider broadening your definition of ROI to encompass business issues (such as those identified in Chapter 3).

3. Size of a company counts, but the 22 adoption steps still need to be followed, regardless of the size of the company.

4. Good adoption means introducing a CM solution successfully, effectively, and optimally.

5. Adopting a CM solution, as with most complex tools, is more than just technical stuff. There are other, more powerful or influential issues in adopting a solution, including managerial, process-oriented, organizational, cultural, political, people-oriented, environment-related, and technical issues.

6. Companies end up doing bad or ugly adoption because they focus just on the technical issues and ignore the others. Then they get surprised as to why no one wants to use the tool.

7. Tool selection and deployment can be broken down into 22 steps.

8. Many lessons have been learned from adoption efforts. There is no need to make the same mistakes.

References

[1]   Rogers, E., *Diffusion of Innovations,* New York: The Free Press, 1983, p. 247.

[2]   Dart, S., "Achieving the Best Possible CM Solution," *Crosstalk,* Sept. 1996, pp. 9–13, on-line at http://www.stsc.hill.af.mil/CrossTalk/1996/sep/achievin.html.

[3]   Dart, S., and J. Krasnov, "Experiences in Risk Mitigation for Configuration Management," *Proc. 4th SEI Conference on Risk,* Monterey, CA, Nov. 1995.

[4]   Dart, S., "Adopting an Automated Configuration Management Solution," *Proc. Software Technology Center (STSC) Conference,* Salt Lake City, UT, Apr. 1994.

[5]   Hall, E. M., *Managing Risk: Methods for Software Systems Development*, SEI
      Series in Software Engineering, Reading, MA: Addison-Wesley, 1998.

[6]   Fayad, M. E., "Software Development Process: A Necessary Evil," *Commun.
      ACM*, Sept. 1997, Vol. 40, No. 9, pp. 101–103.

[7]   Bounds, N., and S. Dart, "CM Plans: The Beginning of Your CM Solution,"
      SEI Technical Report, July 1994, on-line at http://www.sei.cmu.edu/
      technology/case/scm/papers/CM_Plans/CMPlans.MasterToC.html.

[8]   Fowler, P., "Managing Technical Transition as a Project," *Proc. SEI Symp.*,
      Aug. 1993.

[9]   Moore, G., *Crossing the Chasm*, New York: HarperCollins, 1991.

[10] *The American Heritage Dictionary*, 2nd ed., Boston, MA: Houghton Mifflin
      Company, 1982, p. 348.

[11] Bennis, W., *An Invented Life: Reflections on Leadership and Change*, Reading,
      MA: Addison-Wesley, 1993.

[12] Möller, K. H., and D. J. Paulish, *Software Metrics: A Practioner's Guide to
      Improved Product Development*, Piscataway, NJ: IEEE Computer Society Press,
      1993.

[13] Olsina, L., et al., "Specifying Quality Characteristics and Attributes for
      Websites," *Proc. ICSE99 Workshop on Web Engineering, International Conference
      on Software Engineering*, Los Angeles, CA, May 1999, pp. 84–93.

Contents

Case Studies in Configuration Management Automation of Web Systems

"What's miraculous about a spider's web?" said *Mrs. Arable.*
"Ever try to spin one?" asked Mr. Dorian.
—E. B. White, *Charlotte's Web*

This chapter presents simplified case studies about companies using configuration management (CM) tools to manage their Web systems. I attempted to capture the problems they were having that drove them to a CM solution, along with the kinds of processes and emphasis they place on CM. Also, each case study has a lessons learned section. Before presenting the case studies, I discuss what I found and end up with what is really the conclusion of this book: the beginnings of the best practice for Web engineering.

What I did

The companies that participated in the case studies are listed in Table 6.1. They are a mixture of small to large companies doing intranet or full-scale, multiple-site Web development. Some are pure Internet companies and others are bricks-and-clicks companies. I asked all the CM vendors mentioned in Chapter 4 for a case study. A few declined, saying their clients did not want to go public with the details.

The kinds of questions I asked each company are given in the Appendix, Section A.1. I attempted to present uniform information about each company taking into account confidentiality agreements. Keep in mind that the companies view their CM capabilities as a competitive edge so only a certain amount of information or detail can be revealed. Nonetheless, there is valuable information in these case studies. The case studies are presented in alphabetical order by company.

Overall, I wanted to capture the value that each company has received from CM along with their publishing processes and change management processes. There is no attempt on my part to present one tool as better than another because that is not what I believe. It all depends on the preferences and requirements of the company as to which tool is best for them. At the end of this chapter I summarize the key messages that I, and the companies, want to pass onto Web teams, the obvious one being this: Use a CM tool, please!

The messages and best practices

From doing these case studies, various messages become abundantly clear:

Table 6.1
Participants in Case Studies

Company	Vendor	CM Tool
Carclub.com	Serena	eChangeMan
eCampus.com	Rational	ClearCase
EDS	Computer Associates	Harvest
Lockheed Martin	Merant	PVCS Dimensions
Lycos	Perforce	Perforce
NASD	Merant	PVCS Professional
OneSource	Starbase	StarTeam
USinternetworking	Continuus	WebSynergy

1. Web content is software, so treat it as such (rather than as documentation), which means follow good software engineering principles, in particular, configuration management practices. That is, everything we learned from and used to do in traditional software development and maintenance needs to be applied to Web development.

2. The main differences between traditional software development and Web development are concerned with the dramatic increase in the speed of development and maintenance cycles along with the tight synergy between business decisions and technical operations.

3. The speed of change affecting Web systems is amazing. A good balance has to be found between regimented practices and the need to support fast change.

4. The staging or workflow processes that Web systems need are very similar to traditional software ones. We have development (coding, creating content), which is separated from the preproduction work (such as testing and quality assurance) and from the production work (such as publishing). As in software, different people, and often different servers/machines, are used for each stage.

5. Buy the best configuration management tool your company can afford and deploy it properly.

6. Classify the types of changes. Each type will have a particular change cycle or workflow. For instance, a show-stopper bug follows a fast-track cycle, whereas a low-priority bug fix follows a normal change cycle.

7. It is very important to carefully classify changes. Most companies unfortunately treat everything as a show-stopper bug. This quickly overloads a company's ability to respond to changes, which is not sensible. It is wise to carefully classify changes and thus understand the difference between the change cycles such as a show-stopper bug versus a high-, medium-, or low-priority bug. Careful classification along with a judicious choice of change cycle produces the optimal change management solution. Web systems

often have change windows in which changes must happen within designated time frames.

8. Companies need to have development standards to help guide the developers and content authors. For instance, directory naming standards along with component design and reuse guidelines are helpful.

9. A CM manager role is required. That role may be called something different in each company such as QA manager, Web coordinator, release manager, or CM administrator. But the idea is to have someone who is responsible for ensuring that all the development, preproduction and production processes are followed and, if process improvements are needed, that person is responsible for deploying said improvements. This person or set of people needs to have clout—that is, a high level of authority and organizational support.

10. Companies need to set boundaries on their code and content. That is, they need to define the architecture of their Web system and then define partitions that can undergo different rates of change. For instance, most companies pick static HTML script as the Web content and say, "Hey, the marketing group can make all the changes they need to static text." On the other hand, if a change affects code, and bad code can cause the site to crash, then only experienced software engineers can make code changes.

11. Companies need to set boundaries regarding who creates or changes their Web systems. For instance, there are the graphic design artists who are not software people but contribute to the Web system and do not want to know anything about CM. Similarly, there are marketing people who may not be software people but create HTML static text. Then there are the programmers who write the code and definitely need to know about CM. Each role needs to be understood and the appropriate tools and change cycles provided.

12. Easy-to-use, efficient tools are needed to support Web development and maintenance. CM needs to be at the core or foundation of a company's tool suite. The more tightly integrated the tools are, the easier it is to access metadata between repositories and

automate workflow. All this helps speed up the change cycles, not to mention avoid mistakes.

Case study: Carclub.com[1]

The San Francisco-based start-up Carclub.com™ is an Internet company whose Web system supports its automobile club members regarding every aspect of car ownership: from buying, owning, insuring, and maintaining to reselling the car. It is a small, but growing company that employs fewer than 20 developers and content authors to manage its system.

Its CM system and environment

Carclub.com uses Serena's eChangeMan configuration management tool, which supports many of the CM functional areas that I discussed in Chapter 3. The goal of Carclub.com's CM solution is flexibility. Because it is an Internet company, business strategies and, hence, priorities are constantly changing. It wanted a CM tool that supports easy and fast change for its processes.

Initially, Carclub.com started out with simple version control on its Web content using the CVS tool. But it found that version control was not enough to support its Web maintenance needs. More CM functionality, such as process management, was required, so it bought a more substantial tool, eChangeMan. With this increased CM support, it found dramatic improvement in Web development, cost savings, and flexible technology that matched its ever-evolving business strategies. Carclub.com had also considered buying a full-blown, expensive Web content management tool (such as Vignette StoryServer), but found that it did not provide the CM capabilities it needed, such as support for all its staging areas in its development and maintenance processes.

Carclub.com runs its Web-based applications on a combination of Sun Solaris and Microsoft NT SQL server platforms. It uses various languages and technologies such as Perl, HTML, Java, and VBScript.

All of its developers use eChangeMan to control code and content. Its Web system maintenance is divided between code and content. Software

---

1. This case study was written with the assistance of Miguel Navarro, Webmaster for Carclub.com's Web site.

developers work on code. Content authors, such as the marketing group, work on HTML text and multimedia objects.

One of the major business strategies is to partner with other companies, that is, to do cobranding. This results in multiple Web sites that Carclub.com maintains (or variant sites as I discussed in Chapters 2 and 3).

CM process

The change cycles for code and content are very similar, with code going through more formal and stringent testing by the quality assurance (QA) team. A typical cycle begins with a change request (CR) being submitted via eChangeMan. The project coordinator reviews the request to ensure that it is complete and forwards the request to the production or development team depending on the type of request. Some requests span both teams and the role of the coordinator is to divide the tasks. The appropriate team is notified of the new CR.

If it is content, the CR is assigned to the content production team. If it is code, then it is assigned to the appropriate development team. The manager assigns it to a developer or content author. This person checks out the relevant files from the production repository into the development area—their personal workspace (known as the sandbox). When he or she is satisfied with the change edits, he or she uploads them to the test staging area (a separate server) and the QA manager is automatically notified.

The QA manager reviews the change by visiting the test Web site and running any necessary tests. When satisfied, he or she signs off. The initiator of the CR is also notified about this and can also test the changes and sign off on them. In the case of code changes, the QA group is notified and they do their formal regression testing.

Once all the sign-offs have happened, the changes are automatically transferred to the production repository and deployment server, which is very similar to the live Web site. At this point, the systems administrator/build manager is notified automatically and can then run his or her build tests. He or she decides when to publish the changes into the live site. The publishing process is done by switching servers. For example, the deployment server farm may consist of five servers. Two of the servers are taken off-line and the changes are deployed to them. When the systems administrator/build manager is satisfied with the deployment, he or she switches these two servers live and takes the other three off-line since they now have the older version of the Web site.

Minimizing mistakes in publishing

This "farm switching" process provides safety for Carclub.com in that it minimizes mistakes on the live Web site. Carclub.com also enables all the necessary testing and approvals to take place. One of the most difficult things to do is test database changes and enable easy rollbacks of the sites. Carclub.com can very quickly roll back a site from release 2 back to release 1. Of course, it becomes more complex if database records changed between releases 2 and 1. Carclub.com always leaves the previous version of the database schema running in parallel to guard against this situation. It does thorough testing to be fully aware of database changes. This is equally important when releasing a new version of a Web site since the changes must work for all versions of databases that are running at each site.

CM adoption and benefits

Implementing eChangeMan was an easy, fast process. Production implementation took less than 6 hours. User implementation and training of the Web development team was accomplished in less than 1 hour. Fifteen minutes were required to set up the user interface software with only 20 to 30 minutes spent for actual user training.

Carclub.com initially selected eChangeMan because it offered all users (not just the programmers) an interface for supporting and facilitating the management of its Web site. In addition, eChangeMan supports customized workflow. Finally, because the first 10 users were free, eChangeMan was deployed without risk and Carclub.com bypassed the onerous chore of going through purchasing.

Carclub.com feels that its CM solution has enabled it to increase its pace of Web development and maintenance by 20%, which in monetary terms adds up to at least $70,000 in savings per year. It believes that eChangeMan is ideal for Internet start-ups, because of its process management and easy implementation and administration, providing a quick payback in quality, reliability, speed, flexibility, and throughput. One major benefit is the dramatic improvement in communication between teams.

The evolving CM solution

Carclub.com's CM solution is evolving in various ways including supporting true code sharing across sites; providing specialized CM support for business units regarding content maintenance; enabling fresh content in a faster manner; managing versions of database schemas in synchrony with content; and providing more auditing and metrics support.

Messages and lessons learned

Miguel Navarro's messages to other Internet companies are as follows:

- While full-blown Web content management tools appear to offer Web development teams a lot of functionality at a very high price, it is the staging process and baseline management that are vital to the business, which traditional CM tools do well.

- Flexibility in all business and technical aspects is needed to survive and thrive in the Internet world.

- The Internet company's business tactics often drive the development and maintenance practices and technology. Good coordination is needed between business groups such as marketing and all Web development groups.

- Business units need to be given their own CM solution to aid in their content maintenance.

- To minimize the variant explosion problem, good CM is needed along with compatible business strategies, such as recognition that Web sites share content, which requires shared code maintenance on top of normal maintenance.

- Technology has to be a facilitator for Internet companies. It is important to find the right pieces and fit them together. No single tool is a panacea—there is no "silver bullet."

Case study: eCampus.com[2]

eCampus.com is a virtual college bookstore that offers general consumer products and services, textbook and product fulfillment services for traditional and on-line educational providers, an on-line auction, and a book

---

2. This case study was created with the assistance of Ted Willis, director of quality assurance at eCampus.com, and Jule Preston, CM manager, at eCampus.com.

buy-back service. It sells all books in print, school course content in traditional and digitally downloadable formats, imprinted and emblematic merchandise, and apparel. Its Web site has won awards.

Configuration management goals

eCampus.com is a pure Internet company using experienced software developers. As a result, those developers knew the importance of configuration management and instituted CM practices from the beginning using Rational's ClearCase and ClearQuest tools. Hence, they avoided the many development and maintenance problems described in Chapter 3.

eCampus.com believes that its CM solution has saved it 20% to 30% in development and maintenance costs.

The main goals of eCampus.com's CM solution are to ensure the consistent integrity and quality of its baselines. That is, it wants to be absolutely certain that the code and content that are in production (running on the live Web site) are exactly what it expects them to be, that there are no surprises. Similarly, it needs to know for certain all the pieces that make up a particular development and testing baseline. This is vital to its business. It does not wish to publish any errors or surprises.

Development and maintenance life cycles

Much of its development and maintenance schedule is driven by the school year schedule. For instance, for a couple of months the "rush is on"—when students go back to school, eCampus.com sees a dramatic increase in its Web site transactions. Hence, it focuses on keeping content up-to-date and fixing any high-priority bugs during the "rush" season. During the slower periods, lower-priority bugs, enhancements, and new development are done.

eCampus.com has structured all activities related to both Web and internal applications into two divisions:

1. *Technology:* This large division includes development (Java and data management); quality assurance (the CM analysts and testers who manage and test the baselines, and the data steward who manages the corporate knowledge); customer relations (the customer help desk); and operations (the logistics of supporting the company's infrastructure).

2. *Content:* This division is where HTML/XML text and multimedia content are developed by graphic designers, production artists, editors, photographers, and multimedia developers.

The developers and content authors use ClearCase to check out and check in code. Every item that is not actual data stored in the database is placed under version control. Much of the Web site's content is stored in the database, such as each college's (university's) Web site location, class schedule, and textbook requirements. The data in the database is extracted via SQL commands embedded in the Java and HTML code.

The CM manager is the lynchpin—the critical person who brings together, or packages, all the baselines (branches) and passes them onto formal testing group. He or she works with all the developers, content authors, and testers to ensure the correct flow of code through the development and testing staging areas. Code and content are created and changed on development machines and unit tested. They are then transferred to the test staging area (test server) where they are recompiled or reinterpreted in an environment that matches the production site as closely as possible.

Managing changes

For handling changes, change requests (CRs) are logged into ClearQuest. Changes are categorized as defects or enhancements. Each CR is given a priority (immediate, high, medium, or low). Also, a success factor weighting is given to each enhancement CR. For instance, many aspects related to making that change are captured and analyzed in order to set that weighting value. Aspects such as the cost of making the change, the impact of that change to other content and code, the relative risk, the customer satisfaction level, the potential revenue/profit, and corporate strategy are all considered.

Emergency CRs may bypass ClearQuest, but they always go through ClearCase. These typically go from development to production in as short a time as minutes.

Each day, or as required, a triage group (in effect, a change control board) meets to examine the bug and enhancement requests. This group consists of department heads who make key decisions about which changes will happen, when, why, and how. From that meeting, tasks are assigned to the various teams that will make the changes.

After unit testing, development and content teams inform the CM manager that a particular branch has been completed and is ready for formal testing. The QA department performs build verification, use case, load, traffic, and regression testing in the testing area. Defects found in tests are logged and the developers are notified. This cycle continues until testing is completed with successful results and the baseline is ready to be published. That ends the CM cycle for a change. This cycle is applied to bugs as well as enhancements.

Because much of the content of the site is generated from data stored in a relational database, a separate data management team is responsible for publishing new baseline data. This team works closely with the QA department and the database administrator to test and review all data loads and changes to database objects such as functions, procedures, and packages. Once approved, these changes are made directly to the live production site.

Messages and lessons learned

The messages that Ted Willis and Jule Preston want to pass onto you include these:

> ‣ Safe Web development is impossible without formal CM practices, proven CM tools, and the will to enforce them. Without these, the code base will spiral out of control.

> ‣ A good CM manager is required. The CM manager needs to be dedicated to the CM process, take responsibility for it, and work well with the developers, testers, and content authors. He or she needs to be able to move a baseline any time of day from any location through dial-up or a VPN. The CM manager should have a backup too; that is, other CM experts who can do the same job.

> ‣ The deployment of a CM solution requires considerable effort and time but is repaid several times over in the long run.

> ‣ The proper CM solution must become the "heart" of the development and maintenance processes. In addition to the QA department, everyone from development through operations needs to understand the new model and embrace the process.

> ‣ Employing CM in an Internet environment is very different from traditional application development. The time-to-market

requirements dictate that shortcuts be made in the development life cycle, which exposes your site to many risks. Be careful to minimize this by establishing emergency procedures ahead of time and sticking to them.

eCampus.com, like all companies, is continuing to evolve its CM solution in line with its business strategies. It is integrating its CM processes with requirements management tools such as Requisite Pro, along with various testing tools for load and traffic monitoring. Also, it is examining how to place tighter CM controls on its databases along with combining CM with a Web content/site management tool, such as Vignette StoryServer.

Case study: EDS[3]

EDS (Electronic Data Systems), www.eds.com, is a large, global services company that provides process and technology consulting along with ongoing operation of e-business solutions for its clients. In this case study, the typical business model that EDS uses for supporting its large Fortune 500 clients—the Enterprise Business Internet Sites (eBIS) model—is described.

The organization within EDS that supports this business model is comprised of 150 personnel. All are involved in the technical development, management, and operational support of eBIS systems. All content authors are part of external "creative agencies." The software environment consists of Netscape Application Server, Netscape Enterprise Server, Java, Oracle, Perl, CGI, and C tools.

A CM solution was identified as a necessity for supporting internal Capability Maturity Model Integration (CMMI) activities as well as for managing new Java development. The goal of EDS' CM solution was to control the quality of large Web applications. It defines quality in the following terms:

▸ Being able to correctly compile and distribute large Java applications to multiple application servers;

▸ Managing large amounts of graphics content that change on a daily basis;

---

3. This case study was written mostly by Jim Johnston, senior consultant with EDS.

> Auditing the eBIS process and generating reports;

> Providing a solid foundation for achieving level 3 of the CMMI.

The nature of the CM solution

Computer Associate's CCC/Harvest is used for Web content and source code control, builds, version control, approval, and audit purposes. Developers are the primary users of this tool. Computer Associate's Raveler is used for distribution of all content and code assets from a predefined drop zone (a centralized staging area) to preproduction and production servers. The Web hosting group is the primary user of this tool. Hence, all publishing goes through this group.

CCC/Harvest is the primary interface for the management and tracking of all code/content configuration items (CI) that comprise clients' sites. Basic CCC/Harvest functionality has been extended by the addition of several "build scripts" that handle all the compilation and distribution processes for Java, NAS, and Web configuration items. Raveler is the primary distribution tool used for managing and populating preproduction and production servers in the Web hosting environment that EDS operates for its eBIS clients. Raveler also provides a checklist of the tasks that depicts the entire process of gathering content from the drop zone, getting approval for distribution, actually distributing the code, and, finally, running the appropriate scripts. Raveler also provides an audit trail of all the tasks performed in the Web hosting environment.

Code and Web content management for eBIS projects can be broken down into several distinct layers of activities which are discussed in detail next:

> Creation;

> Collection;

> Configuration management;

> Compilation and distribution;

> Deployment.

Creation layer

The creation layer is where the work of creating all the assets that make up eBIS begins. There are three distinct categories of assets:

1. *Code.* Most of the application code for eBIS is written in the Java programming language. This code is created in separate development environments that are maintained by the different development teams who contribute code to eBIS projects. Other code assets such as Perl scripts are also created.

2. *Templates.* To use the Netscape Application Server (NAS), HTML files with special tags (gx tags) are created. These special HTML files are used to link to NAS, which in turn links to Java code objects. Functions such as database searches and e-mail are presented to the user through these special tags. Templates are developed jointly by development teams and creative agencies since they contain both graphic and coding information that must interface with NAS and Java.

3. *Creative.* The navigation and appearance of the Web site is usually created by a special team of graphic artists in an advertising organization called a "creative agency." This team creates the HTML, gifs, jpegs, and so on, that define the look and feel of the Web site. Templates are not considered a creative asset.

Collection layer

The collection layer is where all the assets (excluding database) that make up eBIS projects are brought together and registered in the CCC/Harvest server. There are two ways to get assets into the CCC/Harvest system:

1. Development teams that are not at a facility that has TCP/IP access to the CCC/Harvest server and all creative teams transmit their assets electronically to a mutually accessible computer. This is usually done via the File Transfer Protocol (FTP). This computer is referred to as an FTP server. The operations team has defined several FTP servers to which organizations can send their assets. Once the assets are on the mutually accessible server, the operations team will offload them and check them into the CCC/Harvest CM system. A variant of this method is to send e-mail to a member of the operations team with the assets as an attachment.

2. If a development team does have TCP/IP access to the CCC/Harvest server, then they can use the CCC/Harvest windows client to check their code directly into the CCC/Harvest system.

CM layer

The CM layer is where the traditional tracking, versioning, and configuration management of application assets occur. CCC/Harvest allows registered users of the system to manage these assets. Assets typically flow through the CCC/Harvest system as follows: check-in, test, walkthrough (for code), approval, and promotion.

Compilation and distribution layer

For client applications, all the Java source files that comprise the Web application are compiled. This process is also referred to as a *build*. Once compiled, the Java executables that make up the Web application and all other content/template assets are packaged together (zipped) and shipped to the Web hosting environment where they will eventually be executed. All distributions are placed in a predefined directory called a *drop zone*. This special directory allows for the identification of assets destined for further staging areas: integration and test, preproduction, and production.

Deployment layer

The deployment layer is where all assets are unloaded into their final destination and the application is executed in the Web hosting environment. The Web hosting environment is comprised of three distinct promotion areas with associated functions:

1. *Integration and test lab:* This area is used for system testing of applications that will run in the Web hosting environment. It has the least formal control of the three areas and is only accessible by developers.

2. *Preproduction:* This area is used for all kinds of testing such as user acceptance, Y2K, stress, and durability testing. It is a final checkpoint before applications go into production. It has more process placed on it through the use of Raveler, a workflow-FTP tool. This area is only accessible by developers, testers, and customers.

3. *Production:* This area is used for running the "live" applications on the Internet. It has the highest level of security, which is again controlled through Raveler. This area is accessible by the general public because it is the live Web site.

Each area has a higher level of security as assets move from a testing area to a production area. Asset movement (promotion) is handled within CCC/Harvest and distributed to Raveler.

Once the creative content, code, and templates are deposited in the drop zone, one of two processes is executed depending on the destination of the assets:

1. *Assets bound for integration and test:* These assets are deployed manually by using Perl scripts to extract constituent pieces in either creative (HTML, gifs, and so on) or code (NAS, Java, templates) assets to their respective servers and directory structures.

2. *Assets bound for preproduction and production:* These assets are collected by Raveler and put through a predefined workflow. This workflow indicates FTP targets, approvals, and Perl scripts to execute on target machines.

Figure 6.1 shows how assets flow while in the CCC/Harvest system and the points at which they exit and are distributed to the Web hosting environment. Notice that there are parallel code/content repositories that mirror each other: One is in CCC/Harvest and the other is in the Web hosting environment. The golden code (main code line) is always resident in CCC/Harvest.

Configuration items

For all assets that make up eBIS projects, the following configuration items (CIs) are managed by the CM system:

1. HTML;

2. CGI scripts (Perl);

3. C code (source, headers, makefiles);

4. Data files (text, dat);

5. Graphics (gif, jpeg, mpeg, vrml);

6. Multimedia (QuickTime movies, Shockwave, Real Audio);

7. JavaScript (both client and server);

8. Java applets;

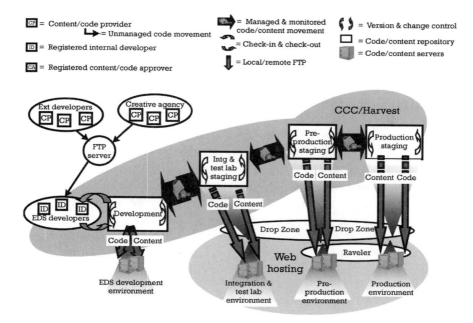

Figure 6.1   EDS eBIS code/content promotion implementation.

9.   Java application code (class, package, jar, both client and server);

10. Netscape Server code (NAS, LiveWire, servlets).

Configuration item life cycle

Each CI goes through five states:

1.   Development;

2.   Integration and test staging;

3.   Preproduction staging;

4.   Production staging;

5.   Closed.

The *development* state (area) represents the entry point for checking in and checking out code/content into the CCC/Harvest system. This area is primarily used by development team members during the development phase of the project. For assets destined for the Web hosting environment, this state is essentially bypassed.

The *integration and test* state represents the staging area for all code/content that will run in the integration and test lab area of the Web hosting environment. Integration and test lab builds are performed and distributed out of this state.

The *preproduction* state is the staging area for code/content that will run in the preproduction area of the Web hosting environment. Preproduction builds are performed and distributed out of this state.

The *production* state is the staging area for code/content that will run in the production area of the Web hosting environment. Production builds are performed and distributed out of this state.

The *closed* state represents the area for storing packages once they are tested and signed off in production. This makes it easier for project leads to identify packages in production, that is, on the live Web site.

Managing changes to client Web sites

A change request (CR) goes to a change control board (CCB). The CCB is the group that is authorized to approve changes to formally controlled assets for eBIS projects. This group has the following responsibilities and authority:

> ▸ Represents the interests of the project manager and all groups who may be affected by changes to the baselines or to individual configuration items.

> ▸ Authorizes changes to the baselines and to individual configuration items.

> ▸ Authorizes the creation and promotion of release from the baseline library.

There are two CCBs for all client projects that will approve promotions at various stages in the development and maintenance process:

1. The CCB that authorizes the promotion of CIs to preproduction from integration and test include the testing coordinator, the operations manager, the project manager, and the customer.

2. The CCB for promoting CIs to production from preproduction include personnel from Web hosting, the operations manager, the project manager, and the customer.

Adoption of the CM solution

The EDS team did a paper evaluation of the leading CM tools on the market. They ended up with four finalists, of which CCC/Harvest was one (which is what they ended up choosing). In their selection process, CCC/Harvest was partnered with Raveler and they were considered together. EDS had representatives come in and give live demonstrations to its evaluation team. Following that, the internal approval process included senior technical personnel in EDS. Their decision included experiences from existing EDS accounts that were using CCC/Harvest as well. Initially, EDS purchased five licenses and did a prototype implementation for 6 months. After the prototype, it reviewed the results and decided to deploy the tool to its team of 150 developers and Web site managers.

Its CM solution was made easier by certain design decisions for its code. For instance, it created standards for how code is designed and how common functionality (across Web sites) is implemented. There are standard functions by which information is accessed or ways that database searches are done. Code is designed for reuse so much that the Java code is reused across sites.

Evolution of its CM solution

EDS plans on extending its CM solution by selecting and deploying a pure Web content management tool that would allow the creative agencies and business customers to approve and promote graphic content (HTML, gif, jpeg) directly to production servers with limited intervention by Webmasters. That is, EDS is fine-tuning its CM solution to ensure "heavyweight CM" on code but "lightweight CM" on creative assets. EDS is also instituting more detailed change management support with finer grained change request classification.

Messages and lessons learned

Jim Johnston has these messages for other companies:

1. CM activities must be planned and staffed as an ongoing part of a Web development environment. They cannot be dumped on development teams as an afterthought. Unless there is a core team

of CM experts who manage the CM system (hardware/software), support developers, and inform management and SQA of CM activities, you are doomed to an endless Web crisis.

2. Define, communicate, and enforce directory and naming standards for your Web site. Next to the organizational issue above, this is the most important aspect of keeping your Web development environment from turning into a chaotic pool of unidentified files.

Case study: Lockheed Martin Aeronautical Systems[4]

Lockheed Martin Aeronautical Company–Marietta has many internal (intranet) Web sites. This case study focuses on the development and maintenance of the intranet Web site for the Environment, Tools, and Software Configuration Management team of the Software Engineering Process Department. The function of this team is to provide support for the development tools, environment, and to provide software CM to several different aircraft development programs.

The environment and CM goals

The intranet site is a small site (about 450 files) that is managed by a team of four developers. This site is accessible by developers and managers within Lockheed Martin in order to find the latest process or standard or daily set of operational metrics. The site provides a major means for intergroup communication. The Web content consists of HTML files, Java code (for metrics collection and reporting), and CGI scripts. Web content is developed and optimized for the Netscape environment, which is the standard Lockheed browsing environment.

The goal of its CM solution is to have all Web artifacts and their related developmental practices under control. To accomplish this goal, it chose PVCS Dimensions from Merant. The deployment of Dimensions as a CM solution at Lockheed Martin Aeronautical Company came about 8 years prior to being chosen to manage this particular effort. That is, since Dimensions was already a "project standard," and the Web developers

---

4. This case study was written with the assistance of Thomas Moore, Webmaster at Lockheed Martin.

had seen its benefits, it was a natural decision to use Dimensions on its Web site.

Lockheed Martin's CM solution not only gave it the capability to roll back to a previous baseline in case of a problem, but the complete history on all files enables it to quickly recall specific historical content without having to recover an entire baseline of the Web site from backup.

CM processes

Because the group is small, the workflow or processes are kept simple. A typical change–publish cycle consists of creating the change document, implementing it, and publishing the changes. A change document is created each week that reflects the list of all changes (bugs and enhancements) to be made. The Webmaster decides which changes will happen that week. Developers are assigned to do the changes, which must be completed by Friday afternoon. The Webmaster then updates the Web site after reviewing all the changes.

The developers all use Dimensions. A change request is filled in using Dimensions. Four key developers are notified immediately and automatically of a new request. Because they all sit in the same room, they decide among themselves how to proceed with that request.

All requests are assigned priorities:

1. Immediate;

2. Adverse effects without a workaround;

3. Adverse effects with a workaround;

4. Annoyance;

5. Informational or enhancement.

Given the nature of the intranet site, it is rare to have bugs that need immediate fixes. Developers make the changes on their own workstations or personal computers. The reviewer/Webmaster then tests the changes on his or her machine. Once the changes pass review and testing, scripts are run that publish the changes to the live site.

Evolution of its CM solution

Its CM solution is being adopted by other Web site development efforts in order to provide for traceability and control. Future evolution of its solution will allow the Web site to be connected directly to its Dimensions repository through the use of CGI scripting and reporting. This will allow real-time access to metrics about its processes, and eventually allow anyone with access to a browser to be able to generate or view a change request against the Web site. This coupling will provide them with a complete change control loop on its Web development efforts.

Messages and lessons learned

For Web teams, Thomas Moore would like to pass on these messages:

1. Use a CM tool. It can provide benefits you cannot even imagine along with saving you a lot of grief.

2. Automate and integrate the complete change cycle. That is, make sure all tools (such as the CM tool and help desk tool) are all integrated in a manner such that you do not need to traverse multiple repositories and tools.

3. The change life cycle is very important. Make sure that review steps are included for each change. It helps to have a "second set of eyes" look at a change. This does not have to take a considerable amount of extra time.

4. Make it easy to improve the change life cycle/processes.

Case study: Lycos[5]

Lycos is one of the leading search engine Web sites and has evolved into a portal offering access to many services such as Web directories, insurance, news, and stock quotes. Lycos uses the CM tool Perforce. Lycos is still evolving its CM solution as its business evolves. Dozens of developers and content authors at multiple locations maintain its sites.

Perforce is the CM tool used by all the developers and Web authors. Each checks out and checks in files to the CM repository (Perforce).

The main emphases for Lycos in its CM solution are accuracy in content as well as high quality in the sense of usability of its Web site. Lycos partners with other companies around the world to provide its

---

5. This case study was written with the assistance of Adam Bellusci and David Markley, software engineers in the Tools Group at Lycos.

international Web sites. Web development is done on Windows and Unix platforms.

In the United States, Lycos maintains multiple data centers. These centers exist to provide fault tolerance of its Web site as well as options for load-balancing during peak performance times. These data centers, which all contain dozens of servers, require stringent replication and synchronization practices; in particular, the centers must be updated simultaneously, the reason being that two different users of Lycos must see the same dynamic page (content) at the same point in time, regardless of which data center is being accessed. Also, a single user may switch servers during his or her on-line session and must be presented with the same set of pages. Otherwise, the user could be presented with links to other pages that may only exist on certain servers. Hence, each data center is carefully updated with the latest release tree and they go live at exactly the same time.

With multiple data centers, updating has to take into account the time lag in updating multiple centers. The data centers are switched over to the updated release tree at exactly the same moment. All servers must have the same release tree before being switched live. One of the challenges is knowing how long the updating will take. Some updates might involve one file; others, 1,000 files.

Lycos provides different ways of publishing updated content to its site. Either a Web developer publishes it directly, or all changes are integrated into an "in-box" branch in Perforce. The change made by this integration is then published to an in-box server for QA review and regression testing and then published automatically to live service by a timed script (daemon). All developers and Web authors use Perforce for version control and configuration items.

Eventually all changes will be controlled with automated change management and release management facilities.

Changes happen via a defect notification, either done by word-of-mouth or via a defect tracking system. Most changes are categorized as exceptions or nonexceptions. Exceptions are typically any defect found in live service. These are corrected immediately in the most expedient manner. Anything else that is not an exception is passed through the normal development process of defect tracking.

Show-stopper bugs (called exceptions), such as a page that does not load correctly or a name that is spelled incorrectly, are acted on immediately. The Operations Department notifies the area manager who assigns the task to a developer or Web author. The code is checked out from the editorial branch (where all changes happen). The fix is made and then it is integrated with all the other changes to the in-box branch.

Changes made to the in-box branch are picked up by any server set up to publish that branch. These servers are the integration staging areas where the QA department can do their testing before publishing. QA testing involves performance, traffic stress tests, and usability testing, along with regression testing. QA is notified automatically by an e-mail whenever a change is added to the in-box.

Configurations, or releases, are defined around the Web site templates. That is, the templates have version numbers so if a site fails, Lycos rolls back to a particular version of the template and can regenerate the content that got published into the templates.

There are only "lightweight" sign-offs and/or management reviews because the CM tool tracks who has made what changes and there is limited time for them in any case. New releases, such as site redesigns, are done in the traditional way by separate development teams.

The content being published using the CM tool consists mostly of the textual content for the site. The content is divided into areas and a team is assigned to each area. Code sharing occurs between the areas. Because all developers and Web authors use Perforce, this is very straightforward.

Lycos sees no need to configuration manage its dynamic content or roll back such, because it can be regenerated for the most part. Also, continuously streaming data is not placed under CM control because it is transitory.

Lycos is very happy with its CM solution and sees ways of improving it by automating more CM activities. Lycos chose Perforce over other CM tools because it:

- Is a lightweight CM tool;

- Had all the features Lycos needed;

- Is easy to use;

- Offers minimal changes in development style;

- Could train Web authors (nonsoftware people) to use it;

- Did not need to hire extra people to administer the CM tool;

‣ Can migrate CM repository from other lightweight CM tools (CVS, PVCS, VSS) into Perforce;

‣ Does not force a certain process or paradigm onto the teams.

A CM solution was originally sought because of the pain: Developers were using FTP to transfer files between machines and servers so, for instance, the last person to submit a page "won." All previous changes to a page were lost. Determining what pages had or had not changed in the tree of files was very time-consuming. Its CM tool addresses these problems because it requires that multiple people making changes to the same page resolve any conflicts. It allows anyone to take a look at the history for a page and determine what changes have been made over time. The CM solution makes it trivial to publish only those files that have been changed. This also makes it easy to see what changes have been made to live service during a given period of time.

Lycos also found that the speed of change was creating insane development patterns and mixups in the FTP files. Getting control over these activities, as well as being able to very easily roll back any Web site in case of a crash or bugs, provided complete payback on its CM solution for Lycos. It believes that its automated CM solution has saved it millions in development and maintenance costs.

Messages and lessons learned

The key messages from Adam Bellusci, David Markley, and their team are as follows:

‣ CM is extremely valuable for Web content management.

‣ Treat Web content just like software so traditional CM tools work very well.

‣ It is not necessary to purchase a large-scale Web content management tool. Traditional CM tools work very well.

‣ Use branching in your CM tool to control the flow of code and content.

Case study: NASD[6]

The National Association of Securities Dealers (NASD) is the largest securities industry self-regulatory organization in the United States. Through its subsidiaries, NASD Regulation, Inc. and the NASDAQ Stock Market, Inc., NASD develops rules and regulations, conducts regulatory reviews of members' business activities, disciplines violators, and designs, operates, and regulates securities markets and services. NASD's development environment supports 6,000 brokerage firms and more than half a million stock brokers.

NASD chose Merant's PVCS Professional, which is a suite of CM tools including Tracker for change management, Version Manager for version and configuration control, and Configuration Builder for build management. Its CM solution is used by more than 2,000 developers and business analysts managing about 500 business-critical applications, including hardware, software, and Web content. This includes the NASDAQ Stock Market, its regulation facilities, and its corporate operational support systems. NASD has implemented a "best practices" CM solution that suits its mission-critical goals.

NASD's goals for its CM solution

For its software systems, NASD has implemented a CM solution that supports its philosophy of "no mistakes." This means that very tight controls are in place to analyze the impact of any change, to review any change that is released or published to the Web site, and to ensure that anyone responsible for releasing or publishing a change (such as a software engineer or administrator) fully understands what they are doing. NASD cannot afford to make mistakes. Its CM solution is very process oriented and provides many checks and reviews throughout. Such a solution easily enables it to meet its CMMI level 2 certification needs and ISO 9001 standardization goals.

CM infrastructure

Anyone creating or changing any software, including Web content authors, uses the CM tools. NASD has a formal CM organization consisting of 34 CM experts who are involved in all projects at corporate headquarters, NASDAQ Stock Market, and its regulatory facilities. These CM

---

6. This study was written with the assistance of Pamela Adams, assistant director of configuration management at NASD.

administrators provide oversight of all CM activities, ensure the integrity of the development and maintenance environments, and are responsible for the implementation of the CM processes and the documentation of CM plans. A CM coordinator has a direct role on every project team and does the day-to-day CM activities.

The development and maintenance of its software is distributed. For instance, the data center is in North Carolina, the disaster recovery center is in Texas, baselines are managed in Maryland, and the stock market is run from Connecticut. It is quite a feat of coordination to manage all of this. Its CM solution makes it possible.

CM processes

NASD defined a corporate CM process. Each project team follows a CM process, which is a tailoring or customization of that corporate process. The CM process is owned by the assistant CM director. It is updated by the official Process Improvement Team that meets every quarter to assess how well CM is being implemented, to examine where improvements can be made, and to review new technology.

All software, hardware, and Web content artifacts are recorded in the CM repository (PVCS Version Manager). The change cycles are implemented in PVCS Tracker and described in the next section. A high-level view of the corporate product life cycle is shown in Figure 6.2. During the initiation phases, the project charter is written and funding assigned. In the solicitation phase, all tools, hardware, and outsourcing needs are resolved. During the analysis phase, the requirements are developed. The product is designed during the design phase and developed during the provisioning phase. It is tested in the acceptance phases and released or published in the deployment phase. After that, it goes into the maintenance phases and eventually goes through auditing reviews in the audit phase.

NASD limits its parallel development paths (number of variants) due to the complexity of merging files. Everything has to be thoroughly checked because there is no room for error, so doing file conflict resolution and merging is a tedious task that they prefer to avoid. NASD limits the number of parallel paths to four, maximum.

Change management

For each project, a maintenance charter is written. This charter defines the number of releases (upgrades) and update cycles for the product. The typical choice at NASD is four releases per year. Bug fixes and

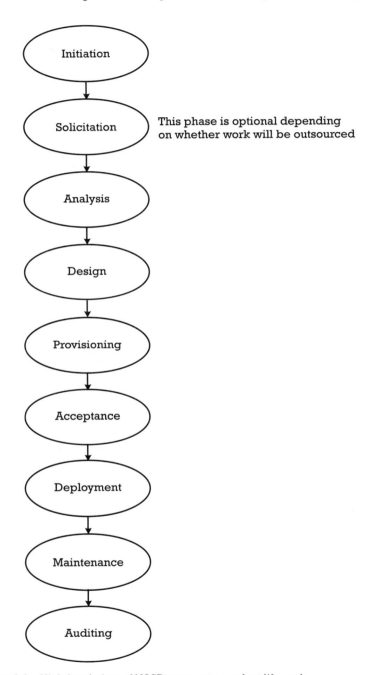

Figure 6.2   High-level view of NASD corporate product life cycle.

enhancements are batched into a quarterly release, although emergency fixes are done immediately.

Because of its strict goals as described earlier, NASD uses a hierarchy of CCBs to authorize changes, as shown in Figure 6.3. Five levels of CCBs have been set up. On average, one or more of the CCBs handles 70 change requests per day. A request for a change can be submitted by any-one via PVCS Tracker, and depending on the nature of a change, it will be submitted to the appropriate CCB and the right people notified of the arrival of a new CR.

A request whose impact is solely within the domain of a project (such as changing a name) goes only to the project level CCB for authorization. A request that affects the entire program (such as adding new functional-ity) goes to the program level CCB for approval. A request that affects the environment or infrastructure (such as porting an application to a new platform or promoting a baseline from development to QC, or QC to pro-duction) requires enterprise level CCB approval. A request that will sig-nificantly affect schedules, budgets, and scope, and have a broad impact on existing code or content, requires sponsor approval. Changes that have been deferred and need to be escalated are approved by the

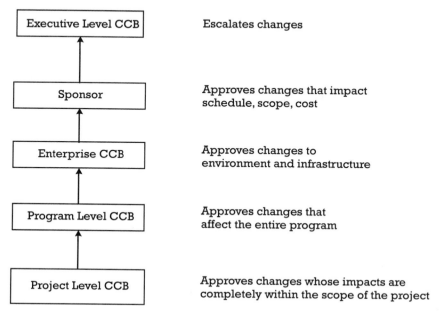

Figure 6.3   Code/content promotion flow.

enterprise level CCB. At any time, any CCB can reassign priorities and severities of requests.

NASD classifies changes into three types:

1. *Turnover changes:* a milestone request that moves a change from development into test, or from test into production;

2. *Change request:* enhancements, new functionality, customer specials;

3. *Problem reports:* bug fixes.

For each type of change, a priority level and severity level are assigned. Three levels of priority (high, medium, and low) and three levels of severity (critical, major, and minor) are possible. Based on these values and doing change impact analysis, the CCB schedules the order of changes.

The CCBs perform their activities by e-mail or by conference calls when necessary. Turnaround times for change approvals vary depending on the type of change. For instance, a high-priority, critical severity Web site problem report can get approval in 10 minutes, whereas Web changes affecting databases may take 3 days because of the heavy-duty change impact analysis that needs to be carried out. The high-priority, critical problem will be "fast tracked" for fixing. Such problems (like hardware malfunction) can generate automatic notifications to the right people via e-mail, along with automatic paging of the people as backup to ensure faster response.

Web content support

The CM support for Web content is an extension of the CM solution for legacy code. Web development is divided into three categories:

1. Static content such as HTML and ASP files;

2. Web databases;

3. Web application code.

For static content, changes go through the following cycle: The change request is submitted; it is approved by the appropriate CCB; edits are made; changes are checked; and then changes are published.

For Web databases, because a physical version of the database is active when it is in production, the change approval cycle takes longer, typically 3 days. This is because of the heavy-duty change impact analysis that needs to be carried out. Database changes need to be made atomic; that is, they must be independent, isolated, complete changes, so the impact analysis must ensure that other, dependent changes are precluded at the same time for this change.

For the Web application code, the approval cycle is typically 7 days for similar reasons as for the databases. NASD is extremely cautious about making changes. It wants to ensure that no change will have a negative impact on their production systems. There is little room for mistakes.

Regarding dynamic content, all the code needed to generate a dynamic page is baselined in the CM repository of PVCS Version Manager. Combined with multiple daily backups, NASD knows that in the event of any kind of server or hardware crash, it can recover instantly either by rolling back to the last day's backup or by regenerating (rebuilding) content based on the information in the CM repository. NASD feels it has some of the best disaster recovery mechanisms in the world and knows that it can recover from a crash within 20 minutes.

Publishing to the live Web site is only done by the systems administrator who understands exactly the nature of the change. Certain groups have permission to publish directly to a live site. For instance, Corporate Communications publishes directly and they only change static content, such as with press releases. Each staging area for changes resides on separate machines, such as the development server, the test server, and the production server.

Problems it was having and benefits that CM brought it
NASD turned to a CM solution to eliminate the chaos and problems it faced without CM. It also wanted to achieve its "no mistakes" goal. NASD wanted to automate manual systems. For instance, it replaced its manual change management system with PVCS Tracker, which resulted in more orderly development and smoother decision-making about changes and releases. NASD now has a single repository of change requests, whereas before requests were scattered all over platforms with some being written on paper and some housed in Access databases. This restricted visibility by not having a global view of the development work. For instance, there was no way of knowing which change requests were being progressed in parallel across the release life cycle and who was working on what code.

NASD's CM solution has increased the quality level of its applications and provides its managers with visibility over all development efforts. The automated reporting capabilities (of the metadata) enable managers to establish measurable quality and schedule objectives and to monitor the progress of the teams. Communication within and between teams has been a big benefit. For instance, automatic notifications are generated for the owner, submitter, and assignee when change requests arrive. The development team always knows the state of all changes, which boosts collaborative development. All changes are now completely documented and authorizations to make changes are no longer subject to guesswork but are now buoyed by thorough impact analysis.

Before its automated CM solution, NASD did not know what versions of code went into builds. Now it knows the contents of all its baselines and can audit them. It can now inform its internal and external customers what code is under development or being tested or already in production.

NASD's CM solution has allowed it to establish common repositories for code. Everyone on the development team is now able to use standard items, which are maintained in one place. CM has been used for disaster recovery at NASD such as when a disk drive went down in production. When this happened, NASD pulled out the latest and the greatest from its CM repository and rebuilt the environment in no time. As a result, it was back in operation in less than an hour.

Further CM evolution

Apart from automating builds and streamlining process controls, NASD is integrating its CM solution with many tools, such as the Mercury suite of tools, Test Director, Load Runner, Win Runner, and with Vantive software and QSS Doors. Its CM solution is also playing a major role in achieving CMMI level 2.

Adoption of the CM solution

NASD staff were careful in developing their requirements for the CM solution. CM functionality issues, user friendliness, performance, ease of tool integration, and cost were major factors in the decision-making. NASD chose PVCS because it met its cost, ease of integration, performance, process, and ease of use criteria. Other tools met some of the criteria, but not all of the criteria.

NASD followed the evolutionary path for its CM solution. As its needs evolved, so did its CM solution. It incrementally added change management, then version and configuration management, and build management to its solution. NASD adopted its CM solution by conducting an evaluation of leading CM tools in the marketplace. Then it took its requirements and mapped them against the functionality of various tools. The final tool selection became obvious. And its tool choice involved all the good steps of technology adoption, such as defining the processes that it wanted to automate. I discuss the four key steps NASD went through in deploying the change management tool (Tracker).

Step 1: Identified the current process for change control

It looked at what NASD was currently doing and not doing, and documented that current process. This was done by interviewing all the people involved: management, project leads, and developers. The key things NASD focused on were how changes were approved, by whom, at what level, and in what time frame. It found out who currently approves changes within each group and who is responsible, and how changes are escalated if they are not addressed immediately. It also examined details concerning the levels of change required, for instance, how cost, work effort, and scheduling issues were resolved. NASD examined whether all changes followed the same approval path and which changes were allowed to be fast-tracked (expedited) for approval, and whether all changes required approval from one or more levels. The next step was to consider what it would like the change process to be.

Step 2: Documented the desired change control solution

In this step, having understood what was currently being done, NASD had a good idea as to what steps were missing or needed improvement. A process action team conducted a roundtable discussion to define their ideal situation. They went through several iterations before they all came to agreement on the best solution given all the requirements. As part of reaching this solution, they addressed some key questions: Do we want an automated system? Do we want an integrated system? Do we want automatic notifications? Who needs to minimally approve changes? What are the desired approval time frames?

With the final process description, they approached senior management for approval and endorsement on the new process. A pilot team was set up to test the new process to make sure it was practical and successful. Once this was done, they felt comfortable selecting a tool.

Step 3: Selected a tool to meet their process

NASD's new process represented the requirements for the new tool. That made it easy for NASD to validate the tool since it completely understood its process. Around the tool, NASD defined the supporting manual procedures (such as file staging and documenting requirements in their version description documents). The change request forms of the tool were customized with fields to capture all the information required for their process. Once this was done, NASD felt comfortable doing a pilot project to thoroughly test the change tracking solution in production mode.

Step 4: Deployed the solution

The tool and related procedures were rolled out to a pilot project group who understood that they were the "guinea pigs" for a new solution. From this pilot project, NASD was able to fine-tune their process and its implementation. It ran the refined solution through another pilot team and achieved all its goals. Then it was time to deploy the solution throughout the enterprise. It developed specialized training courses for the tool and for its processes. All the good momentum and success gained from the two pilots made the deployment to the rest of the company straightforward.

Messages and lessons learned

Pamela Adams's advice to companies is:

1. Make sure you have in place a thorough change approval process that suits your development and maintenance goals.

2. Carefully examine the risk and implications involved for each change. In particular, look at the business implications (such as litigation or revenue loss or corporate liability) in case that change fails. This risk factor needs to be taken into account when authorizing and scheduling changes.

3. When choosing a CM tool, make sure you have a CM process and find a tool that suits that process.

4. Training is vital. Web content authors should be given CM training. Everyone should be given process training so that they understand why they do the things they do.

Case study: OneSource Information Services Inc.[7]

OneSource Information Services Inc., Concord, Massachusetts, is a bricks-and-clicks company that provides corporate market intelligence to corporations. Such intelligence includes company profiles, trade articles, executive profiles, and financial data. Its customers buy a business browser with particular geographical coverage and add advanced functionality as required. OneSource initially provided the information via CD-ROMs and now provides it via the Web, and more than 90% of its income is derived from this Web service. OneSource uses the StarTeam CM tool from StarBase Corp. All 50 developers, content authors, on-line technicians, and quality assurance staff use StarTeam.

Problems solved and benefits gained

OneSource had many goals for its CM solution. The development teams needed to track all changes so that they had a complete change history, which helps them with fixing bugs. Also, OneSource wanted to ensure that all code and content were in one place and that, at any point in time, an entire Web system could be recompiled based on that central repository. The goal was to preserve the integrity of its code—that is, to know exactly what pieces of Web code and content it had, and when and how each piece changes. Another key goal was to support parallel development so that the many small teams could share files and make changes at the same time while generating different (variant) Web systems.

OneSource also wanted to safely update its Web sites once any bugs were found or enhancements required. It needed to roll back to previous versions of Web system. Also, it wanted to control its build process so that it knew exactly want went into each build, along with prohibiting any "rogue" files from accidentally getting into a build. And it also needed to keep track of all changes made on the releases/Web systems.

OneSource found that its workflow processes tended to change often, such as twice a week, and it wanted a tool that supports that. Also, One-Source creates major releases for its Web systems every 4 to 6 weeks. It found a CM solution in StarTeam that met its needs.

---

7. This case study was written with the assistance of Todd Mancini, director of software development for OneSource.

Infrastructure

OneSource supports multiple Web systems concurrently. Each Web site is a separate product dedicated to a specific market niche. Much of the code and content is shared among the sites.

OneSource coordinates its two separate development teams, the Core Platform Group and the Web Applications Group, using StarTeam. The Core Platform Group is responsible for component development and for creating VisualC++ and Active X server components and dynamic link libraries for the connections to its numerous back-end databases that drive the subscription-based services. The Web Applications Group is responsible for creating the look and feel of the products. It creates ASPs (active server pages), HTML, and client-side JavaScript.

Together the groups manage a family of products resulting in multiple Web systems. For instance, they have business browser product versions for the United States, Europe, the United Kingdom, and other countries. With their CM solution, the development teams are able to communicate easily, work on shared and related files in a safe manner without overwriting each other's work, coordinate preproduction activities, and track all changes.

All the Web content/code is dynamic. That is, there is essentially no static content. All Web pages are created dynamically. Hence, all changes to code/content go through the same change cycles.

Workflow and change management

OneSource automates its release process with StarTeam by using separate staging areas:

- Development server for coding;

- Compile server for build and page testing;

- Functional test server for formal functionality and regression testing;

- Performance test server for performance capacity testing;

- Production server for live Web system.

For instance, a developer will make a fix or an enhancement on the development server. Once that is completed, the files that make up the new baseline with the fix/enhancement are transferred to the compile server. The compile server matches exactly the live production server (the live Web site). On the compile server, the developer tests the builds or dynamic compilations as they would take place on the live Web system. Once that is achieved successfully, the baseline is transferred to the test server where the testers go about doing formal testing. Once testing is passed, the changes are published to the live production server where the technicians do the publishing. This complete workflow, along with all files/baselines, is under the control of the CM system.

A change is begun via a change request generated in a Lotus Notes-based system. The QA group verifies the request and then it is sent to the appropriate development manager for analysis. He or she then assigns appropriate developers to fix it or code it. That developer takes the change through the above cycle. On completion, the developer indicates in Lotus Notes that the change has been done and once QA has completed testing, they close the change request.

A CM administrator oversees the entire CM solution, and each development team has its own administrator to ensure the integrity of the development and maintenance cycles.

Deployment

In searching for the right CM tool over a period of 6 months, OneSource had various candidates. After doing a 2-week pilot project with StarTeam on its own data, it was convinced that StarTeam was the appropriate tool. The intuitive interface along with the very easy setup had major influences on this decision. Tool roll-out was straightforward because the developers were ready for it. They knew they needed some unifying tool to help manage all the development and changes.

Messages and lessons learned

Here are Todd Mancini's words of wisdom:

1. Get a good CM tool.

2. Take Web development very seriously by applying all the good software engineering practices to it.

3. Do not be seduced by the ease of Web page creation done without CM controls. Simply churning out Web pages devoid of a solid Web architecture and engineering practices creates serious maintenance problems because it becomes impossible to make changes then to thousands of Web pages in a short time.

4. Web testing requires more effort than traditional software testing. More mature testing tools are needed.

Case study: USinternetworking[8]

USinternetworking Inc., Annapolis, Maryland, is an application service provider (ASP). That is, it hosts, builds, supports, monitors, and manages companies' e-commerce and e-business systems. The goal with its customers is to make the development and maintenance of their complex applications as invisible and as simple as possible for them. Customers do not have to worry about the operational details of their e-commerce or e-business systems. USinternetworking assumes the responsibility guaranteed by service level agreements for each client. It also handles total end-to-end upgrades to hardware and software. The customers focus only on changes to the content because they are ensured by USinternetworking of a certain percentage of uptime for their solution along with a response time to change requests.

USinternetworking operates four data centers in its global networks to manage applications for its customers. A monthly fee is charged to each customer for all of USinternetworking's products and services, which includes the 24-hour uptime monitoring. The products offered include PeopleSoft, Siebel Systems, Lawson, Ariba, BroadVision, and Microsoft.

Problems solved and benefits offered by its CM solution

More than 80 concurrent implementations are being run and maintained by USinternetworking for its customers. Each implementation has its unique combination of operating systems, hardware, and applications running. USinternetworking can implement a PeopleSoft or BroadVision solution in 90 days and a Microsoft Site Server solution in 45 days. It is through the use of a configuration management tool that such schedules are possible. USinternetworking uses WebSynergy from Continuus Software Corp.

All the Web challenges that I have discussed in this book are all the challenges that USinternetworking has encountered. And they are compounded for USinternetworking because it has to maintain many Web

---

8. This study was written with the assistance of Kerry Bailey, vice president of production control for USinternetworking.

systems (more than 150) and because it must also include the customer as part of its development and maintenance processes (that is, customers must be able to update content even though the solution is controlled and maintained by USinternetworking). The e-commerce and e-business systems for the customers are also constantly growing. For instance, during the Christmas rush, the volume of transactions for all the Web systems at least doubles. USinternetworking also has to support each customer's growth rate.

USinternetworking finds that every customer's Web system averages one to four changes every day, with at least 15 minor changes and four major changes each week. As an ASP, USinternetworking has liability issues if it fails to meet the uptime and change cycle requirements specified in the customer contract. Also, it needs to meet all the contracted customer satisfaction requirements. To ensure these, and to protect itself from contract failure, USinternetworking needs automated CM.

The founders of USinternetworking were experienced IT executives, and in their corporate planning, they projected a very fast pace of growth for their company. From its start-up in 1998, it has grown very quickly to more than 1,200 people managing more than 150 customer systems in 2 years. It was very clear to USinternetworking that there was no way it could maintain multiple complex solutions (including the complete network infrastructure, applications, content, databases) without CM automation. Hence, it deployed an automated CM solution up front.

USinternetworking chose Continuus because it felt the vendor could accommodate its pace of work and that Continuus was well suited to its Web needs, especially with its WebSynergy offering. Continuus was deployed throughout the organization to control the preproduction work.

USinternetworking's two major goals were safety and complete change tracking. That is, it wanted everything to be controlled in the CM repository before it went live. Nothing gets deployed or published to a customer's Web system without first being placed under CM control and going through the proper release cycles (such as testing, reviews, authorizations). Also, it wanted everything involved in the change cycle from impact analysis, to the change control board, through the reviews and authorizations, to all be automated, ensuring a quick turnaround of changes, along with having everything tracked and an audit trail kept.

Its CM solution continues to evolve to support the dynamic updating of Web content. For instance, USinternetworking wants customers to have more direct control over daily content updates rather than going through the USinternetworking change process. This means then the customer needs access to the CM solution and needs to be a participant in it so that the necessary change tracking and baseline control can still be established.

Also, USinternetworking has to support whatever volume and frequency of changes that its customers desire, and do that within the budget set by the monthly fees of that customer. Given that USinternetworking decides up front during contract negotiations what the monthly fee will be, USinternetworking needs to keep track of all the efforts involved in making a change along with generating appropriate reports and metrics to help it make better decisions about fees. As a company, it cannot afford to lose money on making changes. It has to be very confident that what it charges a customer on a monthly basis for the lifetime of that contract will cover the costs of making all changes. USinternetworking cannot afford to guess. It needs to have the right metrics. Again, its automated CM solution will generate and track all the data they need.

Change management

Managing changes from all customers and internally within USinternetworking across all Web systems is a major feat, a feat that is made possible via its CM tool. USinternetworking originally used an e-mail system to achieve all the change tracking, but found e-mail systems lacking in many CM features such as workflow support and audit logging.

To generate a change request, a customer or internal engineer or business unit will, through their Web browser, fill in the on-line form. They are unaware that they are using a CM tool to do this but still get all the benefits of using CM.

Changes can come from various avenues:

1. Client-content changes, for example, static content, HTML scripts, or functionality enhancements;

2. Client-platform changes, for example, server changes or .jsp file changes;

3. Internal infrastructure changes, for example, network hardware changes or database changes.

There are two classes of automated changes:

1. *Type 1 changes (HTML files):* The CM system tracks all the details and approval to do the change is automatic. This change will not affect navigation or back-end applications.

2. *Type 2 changes (.jsp files):* A more rigid change control cycle is put in place with change control board approvals and change reviews. This change can affect navigation and back-end applications and resources.

Each type of change has its own change cycles or workflows and the changes are very similar in that impact analysis, change control board review, testing, and so on, are done. They differ in the level of approval required and the amount of peer review carried out.

A change request is received via the CM system in the Client Care Group, which is the first point of contact between USinternetworking and its customers. An account manager reviews the request. Any clarification work is done along with a change impact analysis. The request goes through change approval, the fix gets made, and it is then promoted through various staging areas, such as testing.

Priorities are assigned to changes, such as "urgent" or "emergency." Urgent changes have a fixed change window (the time in which the change happens) such as 1 hour or 1 day. Emergency fixes are the highest severity and all personnel required to fix the problem are assigned immediately.

When the change is completed, the customer reviews the change and closes the change request; all of this is done via the browser.

By allowing customers to participate directly in the change process, the customer effectively becomes part of the change team and release cycle. USinternetworking has found that anyone who is allowed to generate a change request needs to be trained to do this because untrained people may pick an inappropriate type or priority. The customer has to be made CM aware in order for automated CM to work well. You have to feed the right information into the automated system to make sure it works properly. This issue applies to all the partners of USinternetworking as well.

Company organizational layout

USinternetworking has set up key groups to ensure fast and efficient response to customers. Under the executive vice president of operations and client service are these groups:

- Engineering Group for developing new products;

- Client Care Group for supporting the customers;

- Operations Group for maintaining the computing infrastructure;

- Security Group;

- Production Control Group for building and maintaining the customer systems.

USinternetworking's Production Control Center is responsible for managing customer implementations and application testing, and making sure the customer's infrastructure is prepared to link with USinternetworking's service. Production Control has a Systems Assurance Group in which the testing, CM, and performance monitoring are done. The Service Integration Group builds the customer's solution. The Delivery Management Team is responsible for ensuring that all the production and maintenance steps have been carried out and that service readiness—all changes have been through the proper testing, documentation, and so on—has occurred.

Messages and lessons learned
USinternetworking has a tremendous wealth of experience in the Web arena because it is facing all the challenges of Web development and maintenance, but for USinternetworking these challenges are magnified and multiplied because it manages complex applications over the Web for its customers. Some of the lessons that Kerry Bailey wishes to pass on include these:

1. There is very little chance of an ASP staying in business if it does not have CM tools and practices in place.

2. The CM solution must be pervasive; that is, everyone involved in the development and maintenance cycle—from developers to the customer—is part of the CM solution and needs to have their work under CM control.

3. Separate the production from the preproduction activities to ensure the right steps are followed, such as making sure thorough testing was done.

4. Customers are an integral part of the change cycle and must be made aware of the importance of CM as well as how to properly classify and document change requests. Training and education of the customer (as well as internal staff) are often required to ensure the integrity of the change tracking system.

5. Every change request has an effect on the business. It is very important to understand exactly what that effect will be because it could be very costly.

6. Every business decision has an effect on maintenance practices and, similarly, changes in maintenance practices affect business decisions.

APPENDIX A

Contents

This Appendix contains various templates and example documents that will be useful for your company's tool selection and deployment activities. Table A.1 highlights the contents of each section. For a company that is in the process of selecting and deploying a CM solution, or recovering from a failed CM solution, or looking to improve their current CM solution, this Appendix contains invaluable guides and templates to walk you through that process.

Table A.1
Contents of This Appendix

Section	Explanation
A.1 CM questionnaire	List of questions to capture CM status
A.2 CM requirements	Categories of CM requirements
A.3 Categories of risks	List of typical risks found in companies
A.4 Process description	How to describe a CM process
A.5 Levels of process	Different views of processes
A.6 Process model example	How to describe a CM process
A.7 CM status report	Template for CM status

Table A.1 (continued)

Section	Explanation
A.8 Risk management plan	Template for risk management planning
A.9 Pilot project plan	Template for contents of pilot plan

Remember that when you create any documents from these templates, they too must go under configuration management. Hence, each should be given a version number along with a change log to identify the why, who, what, and when of any changes to it.

A.1   Configuration management questionnaire

The following questions and issues can be used as a guide during interviews with management and software engineers to aid you in understanding your company's current CM practices and processes. I use this list of questions and issues with everyone I interview to find out about the way they do CM. I tailor it to suit the audience, of course.

1   Introduction

    1.1   How do you see your role in the organization?

    1.2   How do you see the role of your organization's configuration management (CM) solution?

    1.3   What is your definition of CM?

    1.4   What is the scope of CM throughout your organization?

    1.5   How did CM come about; that is, how and why was it initially introduced into your group?

    1.6   Which groups and which people do you see as being the key players in your CM solution?

2   Current CM Process/Practice

    2.1   Describe the life cycle/stages that a product goes through—a new one versus a reused one versus a changed one:

- Design;
- Creation/manufacture;
- Test (unit, integration, system);
- QA;
- Release (alpha, beta, final);
- Maintenance.

2.2 How would you describe the current state of CM?

- Scope;
- Version control;
- Dependency tracking;
- Change control/problem tracking;
- Status reporting;
- Build management;
- Process management;
- Workspace management;
- Parallel development/concurrent development;
- Remote development;
- Repository management;
- Audit control;
- Produce release planning/scheduling;
- Baseline management.

2.3 How is Web development done?

- What are the classes of change requests?
- How and when are transfers between machines/servers done?
- Who can publish to live sites?
- How many sites?

- What works well?

- What does not work well?

- What improvements do you want to see?

- Why?

- Are "standard" procedures used and followed?

- What is the architecture of the Web system?

- What infrastructure has been set up to support it?

3   Risk Management

3.1 What do you see as the main obstacles/barriers to attaining a better CM solution?

3.2 People issues:

- Champions;

- Favorite tools;

- Resistance;

- Skill set;

- Education level;

- Interest level.

3.3 Management issues:

- Sponsorship;

- Commitment;

- Loyalty;

- Support factor;

- Knowledge/understanding;

- Budgeting;

- Infrastructure;

- Visibility into status of work.

3.4 Cultural issues:

- How does change progress in your culture?
- Who are the key players?

3.5 Political issues:

- Who is for the change or the improvement and why?
- Who is likely to be resistant and why?
- What is the best way to keep people happy?
- What is dangerous or unacceptable?

3.6 Technical issues:

- Platforms;
- Software architecture;
- Tool integration;
- Kinds of objects;
- Scalability;
- Performance;
- Reuse of configuration items.

3.7 Environmental issues:

- Heterogeneous platforms;
- International development.

3.8 Process issues:

- How;
- What;
- Why;
- Who.

3.9 Certification issues:

- Goals (SEI CMMI, ISO 9000, SPICE, BOOTSTRAP, industry audits);
- Drivers;
- Catalysts.

3.10 Customer (internal/external) issues:

- Frequency of change;
- Kinds of change requests;
- Change cycle time (window of change);
- Priority of changes.

3.11 Corporate issues:

- Cost;
- Culture;
- Commitment;
- Schedules;
- Motivation/driver for change;
- Perception of the importance of CM;
- Focus or mission of company (software, hardware);
- Enterprise-wide recognition of software's importance/complexity;
- Appreciation of software;
- Crucial role it plays in business planning;
- Metrics currently captured;
- Values important to management;
- Values important to developers;
- Reports;
- Decision-making factors (that is, who is in power?).

4 Process of Change

4.1 What expectations do people currently have about the prospect of change?

4.2 How can we assist them in achieving a unified perception?

4.3 What is the unified perception?

4.4 What are the current CM problems?

4.5 What is the vision?

4.6 What metrics are currently gathered?

4.7 What expectations have been set?

5 Web-Specific Questions

5.1 Tell me about the kind of business you are in:

- Types of products;
- How they are created;
- Who your clients are;
- How they use the products, for example, scenarios;
- Statistics about company and products, for example, number of products;
- Roles in the organization;
- Size of company;
- Number of developers and Web content people.

5.2 What infrastructure does your company have?

- Types of departments;
- How projects, especially Web ones, are organized;
- How QA and IT fit in;
- Mission statement and vision.

5.3 What Web applications/content are being developed?

- How was the Web system created (legacy, new)?

- What devices are used to access the Web content (browsers, micro-browsers, PDAs, smart phones, pagers, mainframes, SANs, and so on)?

- Are there multiple Web sites?

- Is there an intranet along with an extranet and the public Web site?

- Any merging of sites?

- Difference between content and application?

- Who is responsible for the publishing, for example, technicians?

- Who is responsible for the content, for example, business units?

- Who handles the platform engineering?

- How is the work breakdown structured?

- What skill sets exist?

- What tools and languages are being used?

- What type of Web system (informational, delivery system, customized access, user-provided information, interactive, transaction oriented, service provider, database access, document access, workflow oriented, robots, file sharing) is being used?

- Who owns the Web sites and why?

5.4 What are the main challenges for your company?

- Dynamic content management?

- Variant explosion?

- Changing role of IT department?

- Free-form development processes?

- Performance effect on Web system?

- Scaling content and hardware resources?

- Urgency, frequency, and volume of change?

- Outsourcing and its oversight?

- Politics of who owns what and when and why (responsibilities)?

- Immaturity of skills, tools, languages, processes?

- Site redesign?

- Sharing code across sites?

- Site rollback?

- Fault tolerance and load-sharing management?

5.5 How does your company/group do version control of static and dynamic content?

- Between groups?

- What are the configuration items?

- What objects are under control (data files, documents, images, streaming audio/video, component libraries, code, sources, binaries)?

- What metadata are managed (external and internal structure, hyperlinks, task objects, transactions, security rights, tool relationships, bill of materials, audit logs, generators, validation, and handler rules)?

- Is content separated from representation/templates?

- Who manages the templates?

- How many variants of Web system?

5.6 How does your company do release management?

- Who does the planning?

- What is the workflow?

- How much is automated?

- How is a release defined and identified?

5.7 How does your company do change management?

- What are the sources of change requests (that is, who initiates a CR)?
- What are the categories of change requests?
- How are they prioritized?
- What are the volume and frequency of change?
- Do you have regular change cycles?
- How is an emergency fix handled?
- What is the change cycle for each type of change?
- How is the change control board implemented?
- How are state changes and notifications communicated?
- What is the change escalation process?
- How are deferred changes addressed?
- Do you support change sets or folders and why?
- What types of mistakes can happen (inappropriate content, wrong timing, inaccurate content, top secret, corrupt, unauthorized, untested, stale, inconsistent, sleuthing opportunities) and why?

5.8 How is dynamic content managed?

5.9 How big a role does traffic monitoring play?

- How many user requests and how long to respond?
- What causes site redesign?
- Is dynamic caching done?
- How many hits a day?
- How many pages hit on average?
- Are third-party site ratings of importance to you?

5.10 Is your Web development very different from traditional software development?

5.11 What CM tool was chosen, how and why or why not?

5.12 Who handles the CM solution?

5.13 What benefits have you achieved and why?

5.14 What problems have been avoided or resolved?

5.15 What CM challenges exist, or what are the growth areas?

5.16 How has Web development affected the company?

- Are developers constantly on pagers (sophisticated information devices with remote access capabilities)?

- Instant mobilization; does all work stop to fix a problem?

- Overwhelming workload?

- Nightmarish solutions?

5.17 What lessons have been learned?

- Do you envisage a Web crisis for your systems?

- What skills should developers/content authors have?

- What practices should be put in place for Web teams?

- What guidelines?

- What tools or languages are "must have"?

- How often is a site redesigned or reimplemented?

- How do corporate goals affect the Web system?

- What is the key to managing complexity?

5.18 What kinds of components are under CM and why? What aren't?

5.19 What development and maintenance life cycles are employed?

5.20 What is a configuration item or a baseline or a release for Web content?

6   Conclusion

6.1 What suggestions do you have to make selection, deployment, and certification go well?

6.2 What success criteria should be established?

6.3 What metrics do you want to see collected and why?

6.4 What are the crucial goals of the CM solution?

6.5 What is the vision for a good CM solution?

The list of questions presented in this section can be added to by referring to Chapters 3 and 4.

Once the interviews are done, it is then time to document the results in a status report. A template is given for this in A.7.

A.2   Categories of configuration management requirements

Table A.2 highlights the main categories of CM requirements that a company needs to consider and include in your CM requirements list. A company can develop its requirements list in detail by looking at previous chapters in this book:

▸ Chapter 5 to find out how (the process) to capture a requirements list;

▸ Chapter 3 to see all the CM functional areas and operational elements;

▸ Chapter 4 to find out more about automated CM concepts.

A.3   Categories of risks

This section presents the categories of risks that companies can face when deploying a CM solution.

Risks can be collected into various categories mainly because they are often related to one another. The types I use typically are:

Table A.2
Main CM Requirements Categories

Category	Meaning
Functionality	CM operational aspects; refer to Table 3.3 in Chapter 3
Scalability	Scales to number of users, volume of data
Performance	Responds in the time required under certain loads
Usability	Easy to use, intuitive interfaces, GUI, command-line
Vendor	Solid business background, mature tool
Security	Data will be safe
Network	Runs over all types of networks in efficient manner
Hardware	Has clients for all platforms
Fault tolerance	Will not destroy data in case of crash
Support	Help available when needed
Administration	Maintenance of tool; backups of CM repository

1. Technical;

2. People-related;

3. Organizational;

4. Resource-related;

5. CM skills;

6. Political.

Technical risks concern the technicalities of software development and maintenance. For instance:

▸ How will we deal with the legacy code?

▸ How will we do distributed builds?

▸ What should we do about our multiple bug tracking tools?

▸ How can we improve network performance?

▸ What are our products' architectures?

▸ Can we break up the monolithic code structure?

▸ How can we share code across our Web sites? Across countries?

▸ Should the company use the same CM tool or use what it currently has and integrate them?

▸ If we customize our CM tool, how do we handle upgrades from the CM vendor?

▸ Do we have to switch everyone over to Windows NT before deploying the new CM tool?

People-related risks concern human issues. For instance:

▸ Management has a "silver bullet" attitude toward tools. How can we change that?

▸ Developers do not want automated processes because they fear them as bureaucratic overhead. What can we do?

▸ People have different views of CM. Why?

▸ Managers and developers talk different languages. How are they going to cooperate?

▸ Schedules are tight. Who can we find to be on the deployment team?

▸ Our culture is a bunch of "cowboys." How will we get them to accept change? How do they buy in to this change?

▸ We expect lots of resistance. How can we handle that?

▸ The content authors know nothing about software engineering and CM. What should we do?

▸ People understand version control but not full-process CM. How do we introduce this paradigm shift?

▸ How do we manage resistance to change?

Organizational risks relate to the infrastructure and intergroup cooperation. For instance:

▸ The company is constantly going through reorganizations. How do we fit in this CM improvement?

- Each group has been responsible for its own quality assurance testing. Should we develop a corporate view of QA?

- Which group should be responsible for providing the help desk for the new CM tool? IT or the CM group?

- Who should be allowed to directly publish to the live sites?

- Which group should be the pilot group?

- Should we do multiple pilot projects if we cannot decide between two tools?

- We have a poor track record in adopting new tools so the attitude is generally not positive when we announce a new effort. What can we do about that?

- How should the company be reorganized to aid in more effectively implementing CM?

- How will the responsibilities of the CM group change with the new tool? Will people be fired as a result?

Resource risks relate to the availability of things to carry out tasks. For instance:

- Where do we find time to roll out a new tool?

- Can we find the right change agents to lead the deployment effort?

- How do we get all the hardware we need?

CM skill risks relate to having the right knowledge. For instance:

- How do we select and deploy a CM tool?

- What actually is CM?

- How do we upgrade people's skill sets?

- How can we get the right requirements list?

- How do we prioritize the requirements?

- How do we train everyone?

Political risks relate to managing cultural conflicts. For instance:

> What types of resisters do we have?

> How do we get buy-in for a new tool?

> Can we get each group to agree to a corporate process?

> Who should own the Web content?

> Who owns the processes and who can change them and when?

> How do we elevate the importance of CM?

> How do we get real sponsorship and commitment?

> Why is CM considered a nuisance?

> Why does management not enforce certain policies?

> What metrics should we capture?

> What should we do regarding our subcontractors?

> Some managers believe we should be putting all our focus on better testing rather than CM. How do we counter this?

> Where do we find the office space to do the pilot projects?

> How do we introduce change into our type of culture?

> Will responsibilities and accountability change with the new solution?

> Should the reward system be employed?

A.4   Process description

The process description is a model, an abstraction of the flow of all CM activities, roles, and responsibilities. The key concepts used in the description are:

> *States* are the distinct phases in the life cycle.

> *Transitions* are the act of moving from one state to another.

> *Actions* are the deeds carried out during the state.

- *Trigger conditions* are events that must happen to enable a transition.

- *Roles* indicate who will perform a particular action.

- *Assumptions* are expected events or events taken for granted.

A portion of a process description is shown in Figure A.1. I use this modeling technique when helping groups define their CM processes.

A.5   Types of process or process levels

In a company, several levels of process exist (refer to Figure A.2): the corporate product life cycle, the complete CM process, group processes, personal processes, and life cycles of objects. When automating the CM process, all of these processes have to be taken into account.

I use the levels when speaking to people depending on their job responsibilities. For instance, the Vice President of Engineering and the Chief Technical Officer typically talk at the level of the product life cycle. The CM manager focuses on the complete CM process. Project managers focus on group processes. Developers focus on life cycles.

A.6   Example of a CM process model

This section represents an example of a process model document. I present this example to show what a model looks like and the kind of information that should be captured in a model description.

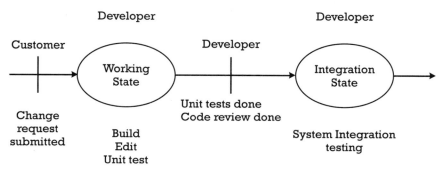

Figure A.1   Portion of a process description.

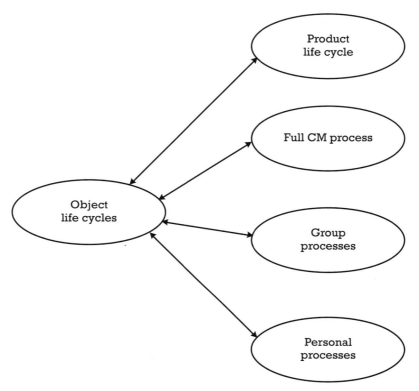

Figure A.2   The different levels of processes.

The process model in Figure A.3 captures the CM life cycle of source code objects. The objects are safety critical source code objects that will be put under configuration management at Company X. These objects include C++ files, Visual Basic files, hardware description language files, class files, and project files, which are considered safety critical. The model presents the entire life cycle for such objects from the time they are created through to the time they are merged into a baseline to the time the baseline is released into the field and subsequently changed due to bug fixes or enhancements.

Objects have to go through certain processing and baselines have to go through certain phases.

A safety critical source object follows exactly the same process as for a source object plus some additional steps:

1. Before a safety critical (SC) object can be created, the documents' requirements traceability inspections must have been done.

2. The SC requirements document must exist.

3. A code review must be done during code development and before integration module testing.

4. Verification and validation (V&V) testing must be done by a special tester.

5. External certification of code may be done, based on the customer's requirements.

6. A release must be approved via sign-off before it is installed in the field.

7. Once the code is released, if any SC bugs are found, they are fixed on site and changes are recorded by SCRs (software change requests).

Figure A.3 shows the life cycle, and Tables A.3 and A.4 provide details about the steps.

Description of the roles in the states
Table A.3 indicates the role responsibilities that apply when a source object is in a certain state; that is, who is responsible for what in which state.

Description of the roles in the transitions
Table A.4 indicates which role is responsible for the actions represented by the transitions.

Description of the states
The following is a description of what happens to the source code object when in a particular state. Only the different states (source objects) are described. The rest are exactly the same as in the process model for source objects compared to normal. Figure A.3 illustrates the state transitions.

CREATE: When an SMRS (Software Module Requirements Specification) exists along with the Safety Requirements, and the requirements traceability inspection has been done, then the SC source object can be created. Information from the SMRS is included as the header of the

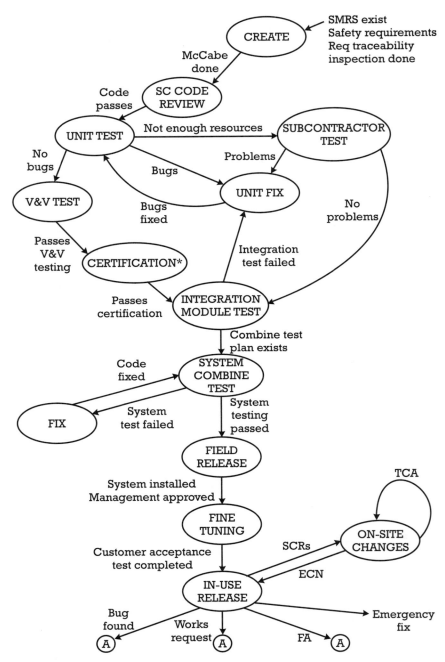

Figure A.3 Process model for safety critical source code objects.

Table A.3
Role Responsibilities for States of Source Objects

State	V&V Tester	Lead Software Engineer	Software Engineer	System Integration Tester
CREATE	–	X	X	–
SC CODE REVIEW	–	X	X	–
UNIT TEST	–	X	X	–
SUBCONTRACTOR TEST	–	X	X	–
UNIT FIX	–	X	X	–
V&V TEST	X	–	–	–
CERTIFICATION	CUSTOMER	–	–	–
INTEGRATION MODULE TEST	–	X	X	–
SYSTEM COMBINE TEST	–	–	–	X
FIX	–	X	X	–
FIELD RELEASE	–	X	X	–
FINE TUNING	–	X	X	–
ON-SITE CHANGES	–	X	X	–
IN-USE RELEASE	–	X	X	–

X means that that role can perform the actions for that state on the source object.

source object. The source object is developed and compiled to the satis-faction of the engineer.

SC CODE REVIEW: Once the McCabe analysis is done, the code is put through an SC code review meeting. If the code passes the review, then it moves onto unit testing.

UNIT TEST: When the source object has been created and run through the McCabe tool (if it is a C or Pascal object), then it goes into unit testing. If bugs are found, then they must be fixed. When the bugs are fixed, unit testing is redone. A situation could occur where there are not enough resources to do the testing, so it is sent to a subcontractor to perform. Unit testing is completed when the engineer feels there are no more bugs or the subcontractor found no problems. Note that at this point, the source object is part of a baseline/configuration item. When there are no more bugs, then the code goes onto V&V testing.

SUBCONTRACTOR TEST: If there were not enough in-house resources to do unit testing, then a subcontractor does it. If no problems are found, then testing is completed and the subcontractor notifies Company X of this. If problems are found, the subcontractor submits a report

Table A.4

Role Responsibilities for Transitions of Source Objects

Transition	Product Line Manager	Lead Software Engineer	Software Engineer	V&V Tester or System Tester
SMRS exists	X	X	–	–
McCabe done	–	X	X	–
Not enough resources	X	–	–	–
Bugs	–	X	X	–
Problems	–	X	X	–
Bugs fixed	–	X	X	–
No bugs	–	X	X	–
Integration test failed	–	X	X	–
No problems	–	X	X	–
Integration test passed	–	X	X	–
System testing passed	–	–	–	System Tester
System test failed	–	–	–	System Tester
Code fixed	–	X	X	–
System installed	–	X	X	–
Changes needed	–	X	X	–
TCA	–	X	X	–
ECN	–	X	X	–
Customer acceptance test completed	–	X	X	–
FAR	–	X	X	–
Work request	–	X	X	–
Bugs found	–	X	X	–
Code passes	–	X	X	–
No bugs	–	X	X	–
Passes V&V testing	–	–	–	X
Passes certification	X	X	–	–
SCRs	–	X	X	–
SC bug	–	X	X	–

X means that that role is responsible for performing the actions represented by that transition.

to Company X detailing the results and any analysis of the problem(s). Fixes must be made before the source objects can move on to integration testing.

UNIT FIX: If any problems are found during unit testing, the source object must be fixed. Once fixed, unit testing continues.

V&V TEST: Verification and validation testing is done by an independent tester. When the tester indicates that testing is completed and the code has passed it, then it is available for customer certification (if required) by transitioning to CERTIFICATION, or goes onto integration testing by transitioning to INTEGRATION MODULE TESTING.

CERTIFICATION*: The asterisk indicates that this is an optional state based on customer requirements. The customers do their certification testing and the program manager is notified that certification passed. The code is then available again for integration and combine testing.

INTEGRATION MODULE TEST: Once unit testing is completed, the source goes through integration module testing. If any problems are found, they must be fixed. The process model shows that the module goes back to unit fixing and testing. If no problems are found, the source goes onto system combine testing.

SYSTEM COMBINE TEST: Once integration testing is completed, and when the combine test plan exists, the system combine testing takes place. If any tests fail, then the system engineer asks the software engineer to fix the problem and then combine testing continues.

FIX: When system combine testing indicates that problems exist, then some quick fixes are made to enable combine testing to continue.

FIELD RELEASE: Once system combine testing is completed, the field release is created and the system is installed at the client's site. Management approves the creation of the release.

FINE TUNING: When the system is installed out in the field at the client's site, some parameters may need fine tuning. If any problems are found, the on-site engineer must fix them. SCRs are generated when problems are found with SC code and the code transitions to ON-SITE CHANGES. If no problems are found, then the customers do their acceptance testing and the code transitions to IN-USE RELEASE.

ON-SITE CHANGES: Changes are made on site as needed as indicated by the SCRs. When all changes are completed, TCA(s) (temporary change approvals) are generated to indicate these changes along with the generation of an ECN (engineering change notice) to ensure that the drawings back at the central office are updated to reflect these changes. Customer acceptance testing is done.

IN-USE RELEASE: When the fine-tuning and customer acceptance testing are completed, the source object is considered to be officially in use in the field release. Any subsequent maintenance is handled via field action requests, work requests, or an informal process of fixing bugs. The maintenance processes are still to be defined. When a problem is found with SC code, an emergency fix process comes into play. This process is still to be defined.

A.7 Template for configuration management status report

(Once I have done the interviews with people to find out the current status of CM, I then use this as a template for writing my CM status report.)

This document captures the typical kinds of topics that would be presented in a CM status report, a report that describes the results of analyzing the current state of CM.

This report was created as a result of a series of interviews done with various customers in order to capture a snapshot of the current status of configuration management on all products.

The purpose of the interviews was to get the perspective of CM from a variety of people involved in the product development and maintenance activities, including developers, managers, testers, build managers, release managers, project managers, upper management, hot-line support staff, and tools support group.

This report identifies:

- People's understanding or definition of CM;

- Problems found in our development and maintenance practices and tools;

- Goals or visions people have for a better solution;

- Why CM is important to this company;

- Recommendations regarding CM.

Executive summary

The executive summary is a one-page synopsis of all the key findings.

People's understanding or definition of CM

This section details how everyone views CM—good or bad, their definition, and corporate versus project view of CM.

Problems found in our development and maintenance practices and tools

This section lists all the problems or weaknesses or pains found in the development and maintenance of the company's products and Web content, along with the tools used to perform all the activities.

Goals or visions people have for a better solution

This section lists all the suggestions for improvements, which will most likely become the CM requirements.

Why CM is important to this company

This section starts to define the benefits and values that the company currently finds, and hopes to find, with its CM solution.

Recommendations regarding CM

This section lists the findings and the recommendations, that is, what the company should do about the findings.

A.8 Template for risk management plan

This document presents a template for a risk management (RM) plan. The purpose of this RM plan is to document all the risks that the CM deployment team perceives as part of implementing the CM solution. This is a working document and is updated as necessary.

RM engenders confidence in the decision-making process and ensures that there will be no "surprises" along the way that could lead to failure of the deployment. RM acts as insurance. Disasters will be avoided. Any problem that could potentially escalate into something bigger is "nipped in the bud."

Eliminating as much risk as possible, or finding an acceptable level of risk, is the goal of RM. Risk needs to be eliminated so that when users switch to the new tool, their work is not negatively affected. Production teams cannot afford new risks in their daily practices.

This plan tracks all the risk resolution and mitigation, along with any contingency plans in case of fallback. This RM plan contains (1) an executive summary, (2) a description of each risk and its attributes, and (3) a lessons learned section.

Executive summary

The executive summary is a short (one page ideally) summary of the status of all the risks. Management will want to receive reports on a regular basis and this summary serves that purpose. It can be easily presented in tabular form, as shown in Table A.5.

Table A.5
Sample of an Executive Summary in Tabular Form

Risk Number	Likelihood of Occurring	Seriousness	Percentage Understood	Percentage Resolved
1	High	High	10%	20%
2	Medium	Medium	100%	100%
3	Low	Low	50%	75%
4	Unknown	Unknown	0%	0%
5	Occurred	High	100%	0%
and so on				

It can be read as follows: one risk has been completely resolved (100% value in the Percentage Resolved column), two new risks were added (0% in the Percentage Resolved column), and other risks still need to be addressed (remaining rows). Risks are typically dependent on each other, so resolving a couple of risks sometimes automatically ends up resolving the related risks.

Following the summary table, a list of the "next steps" to be followed, or the action items, are given. Then a detailed description of risks is given.

Detailed description of the risks

Each risk is described. I prefer to put risks into categories because risks tend to be related to each other. Refer to Section A.3 where typical categories and their risks are described.

Associated with each risk are attributes (or metadata); that is, knowledge about the risk, such as those attributes shown in the executive summary table (Table A.5). The summary attributes that I typically use for that table are as follows:

1. *Risk number:* the unique identity of the risk;

2. *Likelihood of occurring:* the potential that the risk will actually occur; values could be high, medium, low, unknown, or it has occurred;

3. *Seriousness of the risk:* how serious would the situation be if this risk actually occurred? High, medium, low, or unknown are the values;

4. *Percentage understood:* how well understood is this risk? Values are 0% to 100%;

5. *Percentage resolved:* how close to resolution or mitigation is this risk? Values are 0% to 100%.

For the detailed part for each risk, I typically use the following attributes:

1. *Risk name and number:* uniquely identifies each risk;

2. *Meaning of the risk:* a detailed description of what that risk actually is;

3. *Key questions and answers:* risk management is all about asking the right questions and finding the answers. For instance, training was not given to users in the past, so does this same attitude exist today? No, because we have learned from our past mistakes that if we do not take time to train people, then the tool will not be used to its potential and we will waste time as people make errors using the tool;

4. *Strategy for mitigation or resolution:* the action items that need to be accomplished in order to address the risk;

5. *Contingency plan:* if needed (meaning this is a very serious risk), an alternate approach is documented.

Lessons learned
This section lists the lessons learned by doing risk management, or ways in which it can be improved.

A.9 Template for a pilot project plan

This document details the key steps involved in creating a pilot plan for the deployment of the configuration management solution. I have added this template so that you can use it to help you do pilot planning and document that plan. Pilot projects provide the opportunity to resolve risks and to gain complete confidence in the tool. It is a "proof-of-concept" pilot because the idea is to:

- Prove that the tool works in your environment;

- Gain experience in using the tool;

- Get an early success by doing the first roll-out of the tool;

- Uncover any new risks;

- Find out what extra training or documentation will be required for your users;

- Become experts in the tool;

- Test your requirements with hands-on use of the tool;

- Be able to objectively rate the tool using your selection rating system.

Success criteria and expectations

In this section, the success criteria are listed. Any metrics that will be captured are documented here. Two metrics—one pertinent to management's needs and one pertinent to engineers' needs—should be captured that indicate some level of improvement.

Why was this project chosen to be the pilot?

This section describes the reason for the choice of the team to do the pilot and identifies any ramifications for that decision.

Scope of the pilot project

This section describes the scope of the pilot: all the people, data, code, content, applications, platforms, and so on, that will be involved. It discusses the involvement of the deployment team and what role they will play. It describes what test cases or scenarios will be used on the pilot.

Schedule

This section details the schedule of all activities along with who will do them as shown in Table A.6.

Risks and concerns

One of the key purposes of the pilots is to resolve any remaining risks. This section highlights the specific risks that will be addressed during this pilot and lists any new ones that arise. This can be done in tabular form as shown in Table A.7.

Process models

This section describes in detail the process model that will be implemented in the tool.

Training materials

This section details all the training classes and materials that the pilot team used. This is important because one of the goals of the pilot is to determine whether any extra training materials will be needed for new users.

Table A.6
Schedule of Activities

Activity	Who	Schedule
Finalize hardware setup		
Create training materials		
Define process models		
Implement process models		
Train pilot team		
Do data migration		
Execute the pilot with requirements test scenarios		
Review lessons learned		
Refine training materials		
Refine process model		
Prepare for next roll-out		

Table A.7
Specific Risks To Be Addressed

Risk	Comments
Reorganization of company	It could affect decision-making and availability of resources.
London office chose a different tool	Should we go along with London's choice, which is different from ours?
Schedule	The reorganization is likely to affect schedules.
Lack of hardware	No hardware means pilot cannot start.
Migrating data from remote sites	How do we do this with the tool?
Support	Who will be the help desk during the pilot?
Waning CM commitment and sponsorship	Too many delays have affected the level of enthusiasm for the new CM tool.

Vendor interaction

The vendor always plays an important role in the pilots. This section describes who will be the main contact point on the pilot team with the vendor.

Lessons learned and data captured

From the pilots, lots of valuable information will be obtained. In particular, we need to know:

> • What are the most optimal training materials and classes?

> • What preparation of the team is needed beyond training, for example, data migration, process modeling and automation, and customizations?

> • What management issues need to be addressed beforehand?

> • What systems administration issues need to be addressed?

> • Who will provide hot-line support?

> • What new risks need to be addressed?

> • What new policies or procedures need to be considered?

> • Is this the right tool? Do we now have complete confidence in it?

> • What extra training is needed for our staff beyond what the vendor provides?

> • Were our success criteria met? Why or why not?

> • Is the process used sufficient?

> • Are all the risks mitigated?

> • Did new risks arise and why?

> • How does this pilot change the rating values for this tool?

About the Author

Susan Dart has 24 years of experience in software tools and technology adoption and is president of Dart Technology Strategies, Inc. Her experience is unique and all-encompassing across academia and industry. It cuts across all walks of business: software development, management, sales, services, marketing, and research, including Vice President of Process for a leading configuration management (CM) tool vendor. Her main role these days is as a CM evangelist and consultant, helping to shape the role of the CM industry as it tackles the Internet domain. A well-known speaker at international seminars and conferences, and the author of many professional papers and a previous book on CM tools, she received her B.Sc. from the Royal Melbourne Institute of Technology, Australia, and her M.Sc. in software engineering from Carnegie Mellon University, United States. She is a member of the IEEE Computer Society and the ACM and spent seven years at the Software Engineering Institute.

Index

Recent Titles in the Artech House Computing Library

Advanced ANSI SQL Data Modeling and Structure Processing, Michael M. David

Advanced Database Technology and Design, Mario Piattini and Oscar Díaz, editors

Business Process Implementation for IT Professionals and Managers, Robert B. Walford

Configuration Management: The Missing Link in Web Engineering, Susan Dart

Data Modeling and Design for Today's Architectures, Angelo Bobak

Data Quality for the Information Age, Thomas C. Redman

Data Warehousing and Data Mining for Telecommunications, Rob Mattison

Distributed and Multi-Database Systems, Angelo R. Bobak

Electronic Payment Systems, Donal O'Mahony, Michael Peirce, and Hitesh Tewari

Future Codes: Essays in Advanced Computer Technology and the Law, Curtis E. A. Karnow

Global Distributed Applications With Windows® DNA, Enrique Madrona

A Guide to Programming Languages: Overview and Comparison, Ruknet Cezzar

A Guide to Software Configuration Management, Alexis Leon

Guide to Standards and Specifications for Designing Web Software, Stan Magee and Leonard L. Tripp

How to Run Successful High-Tech Project-Based Organizations, Fergus O'Connell

For further information on these and other Artech House titles, including previously considered out-of-print books now available through our In-Print-Forever® (IPF®) program, contact:

Artech House
685 Canton Street
Norwood, MA 02062
Phone: 781-769-9750
Fax: 781-769-6334
e-mail: artech@artechhouse.com

Artech House
46 Gillingham Street
London SW1V 1AH UK
Phone: +44 (0)20 7596-8750
Fax: +44 (0)20 7630-0166
e-mail: artech-uk@artechhouse.com

Find us on the World Wide Web at:
www.artechhouse.com